United States War Department

Business Methods in the War Department

United States War Department
Business Methods in the War Department
ISBN/EAN: 9783744662383

Printed in Europe, USA, Canada, Australia, Japan

Cover: Foto ©ninafisch / pixelio.de

More available books at **www.hansebooks.com**

BUSINESS METHODS

IN THE

WAR DEPARTMENT.

REPORT OF THE BOARD APPOINTED IN COMPLIANCE WITH
THE REQUEST OF THE SENATE SELECT COMMITTEE
TO INVESTIGATE THE METHODS OF BUSINESS
IN THE EXECUTIVE DEPARTMENTS.

WASHINGTON:
GOVERNMENT PRINTING OFFICE.
1889.

17958——1

TABLE OF CONTENTS.

	Page.
Letter of Secretary of War, January 23, 1889, transmitting report of board to Senate select committee (to Appendix 12) with recommendations	1-8

REPORT OF BOARD.

	Page.
Orders of S. of W., March 22, 1888, appointing board on business methods	9
Letter of Senator Cockrell, chairman of Senate select committee, February 10, 1888, to S. of W., submitting extracts from report of that committee recommending the appointment of a commission in War and Treasury Departments to inquire into business methods, &c	9
W. D. circular, April 4, 1888, inviting suggestions	10
List of topics which have been considered and reported upon	11
History and character of work done by board	11
Salaries paid in the Department; payment for overtime work	11
Retired list for employés	12
Stenographers in the Department	12
Appendix No. 1. Requests for requisitions and settlement certificates	13
W. D. circular, April 19, 1888, discontinuing requests for requisitions	15
Appendix No. 2. Rules and regulations of War Department, June 4, 1888	15
Appendix No. 3. Certificates of deposit	16
Exhibit A. Statutes concerning proceeds of Government property	25
Exhibit B. Statement of certificates of deposit received and disposed of in Req. Div. during fiscal year ending June 30, 1887	26
Exhibit C. Army regulations concerning certificates of deposit	26
W. D. letter of June 14, 1888, to Secretary of Treasury concerning C. D	28
W. D. circular of June 21, 1888, publishing letter of Secretary of Treasury of June 19, 1888, concerning C. D., and giving instructions	30
W. D. orders of June 18, 1888, discontinuing books in Req. Div. recording C. D	30
G. O. 52, A. G. O., July 11, 1888, revoking Par. 1608, A. R	30
Appendix No. 4. Army paymaster's collections	31
W. D. indorsement of June 22, 1888, approving recommendations of board	32
Appendix No. 5. Card index record of rolls of Vol. Army	33
Exhibit A. Card showing record of soldier	42
Remarks of A. G. on report of board	43
Order of S. of W. of January 18, 1889, directing the printing of card index of rolls of 164th N. Y. Vols	48
	45
Appendix No. 6. Credit requisitions	46
Exhibit A. Proposed consolidated form of deposit requisition	48
Exhibits B, E, H, L, O, R. Copies of deposit lists	50, 53, 56, 59, 62, 65
Exhibits C, F, I, M, P, S. Copies of deposit requisitions	51, 54, 57, 60, 63, 66
Exhibits D, G, K, N, Q, T. Copies of repay covering warrants	52, 55, 58, 61, 64, 67
Exhibit U. Copy of credit requisition, Q. M. G	68
Exhibit V. Copy of accountable requisition	69
Exhibit W. Copy of accountable warrant	70
Exhibit X. Proposed consolidated form of accountable requisition	71
Letter of S. W., August 9, 1888, to Secretary of Treasury in answer to request that credit requisitions be made out by W. D., and presenting the consolidated form proposed by the board	72
Action taken in W. D. consolidating deposit lists	72
W. D. circular, August 9, 1888, discontinuing requests for accountable requisitions and requiring accountable requisitions to be made in the bureaus	72
Form of accountable req. to be used	73

	Page.
Appendix No. 7. Requisitions on Public Printer	73
W. D. circular, September 11, 1888, discontinuing duplicate requisitions on Public Printer	74
Appendix No. 8. Administration	74
Proposed circular as to disposition of mail, filing of papers, submission of papers to Secretary of War, &c	74
Subject of correspondence to be indicated in upper left hand corner of paper	75
Letter of Q. M. G., August 22, 1873, as to disposition of papers by Q. M. G. and action of S. W., September 9, 1873, thereon authorizing the Q. M. G. to sign certain papers by order of the S. W.	75, 76
Views of present Q. M. G. on method of conducting correspondence	76
Proposed extension of authority given to Q. M. G. to other chiefs of bureaus to sign certain papers "by authority of the Secretary of War"	77
Views of A. G., Q. M. G., C. G. S., and C. of O. in their reports in 1885	77, 78
Amended circular recommended	78
Report on circular required by S. of W.	79
Appendix No. 9. Messenger service	80
W. D. Orders, January 18, 1889, providing half-hour messenger service for delivery of papers, &c.	81
Appendix No. 10. Supply division	82
Table showing expenditures for miscellaneous supplies	83
W. D. circular, July 21, 1884, establishing division, &c	84
W. D. circular, February 19, 1885, publishing regulations to be observed in accounting for supplies furnished to supply div	84
W. D. orders relieving Captain Hoyt from charge of division and assigning M. R. Thorp to charge of the same, and requiring a $10,000 bond, &c	86
Appendix No. 11. Daily reports of work	86
Letter of President Polk to S. W., April 11, 1845	86
W. D. circular of April 25, 1845	87
W. D. circular, April 23, 1887, requiring daily reports	87
W. D. circular, January 21, 1889, rescinding circular of April 23, 1887	89
Letter of S. of W., January 23, 1889, transmitting report of board so far as completed, to Hon. F. M. Cockrell, chairman Senate select committee, with recommendations, &c	89
Appendix No. 12. Correspondence	90
Letters received. Statement showing classes of, whether briefed and entered, &c	92
Letters sent. Statement showing classes of, and whether press-copied or recorded, &c	96
Method of entering and acting on papers	100
Case of transfer of steamer *Success* from Quincy, Illinois, to Plum Point Reach, Mississippi River, traced in detail	100
Proposed circular	110
Copies of papers in pension claim of Thos. W. Taylor	111
Methods of Government Departments and commercial establishments	116
Necessity of recording important papers; duplication of entries to be avoided	117
Receipt of mail, first action on	118
Briefing and indexing	119
Consolidation of record divisions	119
Suggestions of the C. S. O	120
Card-index briefs	121
Acknowledgments	122
Card index	123
Table showing number of pages of record of letters received and sent in W. D. in 1888, and average number of lines of record for each	126
Form of record card	130
File-cases for record cards	131
Index of names on record cards	132
To keep trace of cards and numbers of papers	132
Papers awaiting final action	133
Card index of decisions or precedents	133
Abbreviations	134
Replies to letters	134
General remarks. Cabinet letter files, files, indorsements, letters for immediate attention, lists, notations, papers pertaining to several bureaus, red ink, result of search to be preserved, Secretary's office, unanswered mail	135

	Page.
Miscellaneous, mail chutes	136
Conclusion	137
Letter of S. of W., of February 19, 1889, approving the recommendations and suggestions of the Board on the subject of Correspondence	137
W. D. circular, February 15, 1889, approving report of board, which is to be printed; half-hourly mail service to be put into operation, &c	138
Exhibit A. Instructions for keeping the records, &c., approved October 1, 1870	139–179
Exhibit B. Decisions or precedents, samples of card index	180–185
Exhibit C. List of subjects as shown by index-book of letters received, office of S. of W., 1888	186
Exhibit D. Specimens of cross-reference cards and specimen of record card	190
W. D. circular, February 9, 1889, sample case to be selected in each bureau and action thereon traced in detail	196
W. D. circular, February 13, 1889, relating to correspondence	196
Assignment of business to the bureaus and offices of the Department	197
W. D. circular, February 9, 1889, classes of work belonging to the bureaus to be published, and list of classes of papers belonging to each division to be prepared	206

BUSINESS METHODS IN THE WAR DEPARTMENT.

LETTER OF TRANSMITTAL.

WAR DEPARTMENT,
Washington City, January 23, 1889.

SIR: I have the honor to acknowledge the receipt of your letter of the 11th instant, requesting that if the board on business methods of this Department has performed its work in whole or in part, the Senate Select Committee to Inquire into the Methods of Business in the Executive Departments, etc., of which you are chairman, be furnished at the earliest convenience with a full and detailed statement in regard to the organization of the board and their labors, and what changes have been made or recommended, and the action had thereon, etc., for further consideration either by the committee or by Congress.

In response, I inclose a copy of the report of the board on business methods, dated the 21st instant, and the accompanying appendices.

The first appendix treats of the subject of "Requests for requisitions on settlement certificates." The board recommended that the custom of issuing letters of request upon settlement certificates by the Bureau officers be discontinued, and that the certificates be returned with an indorsement, which may be stamped upon the back of the certificate, showing that it has been "noted," with the name of the office and date; and that should objections exist to the certificate under section 191, Revised Statutes, they should be stated in the indorsement.

In pursuance of said recommendation, on the 19th of April last I issued the following circular:

"Hereafter the custom of issuing 'requests' by the chiefs of Bureaus of this Department for requisition upon Treasury settlement certificates in cases where no objection to payment is known, will be discontinued, and said certificates will be returned to the Secretary of War by indorsement, which may be written or stamped upon the same, showing that it has been noted. If objections are known, they should be indorsed upon the certificate for the action of the Secretary of War, under section 191 of the Revised Statutes."

Appendix 2 treats of the "Rules and regulations of the War Department." The proposed rules were referred to the board, and, after consideration of the laws and rules in force in the War and other Executive Departments, certain amendments were suggested and the present rules and regulations, in which were incorporated the amendments referred to, were promulgated June 4, 1888.

Appendix 3 treats of "Certificates of deposit." With the view of obviating the duplication of work and delay in the disposition of this class of business, and of expediting and simplifying the methods of business in connection with certificates of deposit, the board made certain recommendations which I communicated to the Secretary of the Treasury by letter of June 14, 1888, and having, substantially, received his approval, were, with slight modification, adopted, and were promulgated by circular of this Department dated June 21, 1888, and orders dated respectively June 18 and July 11, 1888.

Appendix 4 treats of "Army paymasters' collections." The board, after reviewing the method of business in relation to this subject, suggested that duplication of work, records, etc., could be obviated by the Paymaster-General designating on the certificate of deposit all the appropriations to which the funds belong. The views of the board met with my concurrence, and on June 22, 1888, I issued the following directions:

"Respectfully returned to the Paymaster-General, who will take the same action in cases of credits for all other appropriations as is now done on account of clothing and ordnance stores.

"The proposed change will obviate the long and, in the opinion of the Secretary of War, entirely unnecessary routine stated in the accompanying memorandum."

Appendix 5 treats of the subject of "Card-index record of rolls of volunteer army." The report of the board upon this subject contains a comprehensive description of the card-index system, points out many advantages which the system is believed to possess, and presents various recommendations respecting the application of the system to rolls and records in the office of the Adjutant-General.

After careful consideration of the subject I deemed it judicious that the merits of the system should be practically tested, and with that object in view I, on January 18, instant, issued an order as follows:

"Having carefully considered the report of the board on the 'Card-index records of the rolls of the late volunteer force,' and the remarks of the Adjutant-General thereon, I am of opinion that a practical test of the value of the system, which has been commenced, can only be made by printing and distributing to the proper officers the card index of the muster-rolls of one regiment.

"It is therefore ordered that the card index of the rolls of the One hundred and sixty-fourth New York Volunteers be printed, and to facilitate search that the cards of said regiment be arranged in one alphabetical list. Requisition will accordingly be made upon the Public Printer for not less than 300 copies of the work. The printed volume to contain a statement on the title page that it is a transcript of the muster-rolls only.

"When printed the book will at once be distributed to all officers of the Government who need a copy in the performance of their duties. Each officer to whom one or more copies may be sent will be requested to report as early as possible whether the book is of value in the dispatch of public business.

"This will enable the Department to report to Congress definite information as to the cost and value of the work."

Appendix 6 treats of the subject of "Credit requisitions." On July 21, 1888, the Secretary of the Treasury communicated to me certain recommendations which had been submitted by the Treasury commission (on business methods), one of which was that the War Department and the Interior Department be requested to make out their own credit requisitions from the lists sent to them from the book-keeper's division of the Third Auditor's office, instead of their being made out in that division, as had been the practice. The subject was referred to the board, who, having considered the same, made recommendations which not only contemplated the devolving upon this Department of the work properly belonging to it which hitherto had been performed in the office of the Third Auditor, but included also the consolidation of certain blank forms then in use by which the work incident to this class of business would be much simplified and lessened.

On August 9, 1888, I communicated these recommendations to the Secretary of the Treasury, whose concurrence therein was necessary in order to carry them fully into effect, and pending his reply I, on August 9, 1888, issued the following circular:

"In order to simplify the business of this Department, reduce the possibility of error, and avoid the duplication of papers containing practically the same information, the Secretary of War directs that the practice in the different Bureaus of writing a separate 'request,' upon which to base an accountable requisition, be discontinued, and that in place thereof the accountable requisition heretofore made in the division of requisitions and accounts, Secretary's office, upon such request, be hereafter prepared in the proper Bureau for the signature of the Secretary of War; and that a note, viz: 'Requested by ——— ———,' signed by the head of the Bureau, be written on the margin of such requisition as indicated on the accompanying form.'

Appendix 7 treats of the subject Requisitions on Public Printer. By an order of the War Department of March 28, 1864, the heads of Bureaus were required to make requisitions in duplicate for printing and binding. In the opinion of the board the concentration of the Bureaus in the War Department Building obviated the necessity for the continuance of this practice, and they recommended that it be discontinued. Accordingly I, on September 11, 1888, issued a circular as follows:

"All the Bureaus of the War Department, with one exception, being now located in the War Department Building, it is no longer necessary that duplicates of requisitions on the Public Printer for printing and binding be prepared; and hereafter only one copy of such requisitions need be sent to the office of the Secretary of War, division of requisitions and accounts, a press copy of the requisition to be retained in the office or bureau in which it was made, for reference therein."

Appendix 8 treats of the subject "Administration." A proposed circular prescribing the action to be taken upon the different classes of letters and papers received at the War Department or any of its Bureaus, having been referred to the board, they reported that such a circular would undoubtedly simplify and hasten the transaction of business; but with a view of making it more complete and to more certainly accomplish the object desired, they recommended that it be referred to each chief of Bureau for his views and for such amendments as in his opinion should be made to it in order to simplify and hasten the work of the Department and do away with unnecessary routine, etc. On January 15, instant, I referred a copy of the circular to the heads of the several Bureaus, with request for their views, amendments, etc., as recommended by the board, and when replies shall have been received the circular, embodying such suggested amendments as may be deemed of value, will be formally promulgated.

Appendix 9 treats of messenger service. The report of the board upon this subject points out the unnecessary delays in the transaction of current business, incident to the manner in which papers are transferred from one room to another for action thereon, and in the delivery of papers between the Bureaus and the office of the Secretary of War; and presents recommendations designed to obviate such delays and thereby effect a more expeditious dispatch of business. The use of reversible mail cards, containing printed addresses, in place of envelopes, in the transmission of papers from one room to another was also recommended as being a simpler and more expeditious manner of transmitting papers intended to go only from room to room by messenger service. These recommendations were formulated into orders and issued January 18, instant, as follows:

"In order to secure frequent and prompt delivery of official papers between the rooms or sections of a Bureau, the chief of each Bureau in which the business transacted will warrant such action is hereby directed to assign an assistant messenger or laborer to the duty of regularly collecting and delivering official papers; collections and deliveries to be punctually made by the designated carrier at all the delivery baskets or boxes in a Bureau every half hour, viz, 8.45, 9.15, 9.45, 10.15, 10.45, 11.15, 11.45 a. m., 12.30, 1.00, 1.30, 2.00, 2.30, 3.00, and 3.30 p. m., the carrier calling at each mail-basket twice each trip, once going and once returning, so as to insure the transmission of completed papers in either direction throughout the Bureau each half hour.

"Similar half-hourly collections and delivery of papers will be made between the several Bureaus and the office of the Secretary by an assistant messenger or laborer, to be designated by the Chief Clerk of the Department; the hours of delivery being 9.00, 9.30, 10.00, 10.30, 11.00, 11.30 a. m, 12. m., 12.45, 1.15, 1.45, 2.15, 2.45, 3.15, and 3.45 p. m.

"In order that the fullest benefit may be derived from this method of communication chiefs of Bureaus will require that all papers delivered be immediately taken up and placed in the hands of clerks engaged upon the work pertaining thereto; and that every paper that has been acted upon in one room and which requires action in another be placed in the delivery-box before or at the time of the next collection. Cases which require immediate action will of course be delivered at once. The half-hourly delivery applies to cases which have been moved at longer intervals.

"Reversible mail cards or jackets plainly addressed will be used for the protection and safe transmission of papers wherever their shape or size will permit. The address of the room or division from which sent to be in red ink on the inside of both folds, and of the room or division to which sent in black ink on the outside of both folds.

"In order to allow time for the preparation of the necessary mail cards, this order will be carried into effect on the 1st of February next.

"In the meantime estimates of the number and sizes of cards will be made by each bureau."

In this connection, and as an illustration of the results which follow efficient administration and the application of practical business methods to the routine work of a public office, your attention is invited to the record and pension division of the Surgeon-General's Office, and the work performed therein during the last two years. As stated in my annual report for 1887, the work of this division—

"Had so far fallen in arrears that 9,511 unanswered calls for information relative to pension and other claims had accumulated in the office on December 13, 1886. Prior to that date a large number of cases were subjected to a delay of two and one-half and three months, and often for a longer period.

"This state of affairs had been brought about by a combination of causes, the most important of which were defective methods of work, laxity of discipline, indifference and lack of interest on the part of some of the clerks, many of whom were inattentive to duty, inefficient, physically or mentally disabled, or otherwise incompetent. A belief seemed to pervade the whole office that no improvement in the old system was either desirable or possible, and that any change made in it must necessarily be for the worse. To such an extent was this carried that the two principal officers responsible for this division were of opinion that, for efficient and constant work, it was necessary to have from two to ten thousand cases always on hand.

"Repeated efforts by the Department to secure greater expedition having failed, it was deemed necessary to relieve the chief of the division and detail another officer in his place, which was done early in December; other changes were also made in the Bureau. In less than three months thereafter the great arrearage which existed was entirely reduced. The methods of work were changed, at once increasing its volume without diminishing its accuracy; the discipline of the force was improved; thirty disabled clerks, who for various reasons were entitled to consideration, were assigned to such duties as they could efficiently perform with comfort to themselves; twenty worthless clerks were discharged, and it is now generally understood that the work of the office is of the first importance, to which personal preference and convenience must yield, and it has been clearly demonstrated that a large number of cases on hand is not essential to the efficient and economical employment of the clerks engaged on pension work. At the close of the fiscal year it was reported by the new chief of this division (Dr. Ainsworth) that any call for information from the records of the Surgeon-General's Office relative to pension claims could be answered in from one to three days from the date of its receipt."

Not only was all this accomplished without increase in the clerical force of the division, but it was soon found that the changes which had been made in the method of work and discipline of the division rendered it possible to keep up the current work, and at the same time to assign a portion of the force to the preparation of a system of index record cards, which would simplify and greatly diminish the future work of the office. In this system the medical history of each soldier as it appears on the hospital register is written on a separate card containing a suitable printed form. The cards are assorted by regiments, then arranged alphabetically by name within the regiment, so that when all the registers shall have been copied, the cards showing the medical history of a soldier, who may have been treated in any number of hospitals and in any part of the country, will by this arrangement all fall together automatically, and his whole medical history can be found by simply turning to the proper letter of the alphabet in the file box containing the cards of his regiment.

The advantages of this system of index-record cards are summed up in my last annual report (1888) as follows:

"They answer all the purposes of a copy or duplication of the valuable records, which, from constant handling, have been fast going to destruction; their alphabetical arrangement in order of surnames under each regiment will obviate tedious, and in some cases unsuccessful, search of the original records; a soldier's medical history can be readily furnished in cases where it is impossible to obtain any data upon which to search other than his name or military organization; and, finally, should it be desired to print the hospital records, the index-cards, which contain everything recorded in the registers, are in the best possible form to send to the printer."

Work was commenced on this system in April, 1887, and has been pushed as rapidly as possible since. At first but a few clerks were available for this duty, but the number so employed has steadily increased as the other work of the division has been lessened by the use of the constantly expanding card files, and the adoption of simpler and more expeditious methods of business, until of the 280 clerks allowed by law to this division, which number two years ago was found insufficient to keep the current work of the office nearer than two or three months from date, now 166 are constantly employed in the preparation of record cards, while with the remainder it is found easy to answer all calls upon the division in from one to three days from the date of their receipt. Over three and one-half millions of cards have already been made and it is believed that within the next fiscal year this great work will be practically completed, including the regimental hospital records now filed in the Adjutant-General office, which in a short time must be transferred to the Surgeon-General's Office to be card-indexed, and thus complete the entire medical history of the soldiers of the late war.

Appendix 10 treats of the Supply division. The board describes the manner in which the stationery and miscellaneous supplies required for the use of the Department have been procured both prior and subsequent to 1882, at which last named date the method was changed, and give a statement of the reasons which, in July, 1884, led to the placing of the business of the supply division in the charge of a bonded officer of the Quartermaster's Department of the Army. They also explain wherein the placing of the business in the charge of an officer failed to accomplish the object in view and, as the officer in charge will go upon the retired list this year, they recommend that the supply division be placed in charge of a clerk in the Secretary's office, who should be required to give bonds. They invite attention to the salaries of like positions in some of the other Executive Departments, and suggest that the salary of the chief of the supply division should equal that of the chief of the stationery division of the Treasury Department, which is $2,500 per annum. The recommendations and suggestions met with my concurrence, and I gave them effect, so far as it was within my power to do so, by issuing orders on January 19th instant, as follows:

"Capt. Charles H. Hoyt, assistant quartermaster, U. S. Army, is hereby relieved from duty in charge of the supply division of this Department, and will report to the Quartermaster-General.

"Mr. M. R. Thorp, chief clerk of the supply division, is assigned to the charge of the supply division. He will give bond in the sum of $10,000 for the faithful performance of his duties and will enter upon his duties after his bond is approved by the Secretary of War.

"He will purchase, issue, and account for all supplies and property in accordance with the regulations contained in the circulars of July 21, 1884, and February 19, 1885, except that portion of the regulations mentioned which requires supplies to be purchased, issued, and accounted for in accordance with the regulations prescribed for the Quartermaster's Department of the Army and the property returns of the officer in charge to be examined in the office of the Quartermaster-General, in lieu of which requirements the books and accounts of the supply division will be hereafter inspected and reported upon by an officer of the inspector-general's department in accordance with the regulations governing that department."

Appendix 11 treats of the subject, "Daily reports of work." The board quote in their report sections 173, 174, and 175 of the Revised Statutes of the United States, enjoining upon chief clerks in the several Departments and Bureaus, and other offices connected with the Departments, certain duties relating to the performance of the duties of the other clerks therein, and quote also a letter upon the subject addressed by the President to the Secretary of War April 11, 1845, and a circular issued thereupon by the latter on April 25, 1845. It appearing that the monthly reports of chief clerks required by section 174 of the Revised Statutes had not been made in writing since December, 1851, I, on April 23, 1887, issued a circular to the heads of Bureaus of the Department, enjoining a strict compliance with the requirements of sections 173, 174, and 175 of the Revised Statutes, and directing them to require each clerk in their respective offices to make a daily report of his (or her) attendance, and of the amount and character of work performed, and to require the respective chief clerks to submit to them a monthly report, compiled from the daily reports, showing the attendance of the clerks, the business transacted in the office during the month, the amount remaining on hand to be disposed of, etc.

The reports thus required have since been regularly made, but in the opinion of the board, based upon reports from some of the bureaus and an examination of the forms used, the circular of April 23, 1887, has been too literally construed, and that in consequence thereof labor and time have been consumed in reporting details of work, without corresponding beneficial results. The board therefore recommended the rescission of the above-mentioned circular, with other recommendations which I approved and issued in the form of a circular, dated January 21st instant, as follows:

"The circular of April 23, 1887, which requires reports to be made of work performed in the several bureaus of the Department, is hereby rescinded.

"Chiefs of bureaus are authorized to exercise their discretion in the matter of reports of work performed in their respective bureaus, having in view the duties required to be performed by chief clerks under sections 173 and 174 of the Revised Statutes."

The report of the board on the subject of "Correspondence," Appendix 12, is still under consideration, and will be transmitted in a few days.

The board in their report refer to unavoidable interruptions which retarded to some extent the progress of their labors, and, in closing, advance certain suggestions relating to the organization of the civilian force of the Department. They refer to the inadequacy of the salaries of employés in this Department, and to the propriety of a re-adjustment so as to equalize the salaries in the War Department with those in the Treasury Department. I invite attention to their remarks upon this general subject and to the views therein presented, in which I heartily concur.

It is but simple justice that employés charged with important and responsible duties, requiring in many cases professional and technical qualifications, should be paid salaries commensurate with the value of their services. The chief clerk of the Department and the chiefs of divisions in the office of the Secretary of War, as also those occupying corresponding positions in the several bureaus, should be paid higher salaries than they now receive, and a reasonable number of the higher grade clerkships (class 4) additional to those now existing should be authorized, so as to provide for the promotion of a corresponding number of clerks of the lower grades who by reason of faithful and efficient service are entitled to an increase of salaries.

I also invite attention to that portion of the report which speaks of the necessity for another stenographer in the office of the Secretary. The reasons advanced why an additional stenographer should be allowed this office are so conclusive, and the economy that would result therefrom is so plainly shown, that I deem it unnecessary to say more than that I fully concur in the views of the board upon this subject.

The necessity for an Assistant Secretary of War, for the performance of a portion of the excessive duties which now devolve upon the Secretary, is becoming more and more imperative, and I shall feel gratified if through your committee these subjects are brought to the attention of Congress.

In transmitting the report of the board, I should feel that I had neglected a duty did I fail to make acknowledgment of the very efficient manner in which the members have discharged the responsible and delicate duties with which they were charged. Their report, which embraces a variety of subjects, shows that their examinations into the methods of business took a wide range, extending to the minute details of every class of business coming under their consideration, and bears evidence of arduous labor well performed. They have pointed the way to many reforms in the business methods which will prove of enduring benefit to the public service, and I regret that I can not do more than record my appreciation of their valuable labors.

Very respectfully, your obedient servant,

WILLIAM C. ENDICOTT,
Secretary of War.

Hon. F. M. COCKRELL,
Chairman of Senate Select Committee to Examine the
Methods of Conducting Business in the Executive Departments.

REPORT OF THE BOARD.

WAR DEPARTMENT,
BOARD ON BUSINESS METHODS,
January 21, 1889.

The board on business methods has the honor to submit the following report. The board was appointed by the following order:

WAR DEPARTMENT,
Washington City, March 22, 1888.

ORDERS:

A board to consist of John Tweedale, chief clerk, War Department; L. W. Tolman, chief of the division of requisitions and accounts, office of the Secretary of War, and Jacob Frech, clerk class 4, Surgeon-General's Office, is hereby appointed to meet on the 24th day of March, 1888, and, after proper examination, to consider and report a practical plan for the more simple, speedy, and efficient transaction of the public business of the War Department and its bureaus. It is desirable that such business shall be finally disposed of with the greatest possible degree of correctness and promptness, with the least possible labor in briefing, notating, and copying, and with the smallest number of record entries and record books. It is also important that there shall be no duplication of work or repetition of copies and records in the Department.

The board will have free access to the records, and chiefs of bureaus are requested to extend such assistance as may be needed in the execution of this order.

Maurice Pechin, clerk class 1, office of the Secretary of War, will report for duty as clerk of the board.

WILLIAM C. ENDICOTT,
Secretary of War.

The board met on the day fixed in the order, and the letter from the chairman of the Senate Select Committee to Inquire into the Methods of Business in the Executive Departments was read. The letter is as follows:

UNITED STATES SENATE,
February 10, 1888.

MY DEAR SIR: The select committee of the Senate required to investigate the methods of business and work in the Executive Departments take the liberty of submitting to you the following extracts from the report to be submitted to the Senate:

The investigations of your committee have forced them to the conclusion that in the Treasury Department, the War Department, and Interior Department, and to a greater or less extent in other Departments, there are more briefings, notations, and record entries made, copying done, and record books kept than is necessary or requisite in preserving proper records of the transactions of the public business or as safeguards and checks against errors, mistakes, or frauds.

They complicate the methods of business, cause unnecessary delays in its transaction, and much unnecessary work, and add to the accumulation of files of papers and record books seldom referred to, and tend greatly to lessen the sense of responsibility on the part of employés.

Likewise, the items of business matters are required to pass through the hands of too many different officers and employés and through the hands of the same persons too often, thus causing the consumption of too much time in the disposition thereof and dividing the responsibility therefor among too many different employés. Some one clerk or employé, too often of the lower grades or classes as to salary, makes the examination and adjustment, and places his initials thereon, and all the others through whose hands the item of business may pass in its routine act simply upon the faith of the initials so made by the one clerk or employé.

Your committee found the labor and time necessary to investigate and determine all steps taken in the transaction of the multitudinous items of business matters coming before the various Departments for disposition under the present methods of business prevailing therein, and to point out the steps or links in the present system which could be left or taken out without detriment to accuracy and safety, too great to undertake with any prospect of completion in any reasonable time.

The most feasible and practical remedy your committee can suggest is for the Secretary of the Treasury and the Secretary of War to select a committee or commission of three competent, industrious, painstaking officers or employés of their respective Departments most familiar with the existing methods of business therein and with correct, prompt, and proper business methods generally, and not wedded to the idea that the age of existing methods has made them the only correct and proper ones or that any change therein will be an improvement.

This committee or commission in each Department should personally trace from inception to final disposition the various classes of public business therein transacted, and ascertain the exact number of persons, officers, or employés through whose hands the same passes, the time, attention, and labor devoted thereto by each, the kind of work done thereto by each, and the entries and records made by each. With this data plainly and fully before them, and understood by them, they ought to be able to determine with certainty, safety, and accuracy exactly what can be omitted, what necessary to be added, and the safe and proper changes to be made, and then devise and prepare judicious, safe, and correct methods for the transaction of the various classes of public business, so that they can be finally disposed of with the greatest possible degree of correctness and promptness, and with the least possible labor, briefing, notating, and copying, and with the smallest number of record entries and record books, and by passing through as few different hands as possible, etc.

When they have completed their work and prepared the report thereof, they should then present the same to the Secretary appointing them, and if approved by him, or when corrected and approved by him, after full consultation, then the Secretary should cause the methods of business so determined upon to be strictly and rigidly carried out in every bureau and division of his Department, and hold the chiefs of bureaus and divisions to a strict accountability for the adoption and enforcement of such methods.

If it should be found that legislation is necessary to adopt or carry out the proposed methods, the requisite legislation should be prepared and submitted to Congress for consideration and action.

Your committee therefore recommend to the designated Secretaries to select such committees or commissions, and give them full authority and power to make the necessary examinations and such assistance as may be proper.

Your committee have addressed letters to the Secretaries of the Treasury and of War, embodying these views and recommendations for their consideration and action.

F. M. COCKRELL,
Chairman of Senate Select Committee.

Hon. WILLIAM C. ENDICOTT,
Secretary of War.

WAR DEPARTMENT, *March 26, 1888.*

Official copy respectfully referred for the information of the War Department board appointed March 22, 1888, to report a plan for the more speedy transaction of the public business.

By order of the Secretary of War.

JOHN TWEEDALE,
Chief Clerk.

The board then proceeded to consider the method to be adopted in performing the work required. It was decided to consider the matters to be inquired into by topics, to investigate each separately, and when a conclusion was reached to report thereon to the Secretary of War, and thus proceed with the work seriatim.

To aid the board the Secretary of War issued the following circular, inviting suggestions upon the subjects to be considered:

[Circular.]

WAR DEPARTMENT,
Washington City, April 4, 1888.

A board has been appointed to consider and report a practical plan for the more simple, speedy, and efficient transaction of the public business of the War Department and its bureaus. It is desirable that such business shall be finally disposed of with the greatest possible degree of correctness and promptness, with the least possible labor in briefing, notating, and copying, and with the smallest number of record entries and record books. It is also important that there shall be no duplication of work or repetition of copies and records in the Department.

Suggestions upon any of the subjects to be considered by the board are invited, with requests that communications be sent direct to the "Chairman of the board on business methods, War Department."

WILLIAM C. ENDICOTT,
Secretary of War.

A copy of this circular was sent to each person in Washington connected with the Department, and in response thereto twenty-one replies were received, containing various suggestions, which were of value in aiding the board in its investigation.

The topics which have been considered and upon which reports have been made are as follows:

(1) Requests for requisitions upon Treasury settlement certificates. (See Appendix No. 1.)
(2) Rules and regulations for the War Department. (See Appendix No. 2.)
(NOTE.—The proposed rules were referred to the board, and after consideration of the laws and rules in force in this and other Executive Departments, certain amendments were suggested.)
(3) Certificates of deposit. (See Appendix No. 3.)
(4) Army paymasters' collections. (See Appendix No. 4.)
(5) Card-index record of the rolls of the volunteer army during the late war. (See Appendix No. 5.)
(6) Credit requisitions for repayment of money into the Treasury. (See Appendix No. 6.)
(7) Requisitions on the Public Printer. (See Appendix No. 7.)
(8) Administration. (See Appendix No. 8.)
(9) Messenger service. (See Appendix No. 9.)
(10) Supply division. (See Appendix No. 10.)
(11) Reports of work done. (See Appendix No. 11.)

The report on "Correspondence," Appendix No. 12, is under consideration.

The board continued in session until it became necessary to take a recess, in order that the members might return to their desks. The work incidental to the preparation of the annual reports and estimates, and other important business delayed reassembling until December 14, 1888. The work of investigation has been further delayed by reason of interruptions during the sessions, caused by the members being frequently consulted upon matters pertaining to their regular official duties, by the chairman being called upon to perform certain duties of the Secretary, including the signing of his mail at times during his absence, and by the occasional absence of the other two members on duty connected with the board of promotion, of which they are members. These interruptions are not peculiar to this board, but would occur with any board composed of members necessarily on duty at the place where their regular duties are performed. They are stated to account for any seeming delay in the business of the board. The investigation had to be made personally to be of value; haste was unwise, for the existing condition must not only be ascertained, but the reason for it; because an apparent improvement may have been tried in the past and found wanting, hence after investigation much study was required to determine what should be done before recommending a change, else a mistake would make all the recommendations doubtful.

With the greatest care mistakes must of necessity occur, especially in dealing with questions which can only be tested in the future, consequently the reasons for each recommendation have been fully stated, and it is hoped if put to the practical test they will prove of actual benefit in hastening the transaction of public business with the least possible expenditure of labor.

In closing this report it is remarked that no matter how perfect the system, success can be assured only through the intelligence, zeal, and fidelity of the working force. To accomplish this there should be reasonable rewards for faithful and valuable service. There should be an appropriation to pay clerks who must work overtime. An appropriation was made to pay the clerks in the Adjutant-General's Office and Surgeon-General's Office who recently worked overtime, but in other offices and bureaus there are clerks who habitually do so in order to keep their work up, and they have never received any compensation therefor. If the heads of Departments were enabled to pay the clerks salaries equal to those paid for like services by corporations and commercial establishments it is believed it would be more satisfactory than the present system; failing that, the pay of employés should be re-adjusted by Congress. There has been no re-adjustment of salaries in the War Department since the war; they should certainly be on a par with those of the Treasury, which Department was reorganized in 1875.

This great Department, with over 1,600 employés, disbursing over $40,000,000 annually, constantly passing upon economic and legal questions, the dredging of rivers, the construction of contracts, the regulation of canals, etc., has neither an assistant secretary nor a legal adviser to assist the Secretary in the determination of the multifarious questions coming before him. The necessity is great; the board can not but refer to it as bearing closely upon the questions it has been required to consider.

While considering the subject of salaries it must be stated that with the rapid growth of Washington the expense of living has increased greatly, while the salaries remain so small as to afford only a bare subsistence. Not being a commercial city, the reputation made is not known where it would be valuable in affording an opportunity to enter civil pursuits outside of Government employ at a compensation commensurate with the ability of those ambitious to succeed. So the employés naturally long for the time when the nation will say to them that having served faithfully at small salaries, they shall be cared for in their declining years. With a retired list for the civil service the *morale* would be vastly improved and every department of the Government would feel the beneficial effects of such wise and beneficent legislation. It would remove temptation, and the day when the faithful employé would be left penniless because no longer of value on account of age would be past forever. It has already been applied to the Judiciary, to the entire Army (officers and enlisted men), to the Navy, and the Marine Corps.

Either one thing or the other should be done; the salaries of competent employés should be raised to a just compensation in order that they may save something for the future, or they should be retired with pay when no longer able to perform efficient service. There are places in all the Departments filled by men who are superannuated; they are retained in service because they have been faithful and it would be a hardship to discharge them. On this subject the Secretary of the Treasury (Hon. John Sherman), in a letter dated April 7, 1880, transmitting to the United States Senate a list of the employés in the Treasury Department, says:

"I am not advised that the removal of any individuals and the appointment of others in their stead is required at this time for the better dispatch of business, except perhaps in a few cases where persons who, on account of old age and physical and mental infirmities, are not as efficient as younger men would be; but these persons have been employed a great many years and have rendered faithful service to the Government. Their removal would be accompanied with great hardship to them personally, and I do not feel justified in making the changes." (See Senate Ex. Doc. 142, Forty-sixth Congress, second session.)

Again, on March 17, 1882, the then Secretary of the Treasury (Hon. Chas. J. Folger), in a letter transmitting a similar list, says:

"There are cases where persons who, on account of old age and physical and mental infirmities, are not as efficient as younger men would be; but these persons have been employed for years and have rendered faithful service to the Government. Their removal would be accompanied with great hardship to them personally, and I do not feel justified in making the changes." (See Senate Ex. Doc. 138, Forty-seventh Congress, first session.)

The board can add nothing to what has been so well expressed, except to say what is self-evident, that the places of employés of the class mentioned could be filled by younger and more efficient men to the benefit of the Government, and to add the recommendation that Congress, by appropriate legislation, may afford relief to the Departments and at the same time provide for this worthy and faithful class of employés.

Finally, the board desires to express its appreciation of the valuable services rendered by Mr. Maurice Pechin, clerk of the board. In addition to clerical ability, he is an excellent stenographer, capable of correctly reporting testimony, and has in consequence been of great service in the investigations of the board. Since October 25, 1888, he has been on duty with the court of inquiry appointed "to examine into and report upon the entire subject of the lining of the tunnel extension of the Washington aqueduct." He has reported much of the testimony taken by the court, and the board is informed that his services have been eminently satisfactory. It is not possible for one stenographer to take testimony for an entire day and have the record ready for the next day, and, therefore, to enable the court to meet on successive days, it became necessary to contract with a firm of stenographers in this city to do part of the work of reporting. When the court adjourns his services are desired by the Board of Ordnance and Fortifications, which Board will be in session for an indefinite time. The foregoing shows the necessity for another stenographer in the office of the Secretary of War. One is now provided by law, but the business of the Department requires two, and it will be more economical to provide for two than to contract for such services when they are needed in a pending investigation. The annual compensation ($1,800) paid to stenographers in the Departments would be exceeded in less than two months at the ruling rate, 25 cents per folio, paid to stenographers employed under contract.

Respectfully submitted.

JOHN TWEEDALE,
L. W. TOLMAN,
JACOB FRECH,
Members of Board.

Hon. WILLIAM C. ENDICOTT,
Secretary of War.

APPENDICES.

APPENDIX No. 1.

REQUESTS FOR REQUISITIONS ON SETTLEMENT CERTIFICATES.

WAR DEPARTMENT,
BOARD ON BUSINESS METHODS,
April 18, 1888.

SIR: Mr. Tolman, chief of the division of requisitions and accounts, brought to the attention of the board on business methods a matter of routine in reference to bureau action on settlement certificates, which in his opinion could be simplified to the benefit of the service.

Settlement certificates are a statement of claims as allowed by the accounting officers of the Treasury. When money is available the certificates pertaining to the appropriations under the jurisdiction of the War Department are sent by the Auditor to this Department for payment. Such certificate is sent to the bureau to which it pertains for appropriate action.

Upon personal investigation by the board it is found that in some of the bureaus a certificate to which no objection is found is returned to the Secretary of War, with a notation on the back of the certificate that it has been "noted" or "verified" in the bureau. In several of the bureaus, however, it is the custom to return the certificate to the Secretary of War with a letter signed by the chief of the bureau, setting forth in detail the information already fully and clearly stated in the certificate, viz, the name and address of the claimant, the number of the certificate, the amount found to be due, and the appropriation to which chargeable, and formally requesting the Secretary of War to issue a requisition on the Secretary of the Treasury for the amount.

In one bureau separate letters are so prepared for each claimant named on a certificate. As certificates sometimes embrace four or five different claims, that number of letters accompany the certificate.

All of the chiefs of bureaus agree that these letters of request are entirely useless and can be dispensed with, and thus save considerable labor.

It is accordingly recommended that the custom of issuing letters of request upon settlement certificates by the bureau officers be discontinued, and that the certificates be returned with an indorsement, which may be stamped upon the back of the certificate, showing that it has been "noted," with the name of the office and date. If objections exist to the certificate under section 191, Revised Statutes, they should be stated in the indorsement.

Very respectfully,

JOHN TWEEDALE,
L. W. TOLMAN,
JACOB FRECH,
Members of Board.

Copies of settlement certificate, letter of request for requisition, and requisition referred to are herewith submitted.

Hon. WILLIAM C. ENDICOTT,
Secretary of War.

Copy of settlement certificate No. 8826.

[No. of claim, 93441.

TREASURY DEPARTMENT,
THIRD AUDITOR'S OFFICE,
April 12, 1887.

I certify that there is due from the United States to John D. Patton for 44,175 lbs. of straw purchased at Fort Meade, D. T., under the provisions of his contract of May 30, 1884, at $4.75 per ton, one hundred and four dollars and ninety-two cents ($104.92).

It is suggested that a requisition now issue, in order that the Secretary of the Treasury may retain said sum of $104.92, under the provisions of the act of March 3, 1875, to await the result of any suit which may be instituted against said Patton to recover damages sustained by the United States by reason of his failure to fulfill said contract of May 30, 1884.

[Vide sett. No. ———, of this date.]

Appropriation: Regular supplies, Q. M. D., 1885.

Payable to ——— ———, as appears from the statements and vouchers herewith transmitted for the decision of the Second Comptroller of the Treasury thereon.

JOHN S. WILLIAMS,
Auditor.

To Hon. SECOND COMPTROLLER OF THE TREASURY.

SECOND COMPTROLLER'S OFFICE.

I admit and certify the above balance this second day of August, 1887.

SIGOURNEY BUTLER,
Second Comptroller.

Issue.

S. B. H.,
Q. M. Gen'l.

Noted: Q. M. G. O., April 9, 1888.

To be reported for appropriation.

JAMES GILLISS.
Major and Qr. Mr., U. S. A.

Copy of "request" for requisition.

$104.92.

WAR DEPARTMENT,
OFFICE OF THE QUARTERMASTER-GENERAL,
Washington City, April 10, 1888.

To the SECRETARY OF WAR:

SIR: Please cause a requisition for the sum of one hundred and four and $\frac{92}{100}$ dollars to be issued in favor of John D. Patton.

To be retained by the Secretary of the Treasury, as per annexed statement of the Second Comptroller and Third Auditor, No. 8826, '87.

To be charged as follows, viz: To the appropriation for regular supplies, Quartermaster's Dept., 1885 and prior years, $104.92.

Respectfully,

S. B. HOLABIRD,
Quartermaster-General, U. S. Army.

12718, '87.
Entered April 11, 1888, Q. M. G. O.

Copy of requisition.

Sett. Requisition No. 437.

WAR DEPARTMENT.

To the SECRETARY OF THE TREASURY:

SIR: Please to cause a warrant for one hundred and four dollars and ninety-two cents to be issued in favor of John D. Patton, the amount to be withheld by the Secretary of the Treasury to await the result of any suit that may be instituted against said Patton, to recover damages sustained by the U. S. by reason of his failure to fulfill his contract, May 30, 1884, to furnish straw at Fort Meade, D. T., due on settlement, as per certificate of Second Comptroller, No. 8326. To be charged to the undermentioned appropriations.

Given under my hand this 14th day of April, 1888.

WILLIAM C. ENDICOTT,
Secretary of War.

$104.92.

Countersigned.

————— —————,
Second Comptroller.

Registered.

————— —————,
Third Auditor.

Regular supplies, Quartermaster's Department, 1885 and prior years, $104.92.

12713—1887.

The action taken by the Secretary of War upon the recommendation of the board appears in the following circular:

[Circular.]

WAR DEPARTMENT,
Washington City, April 19, 1888.

Hereafter the custom of issuing "requests" by the chiefs of Bureaus of this Department for requisition upon Treasury settlement certificates in cases where no objection to payment is known will be discontinued, and said certificates will be returned to the Secretary of War by indorsment, which may be written or stamped upon the same, showing that it has been noted. If objections are known, they should be indorsed upon the certificates for the action of the Secretary of War, under section 191 of the Revised Statutes.

By order of the Secretary of War.

JOHN TWEEDALE,
Chief Clerk.

APPENDIX No. 2.

RULES AND REGULATIONS OF THE WAR DEPARTMENT.

(1) The office hours are from 9 a. m. to 4 p. m., with a recess of half an hour at noon. One clerk at least must remain on duty in each room during recess, and will be permitted to be absent for half an hour thereafter. All other time absent must be with proper permission or satisfactorily explained.

(2) When unavoidably absent, employés must inform their immediate superiors of the cause, in writing, at the earliest practicable moment.

(3) When public business requires the attendance of employés in excess of the regular office hours, they must be present, and note will be made of the number of hours of such extra attendance.

(4) Visits to other rooms, except on public business, are prohibited.

(5) Smoking, discussion, or loud talking is strictly prohibited.

(6) The use of intoxicating liquors to such an extent as to cause unfitness for duty, or other habits having the same effect, will serve as a reason for discharge.

(7) Employés not habitually correct in their work will be recommended for discharge.

(8) A courteous demeanor must be maintained toward all persons.

(9) All files, books, etc., when used, must be immediately replaced in their proper places.

(10) Private business is not to be transacted in the public office, and the reading of books and newspapers will not be permitted except when required in the transaction of business.

(11) Visitors will not be allowed in the rooms in which the clerks are employed, except by permission of the proper officials.

(12) The official records and business of the Department are strictly confidential, and are not to be disclosed or made the subject of conversation out of the office, nor in the office, except so far as necessary to the proper discharge of the public business.

(13) The clerks are expected to study the work upon which they are engaged, and in each branch or division one clerk must be so instructed as to be able to take charge during the absence of his chief.

LEAVES OF ABSENCE.

(14) The act of Congress approved March 3, 1883, provides: * * * "All absence from the Department on the part of said clerks or other employés, in excess of such leave of absence as may be granted by the heads thereof, which shall not exceed thirty days in any one year, except in case of sickness, shall be without pay."

(15) Leaves of absence will be calculated by calendar years.

(16) Only the head of the Department can grant leave of absence, but chiefs of bureaus and the chief clerk of the Department may grant leave by his authority. All applications for leave of absence exceeding sixty days must be submitted to the Secretary of War.

(17) Leaves of absence will not be granted, except in special cases, between the 15th day of November and 1st day of May.

(18) Leaves of absence will be recommended in such order as shall interfere as little as possible with the public business; and chiefs of bureaus will not permit over 25 per cent. of their force to be absent at one time, unless in their judgment a larger percentage can be absent without detriment to the service.

(19) The entire service during the year of those transferred from another bureau or Department will be considered in granting leaves of absence.

(20) Employés who have been in the service of the Government less than one year may be granted leave of absence at the rate of two and one-half days for each month of service.

(21) The days when the Department is closed to business will not be charged when the same are included within the period of any leave of absence, other than a leave without pay.

(22) Leaves of absence for more than one day will be granted for consecutive days only, and not exceeding thirty consecutive days, except in special cases.

(23) Pay will be allowed for absence caused by sickness, if it does not exceed thirty days in any calendar year, provided such absence is explained to the satisfaction of the chief of the bureau or head of the Department.

(24) Pay will be stopped for absence in excess of the time allowed by these regulations; but application may be made for the amount stopped, accompanied by a proper medical certificate. The application must be forwarded through the proper channels, and chiefs of bureaus are requested to express their views thereon for the information of the Secretary of War.

(25) Chiefs of bureaus are authorized to make such rules, not inconsistent with the foregoing, as may be necessary for the government of the employés on duty in their respective offices.

WILLIAM C. ENDICOTT,
Secretary of War.

WAR DEPARTMENT, *June 4, 1888.*

APPENDIX No. 3.

CERTIFICATES OF DEPOSIT.

WAR DEPARTMENT, BOARD ON BUSINESS METHODS,
June 7, 1888.

Hon. WILLIAM C. ENDICOTT,
Secretary of War:

SIR: The subject of routine in regard to certificates of deposit having been brought to the attention of the board, the following report is submitted.

CERTIFICATES OF DEPOSIT.

Certificates of deposit arise under section 3621 of the Revised Statutes (embodied in paragraph 1598 of the Army Regulations of 1881), which directs that "every person who shall have moneys of the United States in his hands or possession shall pay the same to the Treasurer, an assistant treasurer, or some public depositary of the United

States, and take his receipt for the same, in duplicate, and forward one of them forthwith to the Secretary of the Treasury."

Such certificates are issued to officers of the Army in duplicate. The original is sent by the depositor to the Secretary of the Treasury, and by him to the Secretary of War for designation of the appropriation to which the money pertains. The duplicate is retained by the depositor. They embrace two classes of public funds:

(1) Moneys deposited to the credit of the United States or of the Treasurer of the United States, which can not be again withdrawn from the Treasury without a subsequent appropriation by Congress.

(2) Moneys deposited to the credit of the United States or of the Treasurer of the United States, which may be drawn out again upon the requisition of the Secretary of War without a subsequent appropriation.

A synopsis of the several laws governing the disposition of the proceeds of Government property is appended to this report. (Exhibit A.)

Receipts issued by a depositary to a disbursing officer for funds deposited to his credit in his official capacity, and subject only to his check in that capacity, should not be confounded with certificates of deposit referred to in this report. They are more properly designated as "disbursing officers' receipts" (par. 1602, A. R., 1881). They are not issued in duplicate, and are retained by the disbursing officer.

The following statement shows the various steps taken in consecutive order from the beginning of action upon a certificate of deposit pertaining to the Quartermaster's Department to the final disposition thereof:

Capt. A. H. Young, an assistant quartermaster, U. S. Army, on duty at Columbus Barracks, Ohio, in March, 1888, made a sale of fuel and cloth to officers of the Army at that station. Fuel is furnished to the Army out of the appropriation "Regular supplies, Quartermaster's Department," and cloth from the appropriation "Clothing, camp, and garrison equipage," and the proceeds of sales to officers are by sections 3618 and 3692 of the Revised Statutes, permitted to revert to the appropriation out of which they were originally purchased.

The proceeds of sales to officers are usually collected monthly by the officer making the sale, and accordingly, Captain Young collected $36.68, and sent it to the National Exchange Bank, Columbus, Ohio, a United States depository designated by the Secretary of the Treasury, under the authority of section 5155 of the Revised Statutes. Paragraph 1599 of the Army Regulations prescribes that: "The face of each certificate will be made to show, in writing, to what appropriation the deposit belongs, provided the depositor possesses such information as may be necessary to enable the depositary to state the same in preparing the certificate for issue." Captain Young therefore sent with the money information that the same belongs, $34.64, to "Regular supplies," and $2.04 to "Clothing and equipage." The certificate is prepared in duplicate, and reads as follows:

Face of certificate.

Original.
The depositor will forward this, by the first mail, to the Secretary of the Treasury.

[Form 1. National Banks.]

No. 99. The National Exchange Bank of Columbus, Columbus, Ohio, March 31, 1888.

I certify that Captain A. H. Young, Q. M., U. S. A, ...

has this day deposited to the credit of the Treasurer of the United States thirty-six dollars on account of

Regular supplies...................................... $34.64
Clothing and equipage........................... 2.04

for which I have signed triplicate receipts.

C. J. HARDY,
Cashier.

$36.68.   Sales to officers and hosp.

Captain Young is required by paragraph 1600 of the Army Regulations to take note of "the place, date, and amount of deposit, and the number of the certificate, together with the appropriation, if specified, * * * on the account-current or other proper return upon which the depositor desires to be credited with the money."

He then mailed the original certificate direct to the Secretary of the Treasury, and retained the duplicate certificate, as authorized by section 3 of paragraph 1602, Army Regulations. When received at the office of the Secretary of the Treasury it was stamped on the back: Division Public Moneys, April 3, 1888. Received.

When recorded in that division the certificate was placed in a wrapper, the first fold of which reads as follows:

[Form No. 12, first indorsement.]

OFFICE OF THE SECRETARY OF THE TREASURY,
DIVISION OF PUBLIC MONEYS,
———— ————, 188–.

Capt. A. H. Young, inclosing certificates of deposit No. 99, issued Mch. 31, 1888, in his favor by the N. Exchange B'k, Columbus, O., for ———— ————, $36.68.

TREASURY DEPARTMENT, SECRETARY'S OFFICE,
April 3, 1888.

E. B. D. Respectfully referred to the Hon. Secretary of War for designation of the proper appropriation to the credit of which the amount of the within certificate should be covered into the Treasury.

By order of the Secretary:

E. B. YOUMANS,
Chief Clerk.

The certificate and wrapper were inclosed in an envelope addressed to the Secretary of War and sent by mail through the city post-office to the War Department, where they were received at the record division, office Secretary of War (room No. 65, War Department, west wing), at 9 a. m., April 5, 1888. The envelope was opened by the chief of the record division, who, finding that it was a certificate of deposit (which is not entered in the record division), placed it in the box of the requisition division, from which papers are taken at intervals during the day by messenger to the requisition division, and who placed it in the basket on the desk of the chief of the division, room No. 60, War Department, west wing. The chief, or assistant, seeing the character of the case, immediately passed it to the docket clerk, room 59, who stamped it:

"War Department. Division of Requisitions & Accounts. Apr. 5, '88. 6331."

After stamping all such cases on hand, as above, he then stamped the docket number within the circle of the above stamp "6331," giving wrappers and certificates the same docket number, and when all were stamped made the following entry on the "docket book," which is the "letters received" of the requisition division, and contains a brief entry of all cases received in said division:

Page 114 of docket book, requisition division, for 1888.

| Received. | Number. | Name. | Subject settlement certificates, &c. | | Interlocutory. | Sent— | | Number of requisitions. |
			No.	Amount.		To whom.	Date.	
1888. Apr. 5 ...	6329 to 6353.	Certificates of deposit. See Record, &c., Cert. Dep. Book.	*	*	*	R.....	1888. 5	*
*	*	*	*	*	*	*	*	*

This form shows also the printed headings of the columns.

The docket clerk then passed the cases 6329 to 6353 to the clerk in the same room in charge of certificates of deposit, who entered the certificate on the "record of certificates of deposit," giving docket number, date of receipt, number of certificate, where deposited, amount, and date of reference to the bureau to which it pertains.

Record of certificates of deposit.

[Page 104.]

Docket No.	Received. M|D	No. of certificate.	Where deposited.	Amount.	Adj. Gen. Sent M|D	Adj. Gen. Back M|D	Q.M. Gen. Sent M|D	Q.M. Gen. Back M|D	Paym'st'r Gen. Sent M|D	Paym'st'r Gen. Back M|D	Com. Gen. of Sub. Sent M|D	Com. Gen. of Sub. Back M|D	Chief of Ord. Sent M|D	Chief of Ord. Back M|D	Returned to Treasury per indorsement.
1888 6331	4	5.99	Columbus, O.	36.68	...	...	A. H. Young, capt. and A. Q. M. 4|12	4|25	...	...	...	...	...	...	Apr. 28, '88.

This form shows also the printed headings of the columns.

He wrote on the certificate and wrapper "104" (the page which shows the entry), and charged the certificate on the wrapper in red ink to the "Q. M. G." He then placed it in an envelope addressed to the Quartermaster-General, where it remained until the work of the day was completed, when the envelope was sealed and placed in the delivery box on the desk of the docket clerk. The envelope was then carried by the division messenger to the room of the chief clerk, Quartermaster-General's Office, No. 111, third floor, War Department, west wing, who sent it to the clerk in charge of the accounts branch, fifth floor, center wing, No. 69, by whom it was handed to the clerk in charge of the records of certificates of deposit, who stamped on the certificate and wrapper the office stamp, showing date of receipt:

B.	Qr. Mr. General's Office.	
		1888.
119	Received Apr. 12.	

NOTE.—These certificates were until recently first entered on the book of "Letters received" like other communications.

He then examined the certificate to see whether it contained the information necessary to enable him to designate the appropriation. When a certificate does not contain this information (a rare occurrence), he examines the money accounts and property returns filed in the office.

In the case under consideration the certificate bore on its face all the necessary data, and he indorsed upon the back of it the following entry:

```
Regular supplies ..................................................... $34.64
Clothing and equipage................................................   2.04
                                                                       ------
                                                                        36.68
```
1888. [Sales to officers].
And on the second fold of the wrapper:

       [2d indorsement.]   C. G. S.
              WAR DEPARTMENT,
           QUARTERMASTER-GENERAL'S OFFICE,
                 April 24, 1888.

Respectfully returned to the Hon. Secretary of War with the appropriation designated as follows, viz:

```
Regular supplies ..................................................... $34.64
Clothing and equipage................................................   2.04
                                                                       ------
                                                                        36.68
```
1888. [Sales to officers.]

                   S. B. HOLABIRD,
                 Qr. Mr. General, U. S. A.

B. p. 978.

The indorsement on the wrapper containing the certificate was then initialed by the principal clerk of the branch and also by the officer in charge of the branch, and signed by the Quartermaster-General. This indorsement was then type-written on a loose sheet of "letters sent," and the certificate and wrapper returned to the clerk who prepared the indorsement, who then entered the certificate upon one of the records of certificates of deposit, of which there are two kept in this branch; one being for certificates on account of sales to officers and sales at auction, and the other on account of refundments, unexpended balances, and repayments to appropriation.

The certificate in question was entered on the former book, the entry being as follows:

Record of sales of public property to officers and at public auction.

File number.	Character and date of sale.	By whom sold.	Number of C—D.	Where deposited and date of deposit.	Amount of C—D.	Fiscal year designated.	When received.	When returned to War Dept.	Distribution of proceeds recommended.						Remarks.
									Regular supplies.	Incidental expenses.	Cavalry and artillery horses.	Barracks and quarters.	Army transportation.	Clothing and equipage.	
119	To officers, 1st quarter, 1888.	Young, A. H.	99	National Exchange Bank, Columbus, O., March 31, 1888.	$36.68	1888	April 12	April 24	34.64	...	...	...	...	2.04	

This form shows also the printed headings of the columns.

The office stamp on the wrapper and on the certificate was then completed by writing on it the number (119) of the entry on the book of certificates of deposit. He then returned it direct to the division of requisitions and accounts by messenger, and it was passed to the clerk in charge of certificates of deposit, who noted the date of its return on page 104 of the "record of certificates of deposit," first observing that the appropriations were designated on the back of the certificate, and then recorded in a book the following entry:

Moneys repaid or covered into the U. S. Treasury.

No. of inclosures.	Docket number.	Name.	Date of indorsement to Treasury.	Where deposited.	Title of appropriation.	Certificates.			Amount to be covered in and to be credited—		Cover in list.		
						Fiscal year.	Date.	No.	To depositing officer and appropriation as stated.	As "Miscellaneous receipts on account of proceeds of Government property." (see act May 3, '72).	Auditor.	Year.	Number.
1	6331	Young, A. H.	1888. Apl. 28	Columbus, O.	Regular supplies. C. and E.	1888 ...	Mch. 31 ...	99 ...	34.64 2.04				

He then partially filled out the printed form (third indorsement) on the wrapper, placed the same in a basket on the desk of the chief of division, who initialed the same and submitted it for the signature of the chief clerk. After signature the case was returned to the certificate of deposit clerk, who filled in the date of signature and charged the same to the Secretary of the Treasury on page 104 of "Record of certificates of deposit" in the last column thereof, "Ap.:l 28, 1888," placed the same in an envelope directed to the "Honorable Secretary of the Treasury, division of public moneys," to which division it was carried by messenger.

The following is the other form of the record of certificates of deposit kept in the accounts branch of the Quartermaster-General's office, referred to on page 9 of this report:

Record of certificates of deposit, on account of repayments, etc., received at Quartermaster-General's office.

Number of certificate of deposit.	Date of certificate of deposit.	By whom deposited.	Where deposited.	Amount of certificate.		Nature of deposit.	Fiscal year.	Sent to War Department.	Designation of appropriations.															When received.	Remarks.
									Regular supplies.		Incidental expenses.		Cavalry and artillery horses.		Barracks and quarters.		Army transportation.		Clothing.		National cemeteries.		Hospitals.		
				Dolls.	Cents.				Dolls.	Cents.	Dolls.	Cents.	Dolls.	Cents.	Dolls.	Cents.	Dolls.	Cents.	Dolls.	Cents.	Dolls.	Cents.	Dolls.	Cents.	188 .

Certificates of deposit pertaining to other Bureaus of the Department go through the same routine and are entered in the same books in the office of the Secretary before going to the Bureau and after their return from the same, as do those pertaining to the Quartermaster's Department.

The action on such certificates in these Bureaus is briefly described below.

In the office of the Commissary-General of Subsistence certificates of deposit are entered in a book containing the following headings:

Register of certificates of deposit of subsistence funds received at the office of the Commissary-General of Subsistence, Washington, D. C.

Date of deposit.	Name of depositing officer.	Number of certificate of deposit.	Depository.	Amount.	Received from Secretary of War.	Origin of deposit.	Appropriation noted at office of Commissary-General of Subsistence.	Returned to Secretary of War.	Date of cover-in to the appropriation at the Treasury.

But few certificates reach this Bureau, as under the provisions of the act of March 3, 1875 (18 Stat., p. 410), the proceeds of all sales of subsistence supplies are exempt from being covered into the Treasury, and are immediately available for the purchase of fresh supplies.

In the office of the Paymaster-General two classes of certificates of deposit are received; some are in response to the stoppage circular issued by the Paymaster-General, but the majority are for paymasters' collections.

The certificates of deposit arising under the stoppage circular are entered on the book of "Letters received," and returned to the Secretary of War with indorsement suggesting that they be sent to the Bureau or office making the request for the stoppage for designation of the appropriation. This class of certificates should be sent direct to the Bureau requesting the stoppage.

The other class of certificates (paymasters' collections) come directly to the finance division, where they are stamped with date of receipt, and compared with the paymaster's ledger to see whether they agree with the amounts reported on the abstract of collections. The only entry made of the certificate is in the book of "Paymasters' collections," on which are entered number of the certificate, place of deposit, date of receipt, and date when returned to the War Department.

The certificates are held until accounts for the month are in. Paymasters make their deposits at the end of the month; it is about a month after the certificate is issued before it reaches the office, and another month before the deposit requisition is issued.

The appropriations to which the deposits pertain are designated in the office in all cases. Paymasters do not designate the appropriation on the certificates. As a rule the pay-rolls forwarded by the paymaster contain the information necessary to determine the appropriation. When they do not the information is obtained by inquiry from the Bureaus to which the collection pertains.

Upon the completion of the certificate by the designation of the appropriation the wrapper is stamped "Returned," appropriation designated on certificate of deposit, Paymaster-General's office, and the papers returned to the Secretary's office.

In the office of the Surgeon-General the certificates of deposit come direct to the property division for designation of the appropriation.

Certificates of deposit of proceeds of sales of condemned property, etc. (miscellaneous receipts), are recorded in a separate book showing date, name of officer, where sold, character of the property, and disposition of the certificates, all on one line.

This book is referred to in the settlement of property accounts.

The certificates are returned with the following indorsement, which is stamped on the wrapper in each case:

WAR DEPARTMENT, SURGEON-GENERAL'S OFFICE,
PROPERTY DIVISION,
Washington, D. C., ——— 188-.

Respectfully returned to the honorable, the Secretary of War.

The amount of the within certificate of deposit should be covered into the Treasury to the credit of the appropriation for the "Medical and Hospital Department ——— and prior years," as miscellaneous receipts.

Surgeon-General, U. S. Army.

These indorsements are signed by the Surgeon-General.

The medical officers rarely indicate the appropriation on the certificate.

But few certificates of deposit of funds not pertaining to "miscellaneous receipts" are received; they are recorded in "letters received," and treated as ordinary communications.

In the office of the Chief of Ordnance certificates of deposit are entered in a register of the following form:

Date of deposit.	Name of depositor.	Place of deposit.	Amount.	Received from Treasury through War Department.	Returned to Treasury through War Department.	Covered into surplus fund.		Remarks.
						Req. No.	Date.	

The appropriation is designated by the Bureau.

In the office of the Chief of Engineers but few certificates of deposit are received. They are first entered on "Letters received," and then in a separate book of certificates of deposit, which shows the file number, name of officer, appropriation, whether repayment or proceeds of sales, date of return to War Department, ledger folio, and amount.

The amount of the certificate is also entered on the appropriation ledger.

The designation of the appropriation is entered on the back of the certificate, and is also embodied in an indorsement on the wrapper, which is signed by the Chief of Engineers, part of the indorsement being stamped, as follows:

"[―― indorsement.]

"OFFICE OF CHIEF OF ENGINEERS, U. S. ARMY,
"―― ――, 188–.

"Respectfully returned to the Secretary of War.
"This deposit is ―― ―― and pertains to appropriation for ――――.

About ten certificates are received during the month.

In the Signal Office certificates of deposit are received in the examiner's division, are stamped with date of receipt, viz:

Examiner's O. C. S. O. Division.	Received ......

Entered on book of "letters received," and also on record of certificates of deposits of the following form:

Number.	Amount.	Depository.	City	Designation.	Received O. C. S. O.	Date of certificate.	Received from War Department.	Returned to War Department.

The designation of the appropriation is indorsed on the back of the certificate, and the following indorsement stamped on the wrapper:

[―― ―― indorsement.]

SIGNAL OFFICE, WAR DEPARTMENT,
―― ――, 188–.

Respectfully returned to the honorable the Secretary of War, with the information that the appropriation to the credit of which the amount of the within certificate should be covered into the Treasury is indorsed thereon.

―― ――,
Chief Signal Officer.

The indorsement is initialed by the clerk who keeps the record of certificates of deposit, and by the officer in charge of the division, and signed by the Chief Signal Officer. A press copy of the indorsement is kept.

The accounts current of officers making the deposits are checked with the record of certificates, so that the certificates need be retained in the office only a day or two.

It appears from the foregoing that there is duplication of work and delay in the disposition of this class of business, and in order to expedite and simplify the methods of business in connection with certificates of deposit the board recommends as follows:

Let the certificate, after receipt and notation in the Treasury Department, be immediately forwarded to the Secretary of War, without a wrapper, formal indorsement or signature of the chief clerk, a simple stamp on the back of the certificate showing date of receipt at the Treasury, or fact and date of reference to the War Department, without signature, being considered sufficient.

Immediately upon its receipt in the office of the Secretary of War let it be sent to the proper Bureau without entry in any of the three books in which they are now entered in the Secretary's office (division of requisitions and accounts), viz: "docket book," "record of certificates of deposit," and "record of moneys repaid or covered into the Treasury."

Upon its receipt in the Bureau let it be immediately stamped with date of receipt, entered on record of certificates of deposit, and if the appropriation is already correctly stated on the face of the certificate as required by paragraph 1599, A. R., 1881, the indorsement of the words "appropriation designated on face" would complete the certificate; if the appropriation is not clearly stated on the face, then let it be correctly entered on the back, in accordance with information on file in or obtainable by the Bureau, with the remark "appropriation designated." The words "appropriation designated ———" and the name of Bureau can be affixed by stamp in either case, no signature being required.

The certificate should then be forwarded direct from the Bureau to the proper auditor, or if it pertains to "miscellaneous receipts," to the Secretary of the Treasury, in order that it may be "listed."

It is believed that the majority of these certificates need not remain in the War Department longer than two days; whereas under the present methods they remain in the Department a month or more.

The entries in the "record of certificates of deposit" kept in the Bureau will answer for purposes of comparison with the officers' accounts that may reach the Bureau later than the certificates.

Certificates of deposit should not be held in a Bureau longer than two working days, unless the appropriation can not be designated without examination of returns not yet in or correspondence with the depositor or other officer.

The recording of certificates of deposit on "letters received" or on "letters sent" is a duplication of work that can be dispensed with, as the record-book of certificates of deposit would appear to answer all practical purposes.

In the opinion of the board the "record of certificates of deposit" and the "record of moneys repaid or covered into the Treasury," now kept in the division of requisitions and accounts, Secretary's office, should be discontinued, as the information contained in the former book is duplicated in the books kept in the respective Bureaus, and the material information contained in the latter is duplicated in the "register of credit requisitions," kept in the division named.

In order to reduce the number of record-books it is recommended that the two books of certificates of deposit, kept in the office of the Quartermaster-General, be consolidated into one.

The forms of the two books appear on pages 10 and 13 of this report.

It appears from the books of the requisition division, Secretary's office, that during the fiscal year 1887 certificates of deposit to the number of 3,754 were received and disposed of, which required about 7,000 full signatures and as many initials on said papers. (See Exhibit B.)

While it is probably not within the province of the board to recommend a change of the form of the certificate of deposit adopted by the Treasury Department, our investigation has shown the necessity of printing on Government forms, whenever practicable, specific directions, so that it may be readily understood what to insert therein, and what to do with the form when filled out. It should not depend alone on special knowledge or experience, nor upon a search of law and regulations; the form should speak for itself, and thus save time and labor.

The board has searched the law and regulations upon the subject and finds that the regulations conflict with each other, and call for information in greater detail than is actually desired or furnished. Accordingly, we have prepared a form which it is believed will meet all the requirements of this Department, and which we suggest be transmitted to the Secretary of the Treasury for such amendment as may be deemed necessary, and that thereupon it be substituted for the form now in use. The proposed form is as follows:

Certificate of deposit.

No. ——

———————————————— 188-.

Original.

I certify that ———————————— this day deposited to the credit of the Treasurer of the United States————————————————————

dollars, on account of ————————————————————————————

——

for which I have signed duplicate certificates of deposit.

$ ————   ————————————————————————

Margin note (left of face): The depositary will state on the face hereof, from information furnished by depositor, how the money was obtained, and title and year of appropriation to which it pertains. If necessary to make explanation the depositor will briefly indorse it on the back. The depositary will forward this original by first mail to the Secretary of the Treasury without letter of transmittal.

[*Back of certificate.*]

Margin note (left of back): When received at the Treasury Department, the certificate will be stamped with the date of receipt, and sent to the proper department to designate appropriation.

If the money pertains to "miscellaneous receipts," the certificate will be returned to the Secretary of the Treasury; if it reverts to an appropriation it will be sent direct to the proper Auditor.

All stamps and indorsements to be placed hereunder.

The several paragraphs of Army Regulations (1881) relating to certificates of deposit appear as Exhibit C to this report.

Respectfully submitted.

JOHN TWEEDALE,
L. W. TOLMAN,
JACOB FRECH,
Members of Board.

EXHIBIT A.

PROCEEDS OF GOVERNMENT PROPERTY.

Section 3618, Revised Statutes, directs that "all proceeds of sales of old material, condemned stores, supplies, or other public property of any kind, except * * * shall be covered into the Treasury as miscellaneous receipts, on account of 'proceeds of Government property,' and shall not be withdrawn or applied except in consequence of a subsequent appropriation made by law."

The proceeds of sales of the following-named public property pertaining to the War Department are exempt from the provisions of the foregoing section (3618, Revised Statutes).

(1) The Chief Signal Officer may cause to be sold any surplus maps or publications of the Signal Office, the money received therefor to be applied towards defraying the expenses of the Signal Service. (Section 227, Revised Statutes.)

(2) All moneys received from the sale of commissary stores to officers and enlisted men of the Army, or from the sale of materials, stores, or supplies sold to officers and

soldiers of the Army, or to any exploring or surveying expedition authorized by law, shall respectively revert to that appropriation out of which they were originally expended, and shall be applied to the purposes for which they are appropriated by law. (Section 3692, Revised Statutes.)

(3) The proceeds of all sales of subsistence supplies shall hereafter be exempt from being covered into the Treasury and shall be immediately available for the purchase of fresh supplies. (Act of March 3, 1875, chap. 131, 18 Stat., p. 410.)

(4) In the case of sale of useless ordnance material on hand in the War Department the proceeds of which shall be turned into the Treasury an amount equal to the net proceeds of such sale is hereby appropriated for the purpose of procuring a supply of material adapted in manufacture and caliber to the present wants of the war service; and there shall be expended in the War Department, under this provision, not more than $75,000 in any one year. (Act of March 3, 1875, chap. 130, 18 Stat., 338.)

(5) The proceeds of sales of any sunken vessel or craft and cargo and all property therein, removed by the Secretary of War, shall be deposited in the Treasury of the United States to the credit of a fund for the removal of such obstructions to navigation, under the direction of the Secretary of War, and to be paid out for that purpose on his requisition therefor. (Act of June 14, 1880, chap. 211, 21 Stat., 197.)

(6) The Secretary of War is authorized to sell the unserviceable and unsuitable powder and shot on hand, and purchase similar articles with the proceeds of the sales. (Act of March 3, 1881, chap. 135, 21 Stat., 468.)

(7) All funds arising from the rent of hotel on Academy grounds, and other incidental sources, are made a special contingent fund, to be expended under the supervision of the Superintendent of the Academy, who will be required to account for the same annually, accompanied by proper vouchers, to the Secretary of War. (Mil. Acad. appropriation act of May 1, 1888, chap. 212, 25 Stat., 112.)

EXHIBIT B.

Statement of certificates of deposit received and disposed of in the requisition division, office of the Secretary of War, during the fiscal year ended June 30, 1887.

Office.	Number of certificates.	Pertaining to—		Total.
		Appropriations.	Miscellaneous receipts.	
Quartermaster-General	2407	$398,192.03	$262,131.40	$660,323.43
Paymaster-General	516	325,668.00	10.20	325,678.20
Chief of Ordnance	321	22,872.31	42,903.77	65,776.08
Signal Office	170	30,732.64	19,271.55	50,004.19
Engineer's Office	137	63,687.85	22,078.68	85,766.53
Surgeon-General	93	14,978.59	2,106.85	17,085.44
Subsistence Office	75	210,462.59	64.27	210,526.86
Office Secretary of War	20	15,171.90	8,387.70	23,559.60
Adjutant-General	15	7,054.42	16.10	7,070.52
Total	3,754	1,088,820.33	356,970.52	1,445,790.85

EXHIBIT C.

PARAGRAPHS OF ARMY REGULATIONS (1881) RELATING TO CERTIFICATES OF DEPOSIT.

1598. Every person who shall have moneys of the United States in his hands or possession shall pay the same to the Treasurer, and assistant treasurer, or some public depositary of the United States, and take his receipt for the same, in duplicate, and forward one of them forthwith to the Secretary of the Treasury. (R. S., sec. 3621.)

1599. The face of each certificate will be made to show, in writing, to what appropriation the deposit belongs, provided the depositary possesses such information as may be necessary to enable the depositary to state the same in preparing the certificate for issue. (G. O. 65, 1871.)

1600. The place, date, and amount of deposit, and the number of the certificate, together with the appropriation, if specified, will be noted on the account current or other proper return upon which the depositor desires to be credited for the money. (G. O. 65, 1871.)

1601. Whenever repayments are made into the Treasury from funds belonging to appropriations, the balances of which have been carried to the surplus fund under section 5 of the act of June 20, 1874, and prior acts, the accounting officers of the

Treasury will credit them to the appropriations from which they were drawn, under the designation of the year for which balances were last carried to the surplus fund, or were liable to be so carried, adding thereto the words "and prior years." (Treas. Cir. 132, 1879.)

1602. As the certificates of deposit constitute an important check upon the transactions of the different Government depositaries, and are required at the Treasury Department at the earliest possible moment for verification with the accounts of said depositaries, the following regulations concerning their future disposition are prescribed, which, as they are based upon express provisions of law, will be expected to be strictly complied with:

(1) The originals of all certificates of deposit of any and all public moneys of every character and description *except as stated in the next succeeding paragraph*, should be forwarded to the Secretary of the Treasury immediately upon their issue by the depositors [not the depositaries], who, before transmitting them, should see that their amounts correspond with the amounts actually deposited by them. No letters of transmittal will be forwarded with these certificates unless in cases where an explanation or statement of facts, which could not otherwise appear, is actually necessary. (G. O. 7, 1888.)

(2) Those issued to disbursing officers for disbursing funds deposited to their own official credit, subject to the payment of their checks, and more properly called disbursing officers' receipts, should be retained in their own possession; those issued for the transfer of funds from one Government depository to another should be forwarded to the Treasurer of the United States.

(3) Certificates of deposit issued to military officers, either on account of repayments, sales of public property, or otherwise, should be *in duplicate*, the duplicate to be retained by the depositors.

(4) In no case are certificates of deposit required to be filed with accounts rendered by Government officers to the accounting officers of the Treasury Department, nor does such a disposition of any certificates of deposit secure to the officers transmitting them proper credits in their accounts. Credits are only given officers in the settlement of their accounts upon warrants, which warrants are issued by the Secretary of the Treasury, and based upon the original certificates of deposit. In taking credit in their accounts current, however, for deposits made, officers should state specifically the date of the deposit, and the designation and location of the depository in which the deposit was made, as well as the source, etc. All original certificates of deposit in favor of military officers, the amounts of which are required to be listed and recorded in the offices of any of the heads of the Bureaus of the War Department, will immediately, upon their receipt—a record having first been made of them for verification with the proper depositary accounts—be forwarded to the head of the respective department to which the deposits pertain for designation of the proper appropriations, etc. (G. O. 10, 1874.)

1605. All officers of the Army who shall make deposits of Army funds to the credit of the Treasurer of the United States will file with the original certificate of deposit, to be forwarded to the Secretary of the Treasury, a statement showing distinctly from what source the money was derived, that is to say:

(1) If the balance of funds for disbursement, it should be so stated, and the appropriation and fiscal year correctly named.

(2) If a refundment of an overpayment, it should be stated when, by whom, and definitely upon what *money* voucher the said overpayment was made.

(3) If from stoppages on pay-rolls on account of loss, damage, etc., of property by employés, or of sales to them, for which property the depositing officer is himself responsible, the character of the property should be mentioned, the date of loss, etc., given, and a reference made, as definite as practicable, to the officer's *property* voucher accounting for the stores involved.

(4) If from stoppages on account of loss, damage, sale, etc., of property for which some other than the depositing officer is responsible, the name of the responsible officer should be given, together with a list of the persons from whom deductions were made, stating the character of the property and the amount deducted in each individual case.

(5) In like manner, deposits of funds received from other collections, from sales of supplies to officers and soldiers of the Army, or on account of losses, forfeitures, etc., will be specifically and fully explained. (G. O. 93, 1879.)

1606. A disbursing officer of one staff department or Bureau making stoppages from pay-rolls and vouchers on account of the funds or property of another staff department or Bureau will, in the absence of special instructions to the contrary, deposit the funds so received, and not leave them to be transferred upon settlement of his accounts at the Treasury. (G. O. 93, 1879.)

1607. Nothing in the foregoing paragraphs will be construed to affect the system of deposits of collections by paymasters of the Army. (G. O. 93, 1879.)

1608. Every officer who takes out a certificate of deposit for funds obtained from any sale of public property will forward, with each original certificate, a detailed statement of the articles sold and the appropriation from which they were originally purchased in the following form:

[To accompany certificate No. ——, dated ——.]

Proceeds of Government property.

Class.	Character.	Purchase appropriation.	30 June.	Amount.
1.	2.	3.	4.	5.
Total miscellaneous receipts				$

——— ———, *Depositor.*

NOTES.

1. Old material, condemned stores, condemned supplies, etc.
2. Lumber, subsistence stores, forage, instruments, etc.
3. If unknown, so state it.
4. Here state the year.
5. Amount received for item mentioned in second place.

[Circ. A. G. O., April 12, 1873.]

1624. For all such deposits (proceeds of sales) certificates of deposit in duplicate or triplicate should be issued by the several depositaries, giving the name and official title of the depositor, and stating that they are on account of "proceeds of Government property." The bureau or office to which the property appertains should also be given on the face or back of each certificate, and an explanation of the kind and amount of property sold, and the original of these certificates should always be forwarded to the Secretary of the Treasury as soon as they shall have reached the depositor. (G.O. 81, 1872.)

1626. The furnishing of stores or public property from one Bureau or Department of the Government is not regarded as a sale. If money is received therefor, it can be used to replace such stores, and will be reported for cover-in to the credit of the appropriation from which the stores were originally purchased. (G. O. 20, 1874.)

1681. All funds received from sales, refundments, or miscellaneous sources, except as hereinafter provided, will be at once deposited in the nearest United States depository to the credit of the Treasurer of the United States on account of the appropriation to which it belongs, if any, and receipts taken therefor. The original receipt will be forwarded forthwith to the Secretary of the Treasury, and should show, if possible, to what particular appropriation the money belongs, and for what year. For funds thus deposited officers will take credit on their accounts current. (G. O. 14, 1882.)

The action taken by the Secretary of War and the Secretary of the Treasury upon the recommendations of the board, relative to certificates of deposit, appears in the following letter dated June 14, 1888, circular of June 21, 1888, and orders of June 18, and July 11, 1888.

WAR DEPARTMENT,
Washington City, June 14, 1888.

SIR: With reference to "certificates of deposit" which are referred by you to this Department "for designation of the proper appropriation to the credit of which the amount of the within certificate should be covered into the Treasury," it seems possible to simplify the routine pursued with advantage to the speedy transaction of business, and without detriment to the public service; accordingly I have the honor to invite your attention to the following extract from the report on the subject of the War Department board on business methods:

"Let the certificate, after its receipt and notation in the Treasury Department, be immediately forwarded to the Secretary of War, without a wrapper, formal indorsement, or signature of the chief clerk; a simple stamp on the back of the certificate, showing date of receipt at the Treasury, or fact and date of reference to the War Department, without signature, being considered sufficient."

When the appropriation is designated on the back of the certificate in the proper bureau of this Department, it should "be forwarded *direct from the bureau to the proper Auditor* in order that it may be listed."

Upon investigation the board finds that the wrapper which is placed on the certificate of deposit in the Treasury Department receives in this Department two signatures and two sets of initials; is noted on five different books, and the wrapper indorsement on one additional book, and that from three to six weeks elapse before the certificate is returned to the Treasury Department.

Besides the signatures in this Department, three signatures are placed on the wrapper in the Treasury Department before the deposit requisition is issued.

If the proposed change meets with your approval, it is believed that a considerable saving of time and labor (in both Departments) can be effected without sacrifice of accuracy, as it is intended to dispense entirely with the signatures and initials and the entering on five record books in this Department, and in lieu thereof to note the proper appropriation on the back of the certificates, unless it already appears on the face thereof, and to at once forward them direct to the proper Auditor, or, if "miscellaneous receipts," direct to the office of the Secretary of the Treasury within a few working days after their receipt in this Department.

Your attention is also respectfully invited to the following extract from the report of the board suggesting a change in the form of the certificate of deposit:

"While it is probably not within the province of the board to recommend a change of the form of the certificate of deposit adopted by the Treasury Department, our investigation has shown the necessity of printing on Government forms, whenever practicable, specific directions, so that it may be readily understood what to insert therein and what to do with the form when filled out. It should not depend alone on special knowledge or experience, nor upon a search of law and regulations; the form should speak for itself, and thus save time and labor.

"The board has searched the law and regulations upon the subject and finds that the regulations conflict with each other, and call for information in greater detail than is actually desired or furnished. Accordingly, we have prepared a form which it is believed will meet all the requirements of this Department, and which we suggest be transmitted to the Secretary of the Treasury for such amendment as may be deemed necessary, and that thereupon it be substituted for the form now in use. The proposed form is as follows:

Certificate of deposit.

No. ——

————————————————, 188 .

Original.

I certify that ———————————— this day deposited to the credit of the Treasurer of the United States ————————————
dollars on account of ————————————

for which I have signed duplicate certificates of deposit.

$ ——

[Back.]

Very respectfully, your obedient servant,

WILLIAM C. ENDICOTT,
Secretary of War.

The SECRETARY OF THE TREASURY.

[Circular.]

WAR DEPARTMENT, *June* 21, 1888.

The following letter of the Secretary of the Treasury, concerning the action on certificates of deposit, is published for the information and guidance of all concerned:

TREASURY DEPARTMENT, OFFICE OF THE SECRETARY,
Washington, D. C., June 19, 1888.

SIR: I have the honor to acknowledge the receipt of your letter of the 14th instant suggesting, as a means of simplifying the routine pursued relative to certificates of deposit referred to your Department for designation of appropriation, that the certificate, after its receipt and notation in this office, be immediately forwarded to the Secretary of War, without a wrapper, formal indorsement, or signature of the chief clerk; that when the appropriation is designated on the back of the certificate by the proper bureau of your Department it be forwarded direct from the bureau to the proper auditor in order that it may be listed, and that when the *whole or any part* of the amount of the certificate of deposit is to be covered into the Treasury as a miscellaneous receipt such certificate be returned direct to this office, the miscellaneous receipt to be listed here and the certificate then referred to the proper auditor, when a part is to be listed by him.

The suggestion meets with the approval of this office; the loss or mislaying of a certificate occasions considerable delay and annoyance, and it is thought the wrapper is a safeguard against such possible loss, but if it is fully understood in the several bureaus of your Department that prompt action be taken whenever the certificates are received, and that the certificates will be promptly indorsed and forwarded to their destination, the wrapper may be dispensed with, and in lieu thereof the certificates be sent to your office each day in an envelope, without any official signature, but with simply a notation on the envelope of the number of certificates contained therein. A note, however, will be made each day on the books of this office opposite each certificate entry, showing date of reference to the War Department.

It is not deemed practicable to change the form of certificate by printing thereon the instructions as suggested.

Respectfully, yours,

C. S. FAIRCHILD,
Secretary.

The SECRETARY OF WAR.

Upon receipt of the certificates in a bureau they will be examined, and if the appropriation is correctly stated on the face, they will be stamped on the back "appropriation designated on face," with name of bureau. If not correctly stated on the face the appropriation will be designated on the back; in this case the stamp should read "appropriation designated."

Except in unavoidable cases certificates of deposit will be sent to the proper auditor or returned to the Secretary of the Treasury within two working days after their receipt in the bureau.

By order of the Secretary of War:

SAML. HODGKINS,
Acting Chief Clerk.

WAR DEPARTMENT,
June 18, 1888.

ORDERS:

From and after this date the books "Record of certificates of deposit" and "Moneys repaid or covered into the Treasury," heretofore kept in the division of requisitions and accounts, will be discontinued.

By order of the Secretary of War:

SAM'L HODGKINS,
Acting Chief Clerk.

GENERAL ORDERS, } HEADQUARTERS OF THE ARMY,
No. 52.   } ADJUTANT-GENERAL'S OFFICE,
Washington, July 11, 1888.

By direction of the Secretary of War paragraph 1608 of the Regulations is revoked.

By command of General Sheridan:

R. C. DRUM,
Adjutant-General.

APPENDIX No. 4.

ARMY PAYMASTERS' COLLECTIONS.

[Memorandum.]

WAR DEPARTMENT,
BOARD ON BUSINESS METHODS,
June 22, 1888.

In considering the subject of certificates of deposit the board noticed that in paymasters' collections funds pertaining to appropriations other than "Pay, etc., of the Army," with two exceptions, are covered into the Treasury to that fund, and after such cover-in are, through a long routine of labor, drawn out of that appropriation and covered into the appropriation to which they belong. The course pursued is shown in the following statement:

Private Charles Goodrich, engineer battalion, having received transportation from Fort Leavenworth to New York City at a cost of $28, that amount is made a charge against him, and is collected by the paymaster, F. S. Dodge, who deposits the same with other collections for April, 1888, the whole amounting to $750.93, to the credit of the Treasurer of the United States. The paymaster reports said collection in his "Abstract of collections," which he forwards monthly with his accounts to the Paymaster-General. Upon receipt of the certificate of deposit in the Paymaster-General's Office, an examination is made of the "Abstract of collections" for April, 1888, and the amount of the certificate ($750.93) is designated as pertaining to "Pay, etc., of the Army, $403.36," "Clothing and equipage, $346.40," and "Arming and equipping the militia, $1.17." The $28, although belonging to "Army transportation," is designated as belonging to "Pay, etc., of the Army," and is covered into the Treasury by deposit requisition to the credit of said appropriation. The Paymaster-General then writes to the Quartermaster-General as follows:

[Letters sent. Form 11.]

WAR DEPARTMENT,
PAYMASTER-GENERAL'S OFFICE,
Washington, June 13, 1888.

SIR: The appropriations subject to control of your office are entitled to the benefit of the sums collected, as stated below, in the account of Maj. F. S. Dodge, paymaster, U. S. Army, for April, 1888, and included in the amount of his "Abstract of collections" deposited by him to the credit of the Treasurer United States. The same having been designated on the deposit certificate for cover-in to "Pay, etc., of the Army, 1888," I have the honor to request that you take the steps necessary to transfer the amounts to the credit of the appropriation to which they belong.

Voucher.	Name.	On what account.	Amount.
1157	Charles Goodrich, second-class private, Company C, Engineers.	Transportation from Fort Leavenworth, Kans., to New York City.	$28.00

Very respectfully, your obedient servant,

WM. B. ROCHESTER,
Paymaster-General, U. S. Army.

The QUARTERMASTER-GENERAL, U. S. ARMY.

And the Quartermaster-General indorses this letter as follows:

[First indorsement.]

C. G. S.

WAR DEPARTMENT,
QUARTERMASTER-GENERAL'S OFFICE,
June 15, 1888.

Respectfully submitted to the honorable the Secretary of War, recommending that the amount be transferred from the appropriation "Pay, etc., of the Army, 1888," to "Army transportation, 1888," $28.

The paper is then sent to the office of the Secretary of War, where it is taken up on the docket book, division of requisitions and accounts, as No. 11305, received June 19, 1888, and indorsed with a stamp.

[Second indorsement.]

WAR DEPARTMENT,
June —, 1888.

Respectfully forwarded to the Second Auditor of the Treasury for settlement, as recommended by the Quartermaster-General.
By order of the Secretary of War.

————— —————,
Chief Clerk.

After being initialed by the chief of the division and signed by the chief clerk, the indorsement is press-copied in the requisition division and the paper placed in an envelope for delivery to the Auditor. The Second Auditor then prepares a settlement certificate that there is due from the appropriation for "pay, etc., of the Army, 1888" to appropriation "Army transportation, 1888," the sum of $28, for which a transfer requisition will be issued to draw the amount from the first named appropriation, and a counter requisition to credit the same to the last named appropriation. The certificate is then sent to the Second Comptroller, who admits and allows "the above reported balance" and signs the same. The settlement is then returned to the Second Auditor's office, where it is registered, and it is then sent to the office of the Secretary of War, and taken up on the docket book of the requisition division. The amount being a charge against the appropriation "pay, etc., of the Army," the settlement is sent to the Paymaster-General's office, who stamps the same, notes the charge, and returns it to the requisition division. The amount being also a credit to "Army transportation, 1888," the settlement is sent to the Quartermaster-General's office, where it is stamped, noted, and returned to the requisition division.

The settlement, after being checked by the book-keeper, is then ready for requisition, and the requisition clerk makes out two requisitions, "transfer" and "counter," and after these are compared they are placed in a basket for the Secretary's signature. After signature the "transfer" is entered in the "Second Auditor's register of pay requisitions" and the "counter" in the "register of credit requisitions," compared, and charged on the docket book to the Second Comptroller. Similar entries are made on the registers of requisitions in his office. The requisitions are initialed by a clerk and signed by the Comptroller. The settlement and transfer requisition is then sent to the Second Auditor's office for registry and signature of the Second Auditor, where the settlement is filed. The counter requisition is sent to the Third Auditor's office, where it is registered and initialed by the chief of division and signed by the Auditor. The transfer and counter requisitions next meet in the warrant division, office Secretary of the Treasury, where transfer and counter warrants are prepared and attached to the requisitions, initialed by the chief of division, signed by the Secretary or Assistant Secretary, and registered. They are then sent to the First Comptroller for counter signature, "if warranted by law," and then to the Register of the Treasury to be registered.

The further steps, before the funds are drawn from and repaid to the respective appropriations, it is not necessary here to follow. It is sufficient to state that all the duplication of work and records, initials and signatures can be obviated if the Paymaster-General will designate on the certificate of deposit all the appropriations to which the funds belong.

Respectfully submitted to the honorable Secretary of War.

JOHN TWEEDALE,
L. W. TOLMAN,
JACOB FRECH,
Members of Board.

The views of the board were concurred in by the Secretary of War, who issued the following directions:

Respectfully returned to the Paymaster-General, who will take the same action in cases of credits for all other appropriations as is now done on account of clothing and ordnance stores.

The proposed change will obviate the long and, in the opinion of the Secretary of War, entirely unnecessary routine stated in the accompanying memorandum.

By order of the Secretary of War.

SAM'L HODGKINS,
Acting Chief Clerk.

WAR DEPARTMENT, *June* 22, 1888.

APPENDIX No. 5.

CARD-INDEX RECORD OF ROLLS OF VOLUNTEER ARMY.

WAR DEPARTMENT,
BOARD ON BUSINESS METHODS,
July 24, 1888.

The board having examined into the subject of copying the regimental muster-rolls on file in the Adjutant-General's Office, find that on the 22d of March last the work of copying the military history of each officer and enlisted man from these rolls on a card-index record was commenced.

The method of work adopted is as follows: The rolls of a regiment, consisting of the field and staff, and of the several companies, covering the entire time of service, are withdrawn from the files and turned over to the clerks engaged in copying in the register (or card-index record) division, under the charge of Mr. E. A. Woodward. All the rolls of a company, consisting of the muster-in, current or bi-monthly, and muster-out rolls, together with individual and detachment muster-out rolls, are issued at the same time to a copyist, who copies on a printed form (card-index record) as much of the history of the first man named on the earliest roll as it contains. (This form, which is 11¾ inches long and 9¾ inches wide, is appended to this report as Exhibit A. For the sake of brevity it will be spoken of hereafter as a "card." In the office it is called a "slip.")

The copyist then takes a separate card for the next name on the roll, and so on until he has commenced a separate card for each man borne on the first roll. The cards are placed successively together, face down, as the entries are made, until the entire roll is copied. He then lays the copied roll aside and takes up the next in order of date, turns his set of cards face up, and copies the entry opposite the first name found on the second roll on the card pertaining to that name, and in the same manner the entry opposite the second name is copied on the card pertaining to that name, and so continues until all the entries on the second roll are copied on the appropriate cards. As a rule the names appear in the same order on successive rolls. When any roll contains a name not found on a prior roll, a card is commenced for such name. In this manner all the rolls are copied, and the entries for the same soldier all brought to one card with only one handling of each roll.

After the rolls of a company are copied they are carefully compared by two clerks, one reading from the original roll and the other examining the cards. Errors found on the cards are corrected by the comparers.

All the information on the rolls concerning a soldier is copied on his individual card except the name of the paymaster who paid him, whose surname only is usually given on the rolls.

The rolls of three regiments (the 152d, 164th, and 177th, N. Y. Vols.) have been copied as above described, and the rolls of nine other regiments (the 155th, 157th, 161st, 162d, 168th, 169th, 173d, 182d, and 186th, N. Y. Vols.) are in the hands of copyists. The cards of the 152d regiment have been bound in three volumes, averaging three hundred and forty cards each. Part I contains the field and staff, and Companies A, B, and C; Part II, Companies D, E, and F, and Part III, Companies H, I, and K. The cards are arranged in separate alphabetical order by field and staff, and by each company, making eleven alphabetical lists for the regiment.

These three volumes are now used in place of the original rolls of the regiment in furnishing information called for by the Commissioner of Pensions, Second, Third, and Fourth Auditors, Second Comptroller, Commissioner of the General Land Office, Commissary-General of Subsistence, Quartermaster-General, adjutants-general of States, Loyal Legion, Grand Army of the Republic, and individuals, for various purposes. The search for the military history of a soldier is by their use reduced to a minimum, and the original worn and tattered rolls need not be handled again for that purpose.

In view of the fact that calls for transcripts from the rolls are received at the Adjutant-General's Office from so many sources, it is the opinion of the board that a large amount of clerical work and much dpay would be saved by the printing of these card-index records as fast as a regiment is completed, and the distribution of copies to the different Bureaus requiring the information; as in that case no calls for that particular information need thereafter be made on the Adjutant-General, and the clerks now engaged in answering such calls could be relieved, one after another, and assigned to the pressing work of copying the worn muster-rolls of other regiments.

The board is also of opinion that all the cards for a regiment should be arranged in one alphabetical series instead of eleven, the order in which the One hundred and Fifty-second Regiment is bound, thus greatly facilitating the search for the record of a member of a regiment whose company or rank is not definitely known; cases which must increase in frequency with the lapse of time.

In answer to any objection that may be raised to the publication of the information borne on these rolls, on the ground that it might form a basis for the prosecution of claims against the Government, it may be stated:

(1) Nearly every State has published the military record of its soldiers who enlisted in the Union Army during the late war; and this record has been compiled in part from the rolls in the Adjutant-General's Office.

(2) The War Department has published the roll of honor, showing name, date of death, and place of interment of all soldiers buried in national and other cemeteries.

(3) Under joint resolution of March 2, 1865 (13 Stat., 570), the War Department published the Volunteer Army Register, containing the names of all volunteer officers, and showing casualties; and,

(4) In February, 1867, the Senate of the United States authorized the publication of the military history of the Union soldiers who served in regiments raised in the State of Arkansas, showing name, rank, date of enlistment, muster, discharge or desertion, date and cause of death, date and nature of wound, and the action in which wounded. (See Senate Mis. Doc. 53, Thirty-ninth Congress, second session.)

The fact that so much of the military history of soldiers of the late war has already been published, seems to remove all ground for objection to printing the record of all soldiers for the information of the officers of the Government charged with the adjudication of the claims of soldiers or their heirs. There can be no doubt whatever that the distribution of such printed copies to the different Bureaus of the Government would materially expedite the public business, and save clerical labor which is now expended in making calls in one office, searching the rolls in another, writing up the information thus found and sending it to the office making the call; while in the mean time clerks must be constantly employed on the work of mending and copying, first, the originals, and then the copies of these rolls, to prevent them from actually falling to pieces from incessant wear and tear.

When the rolls of a State have been printed in the form proposed, it will be practicable to arrange the cards in one alphabetical series for the State, thus making it possible to find the record of a soldier whose regiment may be unknown; and with the alphabetical arrangement for each State, it would not be a matter of great difficulty (except in case of common names) to find the record of a soldier whose State is unknown, by searching the alphabetical cards of each State.

In a report of the Senate Select Committee on Business Methods (Report No. 507, Fiftieth Congress, first session, pp. 182 to 192), the question of continuing the compilation of regimental registers of the volunteer forces from the muster-rolls, a work that was begun in the Adjutant-General's Office years ago, as also the question of reproducing the rolls by photography, by the platino-type process, and by printing, is fully discussed. The reasons for discontinuing the compilation of the regimental registers, and for rejecting the proposition to reproduce the rolls by any of the means suggested, are clearly and fully set forth in said report, and need not therefore be repeated here. In that report the Senate committee recommend the application of the card-index record system to these rolls, and of finally printing these cards in a condensed form and furnishing copies to all divisions and Bureaus requiring the same. The report concludes as follows:

"In the opinion of your committee this card-index record system is the solution, and the only practical, feasible, and economical solution, of the vexed question in regard to the preservation of these rolls without further wear and destruction, and the placing of the data contained in them in an easily accessible and convenient condition for use, without the handling of the rolls.

"Your committee, therefore, unhesitatingly recommended the adoption of this system to the Secretary of War and the Adjutant-General, and recommend that the work upon the volunteer regimental registers be discontinued, and all the available force of employés be placed at work in compiling from the rolls upon these card records the military history and services, etc., of the officers and soldiers whose names are borne thereon, the rolls to be taken by States, and as soon as the rolls, reports, records, etc., relating to the soldiers of any one State are completed upon these card-index records, then that the card-index records, arranged alphabetically by regiments, without regard to rank, be printed in sufficient numbers to furnish copies to all the divisions and Bureaus of all the Departments having any occasion to call for the military history, services, etc., of soldiers for any purpose in the work of such divisions and bureaus, and be prosecuted as rapidly as possible until completed as to all the States, then printed and distributed as above indicated.

"When so completed, printed, and distributed, then all the labor in the various divisions and Bureaus of all the Departments in writing applications to or calls upon the Adjutant-General for information in regard to officers and soldiers, and all the labor in the office of the Adjutant-General in searching these rolls and answering such calls can be dispensed with, and the further use, wear, and tear of the rolls will cease, and there will be no occasion to refer to or use the rolls except in case of a dispute as to the correctness of such card-index record, when the card-index record will show the particular rolls to be referred to for verification."

"The employés in any office desiring any information in regard to any soldier can by knowing his regiment and State, quickly take the printed book containing the names, record, etc., of the soldiers of that regiment and State, and find the information desired as easily and quickly as he could take a dictionary and find the definition of any word.

"This work is so important that it should be prosecuted with the greatest vigor and by every available employé, and, if necessary, there should be an additional force provided for."

It has been estimated in the Adjutant-General's Office that there are 402,916 separate rolls, or 22,384 sets of successive rolls of companies or equivalent organizations, averaging 18 rolls to a set. The total number of men furnished during the late war under the different calls of the President is reported to be 2,778,304, and there were organizations in service equivalent to 2,047 regiments of 10 companies each. (Phisterer's Statistical Record, p. 23.) Estimating that the total number of cards to be made will nearly equal the total number of men furnished, there would be 1,356 cards to each average regiment. It is thought that from 6 to 7 average cards can be printed in brevier type, in solid form, upon an octavo page (7¼ by 4½ inches); that all the cards could be printed on 463,051 such pages. To print each regiment separately will require about 2,047 volumes of 212 pages each.

The following estimate shows the cost of printing each volume:

Estimated cost of printing 300 copies of a book of 212 pages, brevier type, octavo size, 100 copies interleaved, and bound in half sheep, and 200 copies stitched and trimmed:

Composition	$416.00
Stereotyping	76.80
Press-work	13.33
Folding	6.40
Paper for 200 copies (48 pounds)	7.20
Paper for 100 copies (interleaved; 48-pound paper)	7.20
Binding and interleaving	75.00
	601.93

The cost of printing and binding the entire 2,047 volumes, at an estimated cost of $600 a volume, is $1,228,200. Omitting the cost of binding will reduce the estimate $150,000 in round numbers.

In order that the precise cost and utility of the printing of these card-index records may be practically tested, the Board recommends that the cards of the One hundred and sixty-fourth Regiment of New York Volunteers, just completed, be printed as soon as possible, and copies distributed to the various divisions and bureaus of the Departments now making calls for information from the rolls. This will cost about $600.

With the view of facilitating the work of the copyists in the preparation of the cards, the following remarks and recommendations are also respectfully submitted for consideration:

In the operation of copying a roll it was observed that the copyist unfolds it and lays it flat on his desk before him. As it is quite large, being 21 inches from top to bottom and varying in width from 22 to 31 inches, it is difficult to read all the entries on it, especially where they are closely written or obscured by blots, and the roll must consequently be frequently picked up from the desk and brought closer to the eye or the clerk must get up from his seat and lean over his desk to decipher the entry. To avoid these frequent interruptions to the progress of the work, it is suggested that a suitable cylinder be provided for each copyist, to be made of light material and of such dimensions that a whole roll can be spread out on its surface and clamped to it; the cylinder to be erected on a stand, and to be so attached that it will easily revolve; a horizontal bar or guide to be fastened to the stand, or the cylinder, on the side facing the clerk, so that he can always have the entry he is copying appear immediately above the guide. It is believed that such device will materially facilitate the work of the copyists. Possibly two small cylinders would answer the purpose better than one large one; this can be best determined by actual experiment.

It is also recommended that hereafter, when a call is received for the full military history of a soldier from the rolls of a regiment which has not yet been carded, that the searchers fill up a card for such soldier similar to and containing as full information as those prepared in the card-index record division, adding thereto, of course, the result of the search made of any other record to answer the call, and further, that a mark be then placed opposite the name of such soldier, say on the muster-out oll, to indicate that his record has been carded. These card forms should be printed in copying-ink, the record inserted in copying ink, and then press-copied, the press copy to be sent to the office making the call, with a statement stamped thereon in these or other suitable words: "This is the full military history of the soldier named herein, and is furnished in answer to the call of the Commissioner of Pensions of ———— ————.

"R. C. DRUM,
Adjutant-General."

Similar stamps should be prepared for other offices making similar calls.

After being press-copied the cards should be filed alphabetically by regiments, and when another call from any office for one of these soldiers comes in, his history need not again be searched, but the call can be answered directly from the card.

The benefit is obvious. The card-index will immediately be commenced with a large force, and what is more important, a force of skilled men. The board is informed that the copying force at present engaged on the card-index is not a skilled force, and that many mistakes are made, to be finally corrected by the comparers.

To the objection that cards made as above recommended would not be compared, we would answer that the replies now made to the Commissioner of Pensions and others are not now compared, or researched, but the call is answered upon the one search made by the skilled searcher. So the card now recommended will be made upon the one search of the skilled searcher; it will be just as accurate, just as valuable as the present system, and moreover the labor expended in the search is preserved for future use, which is a great gain. Under the present system each subsequent call received requires another original search of the rolls.

When the rolls of a regiment are taken up to be copied in the card-index record division these cards can be taken from the temporary file in the roll-room and placed with those to be made by the copyist.

During the three years, 1884-'85-'86, there were received in the Adjutant-General's office 1,106,907 calls for information from the volunteer rolls. At this rate the rolls are searched for every man in service during the war once every eight years. It will therefore be readily seen that during the past twenty years the rolls have been searched over and over again for the same information in many cases. In one case it was ascertained that there had been 15 calls at different times for information about the same man. While the time required to make a separate index-record card for a soldier, when his case is being reported on, may delay the reply to such call to some extent, there is no doubt that in a comparatively short time this delay would be compensated for by the facility with which all subsequent calls in such cases can be reported on.

ESTIMATE OF TIME REQUIRED TO COMPLETE CARD-INDEX.

The law requires 200 of the clerks in the Adjutant-General's office to be "exclusively engaged in preparing and making reports to expedite the settlement of pension applications and soldiers' claims."

There were in the Army during the war of the rebellion an equivalent of 2,047 regiments. (See Statistical Record of the Army of the United States; Phisterer, p. 23.)

Assuming that 200 clerks are engaged on the rolls of 2,047 regiments and records connected therewith, the proportion for each clerk is the rolls of ten regiments; so when the rolls of ten regiments are carded 1 man of the 200 could be spared to work with the men engaged in making the card record index if he was at work all the time on the rolls, but half of the time he is searching other records; therefore one man can not be spared until about 20 regiments are carded.

In other words, if one man is engaged half of his time in searching 10 regiments, then when 20 regiments are carded half of the time of 2 men can be spared, which is equal to the entire time of 1 man. This is more apparent when we consider that such calls as are made by the Pension and other offices, when the card-indexes are printed, will be for information from the other records of the Adjutant-General's office, and not from the rolls which have been printed. The following table shows the average number of calls received every month in the two divisions of the volunteer-roll rooms, Adjutant-General's office:

Year.	Average number of calls per month.	Number of employés.	Average number of calls answered by one clerk in one month.
1884	25,276	192	131.6
1885	28,791	176	163.6
1886	34,850	168	207.5
1887	36,794	182	202.1
			704.8
Total average number of calls answered by one clerk in one month			176.2

These calls now require a search not only of the rolls, but of other records which, it is stated, take as long to search as the rolls; consequently, when 10 regiments are carded and printed the work on 176 of the calls will be reduced but one-half, and not until about 20 regiments are carded can the services of one clerk be spared from the roll-rooms for work on the card-index record.

This conclusion agrees with the conclusion arrived at above. It introduces, however, a new element into the calculation, viz, whether there will be any falling off in the number of calls after the card-index record is printed. It would seem reasonable to conclude that there would be a large reduction, but the clerks who have been questioned answer in the negative. They say the field of inquiry or search will be reduced about 50 per cent. when the index is printed, but that the number of inquiries will remain about as at present. This impression is based upon their present experience, and while it may be correct, actual experience after the index is printed can alone determine the fact.

For the purpose of this calculation it will be assumed that one clerk can be transferred from the rolls to the card-index work when about 20 regiments are carded. He can be spared whether the index is printed or not. When carded the information in an individual case is at once available without further search.

There are 34 men engaged now (July, 1888) in making the card-index record. There were 30 engaged in the work in June (part engaged in copying and part comparing), and it is reported to the Board that this force can complete 3 regiments of infantry, equal to 30 companies, each month; so that 1 company is completed each month for each man employed. The 30 men engaged on this work in June can complete 36 regiments, equal to 360 companies, in a year. At the end of the first six months one man is added for the 18 regiments then completed.

With these elements as a basis, the following computation shows how the work will progress:

38

Force employed.	Men.	Months employed.	Companies carded.	Regiments carded by 30 men with accretions.	Regiments carded by 60 men with accretions.	Regiments carded by 90 men with accretions.	Regiments carded by 120 men with accretions.	Regiments carded by 150 men with accretions.	Regiments carded by 180 men with accretions.	Regiments carded by 210 men with accretions.	Regiments carded by 240 men with accretions.	Regiments carded by 270 men with accretions.	Regiments carded by 300 men with accretions.
Commencing with	30	6	189	36.6									
Add one man for 18 regiments carded	31	6	186	3									
Deduct one month's work for leave of absence to force													
Total for first year				33.6	67.2	100.8	134.4	168	201.6	235.2	268.8	302.4	336
Add one man for 18.6 regiments carded	32	6	192	36									
Add one man for 19.2 regiments carded	33	6	198	3									
Deduct one month's work for leave													
Total for second year				36	72	108	144	180	216	252	288	324	360
Add one man for 19.8 regiments carded	34	6	204	41.4									
Add one man for 20.4 regiments carded	35	6	210	3									
Deduct one month's work for leave													
Total for third year				38.4	76.8	115.2	153.6	192	230.4	268.8	307.2	345.6	384
Add one man for 21 regiments carded	36	6	216	43.8									
Add one man for 21.6 regiments carded	37	6	222	3									
Deduct one month's work for leave													
Total for fourth year				40.8	81.6	122.4	163.2	204	244.8	285.6	326.4	367.2	408
Add one man for 22.2 regiments carded	38	6	228	46.2									
Add one man for +22.8 regiments carded	39	6	234	4									
Deduct one month's work for leave													
Total for fifth year				42.2	84.4	126.6	168.8	211	253.2	295.4	337.6	379.8	422
Total in five years														1,910
One-half year													200.7	
Total in five and one-half years													1,017.7	
Add one man for +23.4 regiments carded	40	6	240	48.6									
Add one man for +24 regiments carded	41		246	4									
Deduct one month's work for leave													
Total for sixth year				44.6	89.2	133.8	178.4	223	267.6	312.2	356.8		

One-half year								188
Total in six and one-half years								2,072.8
Add one man for + 24.6 regiments carded	42	6	252					
Add one man for + 25.2 regiments carded	43	6	258					
Deduct one month's work for leave								
Total for seventh year			47	94	141	188	235	282	329
								1,978.2
Total in seven years								
Add one man for excess (20) over 20 regiments carded, marked +, and one man for °25.8 regiments carded	45	6	270	54.6				
Add one man for °27 regiments carded	46	6	276	4				
Deduct one month's work for leave								
Total for eighth year			50.6	101.2	151.8	202.4	253	303.6
								1,999.2
Total in eight years								
Add one man for °27.6 regiments carded	47	6	282	57.6				
Add one man for excess (30.4) over 20 regiments carded, marked o, and one man for x 28.2 regiments carded	49	6	294	5				
Deduct one month's work for leave								
Total for ninth year			52.6	105.2	157.8	210.4	263	
							1,929	
Total in nine years								
Add one man for x 29.4 regiments carded	50	6	300					
Add one man for excess (17.6) over 20 regiments carded, marked x, and one man for ⊙ 30 regiments carded	52	6	312	61.2 5				
Deduct one month's work for leave								
Total for tenth year			56.2	112.4	168.6	224.8		
Add one man for ⊙ 31.2 regiments carded and one man for excess (21.2) over 20 regiments carded, marked ⊙	54	6	324	61.4				
Add one man for ± 32.4 regiments carded	55	6	330	5				
Deduct one month's work for leave								
Total for eleventh year			60.4	120.8	181.2	241.6		
						2,009.6		
Total in eleven years								
Add one man for ± 33 regiments carded and one man for excess φ (23.4) over 20 regiments carded, marked ±	57	6	342	60 5				
Add one man for φ 34.2 regiments carded	58	6	348					
Deduct one month's work for leave								
Total for twelfth year			64	128	192			

40

Force employed.	Men.	Months employed.	Companies carded.	Regiments carded by 30 men with accretions.	Regiments carded by 60 men with accretions.	Regiments carded by 90 men with accretions.	Regiments carded by 120 men with accretions.	Regiments carded by 150 men with accretions.	Regiments carded by 180 men with accretions.	Regiments carded by 210 men with accretions.	Regiments carded by 240 men with accretions.	Regiments carded by 270 men with accretions.	Regiments carded by 300 men with accretions.
	60	6	360										
Add one man for excess (19.0) over 20 regiments carded, marked *, and one man for *34.8 regiments carded													
Add one man for excess (20.8) over 20 regiments carded, marked *	62	6	372	73.2 6									
Deduct one month's work for leave													
Total for thirteenth year				67.2	134.4	201.6							
Regiments carded in thirteen years				633.6	1,267.2	1,900.8							

From this table it appears that, commencing with 30 clerks, the average accretions have been one man every five and one-fifth months, that the force has doubled in thirteen years, and in that time the rolls of 633.6 regiments have been carded.

With 90 clerks the work can be completed in thirteen years; with 120 clerks, in eleven years; with 150 clerks, in nine years; with 180 clerks, in eight years; with 210 clerks, in seven years; with 240 clerks, in six and one-half years; with 270 clerks, in five and one-half years; with 300 clerks, in five years.

The work has been in progress but four months; with time the clerks will become more expert and the time for completion of the work can doubtless be shortened. If it should be decided to print the card-index the board is of opinion that there will be a falling off in the number of calls, which will be felt in every branch of the office where such calls are noted, searched, answered, or initialed, and the expedition with which the calls can be answered will largely reduce the inquiries made with reference to cases which have been delayed.

It is admitted that something must speedily be done to preserve the rolls. They are now so dilapidated that many of them crumble to pieces at the folds whenever they are opened. How long they will last can not be determined accurately; with the present handling, perhaps not more than eight years. To make a card-index of the rolls in eight years 180 clerks should now be put upon the work, or 150 more than are now employed. Can that number be spared without delaying other work?

To answer this question we must consider for a moment the work in the record and pension division of the Surgeon-General's office. There the card-index of hospital registers of the war period will be completed within a year, and 100 clerks can then probably be transferred to the work of card-indexing in the Adjutant-General's office. Within a year, therefore, the work can be commenced in the Adjutant-General's office with 130 clerks, and no doubt sufficient force can be added to complete it in eight years, and without any increase of appropriations.

There is another alternative which will relieve a number of clerks in the Adjutant-General's office and tend to simplify the records. In March, 1884, the Surgeon-General transferred to the Adjutant-General "all hospital registers and prescription books, and all field registers and prescription books, so called, of State and Territorial regimental volunteer organizations, also of United States white and colored troops serving as complete regiments or battalions." These were added to a mass of similar records in the Adjutant-General's office. These records contain much valuable information, but are difficult to search and take much time of the searchers. The information they contain is analogous to the information in the Surgeon-General's office, and which is now being carded. If these records were transferred to the Surgeon-General's office the information they contain could be added to the card-index now approaching completion. The transfer of these records would enable a clerk in the Adjutant-General's office to answer many more calls than at present, and consequently a number of clerks could at once be available for work on the cards.

While the board has not yet traced in detail the different classes of cases through the office, it finds that in the pension-record division 9 clerks are employed in recording calls for information from the volunteer rolls and records, and distributing them to the two divisions of rolls and records for search. This record is kept in order that the number of calls received and answered may be known, and that inquiries regarding their status may be replied to. If the 9 clerks in this division were assigned to the work of answering calls, about 70 more cases a day could be reported upon; thus lessening the number of inquiries concerning delayed cases, saving the delay of two days now caused by entering and charging out the cases in the seven books, increasing the output of the office by about 1,700 cases a month, and hastening the transfer of clerks from the work of searching the rolls to that of making index-record cards. To readily find a case the date of the call must be given, otherwise the search must be made in three books for a case one year old. If all calls were answered promptly (say within one week) it is apparent that there would be but very few inquiries about delayed cases. After the calls have been answered the records are of no use, as a second call for information concerning the same man is entered anew, the previous entry not being looked up.

In the Paymaster-General's office no record is kept of the calls (about 2,400 a month) for information from the volunteer records in his office, for the reason that to do so would delay the answering of calls. They are now simply stamped with the date of receipt and counted. If in place of the date of receipt stamp now used in the pension record division, Adjutant-General's office, an automatic numbering and dating stamp were used, it would both show the date of receipt and accurately count the cases at one operation.

The board recommends that the pension-record division of the enlisted volunteer pension branch be discontinued, and that the clerks employed therein be assigned to answering calls from the pension and other offices

The unanswered calls in the first and second divisions of the volunteer rolls and records on hand July 1, 1888, were 11,986, some of the uncomplicated pension cases being three weeks old, while some complicated pension cases are two months old, and the calls from the Second Auditor's office three months old. The board is of opinion that measures should be at once taken to bring this work up so that no calls shall remain unanswered longer than one week.

Respectfully submitted.

JOHN TWEEDALE,
L. W. TOLMAN,
JACOB FRECH,
Members of Board.

Hon. WILLIAM C. ENDICOTT,
Secretary of War.

EXHIBIT A.

Bosworth, Clement A. rank, private Co. A, 182d Reg't, New York Infantry (69th N. Y. S. N. G. A.).

Co. M. I. roll, dated.*	Age.	Rank.	Day.	Month.	Year.	Where.	By whom.	Term.
Enrolled		Private	12th	Sept	1862	New York	Capt. Sullivan	3 yrs.

* Mustered in Newport News, Va., Nov. 17th, 1862.

Remarks: On detached service in New York since Nov. 8th, 1862, by order of Col. Murphy. No. and date order unknown.

Muster roll for—	Last paid.	Bounty.		Clothing.		Remarks.
		Paid.	Due.	Date of last settlement.	Drawn since.	
1862. Nov. 17		*Dolls.*	*Dolls.*		*Dolls.*	Present. On detached service at New York since Nov. 8, 1862, by order of Brig. Gen. Corcoran. No. and date of order unknown.
Nov. 17 to Dec. 31.						Present. Not yet mustered into U. S. service. Received no pay.
1863. Jan. and Feb.						Present. Not mustered into U. S. service.
Apr. 10						Present.
Mar. and Apr.						Present. Never received any pay from date enlistment. Mustered in Apr. 29, at Suffolk, by Lient. Hunt.
May and June	Apr. 30					Present.
July and Aug.	June 30, '63					Absent. Detached in New York for conscripts by order of Gen. Heintzleman.
Nov. and Dec	June 30					Absent. Detached in New York for conscripts by order of Gen. Heintzleman.
1864. Jan. and Feb.	June 30					Absent. Detached in New York for conscripts by order of Gen. Heintzleman.
Mar. and Apr.						Present. Returned from detached service in New York and arrest for desertion therefrom. Due U. S. for clothing, $9.54; for arrest, $30.00.
May and June						Absent. Wounded May 22.
July and Aug.	Dec. 31, '63					Present.
Sept. and Oct	Aug. 31					Present. Due U. S. bounty, $27.00. Due by U. S. for clothing not drawn, $16.39.

Bosworth, Clement A., rank, private Co. A, 182d Reg't, New York Infantry (69th N. Y. S. N. G. A.)—Continued.

Muster roll for—	Last paid.	Bounty.		Clothing.		Remarks.
		Paid.	Due.	Date of last settlement.	Drawn since.	
1864. Nov. and Dec.	Aug. 31	*Dolls.*	*Dolls.*		*Dolls.*	Present. Due U. S. bounty $27.00. Due by U. S. for clothing, $16.39.
1865. Jan. and Feb.	Dec. 31, '64					Corporal. Presence or absence not stated. Charge for one cartridge-box belt.
Mar. and Apr.	Dec. 31, '64					Present. Due U. S. for clothing overdrawn $2.37. Charge for one cross-belt.
May and June	Dec. 31, '64					Present. Due U. S. for clothing overdrawn $2 37. Charge for one cross-belt.

Mustered out: With company.

Rank.	When.			Where.	Last paid.	Clothing.		Bounty.		Equipments lost, etc. Retained.
	Day.	Month.	Year.			Last settled.	Drawn since.	Paid.	Due.	
Corporal.	15	July	1865	Near Washington, D. C.	Dec. 31, 1864	Sept. 1, 1864	$54.50	25	75	$6.00

Remarks: Charge for one cross-belt. Age 27 years.

Month.	Regimental returns.	Month.	Regimental returns.

REMARKS ON REPORT OF THE WAR DEPARTMENT BOARD ON BUSINESS METHODS.

CARD-INDEX RECORDS OF ROLLS OF THE LATE VOLUNTEER FORCES.

The narrative portions of the report is an accurate description of the minutiæ of the work of transcribing on printed forms of "card-index record" all the information the rolls afford concerning the military history of a soldier.

The first recommendation of the Board is for printing the card-index records "as fast as a regiment is completed, and the distribution of copies to the different Bureaus requiring the information."

I can not concur in this recommendation, for the following reasons:

1. The time that would be required in reading and correcting proofs would necessarily retard the prompt preparation of answers to calls for information from the Pension and other Bureaus.

2. The record given in the cards, while correct so far as the rolls are concerned, is not absolutely reliable, as in many instances the entries on the rolls are reliable only when verified by other records not entered at present on the cards. As the dual primary objects of the card system are to obviate the handling of the rolls and to record in compact form the information they contain, hence no part of the record of the soldier contained in company and regimental books, and other records, is now entered on the cards, as to do so would greatly retard the copying of the rolls, which is the primary object. I desire to emphasize this fact to correct a widespread opinion that a correct abstract from the rolls furnishes a complete military history of any given man.

In view of this fact the printing of the card-index record at present would not be of benefit and the distribution of the record cards to other Bureaus would be open to serious objections and tend to confusion.

The supposed objection to the recommendation of the board, that such publication might afford the basis for the prosecution of claims is, as represented by the board, without valid ground, and is not considered.

The real objection is that the record given by the cards, while correct as to the rolls, is incomplete, and, as stated above, in many cases the entries on the rolls are shown on investigation of other records to be erroneous; while, as stated by the board, many of the States have published the military records of their troops during the late war, based, in part, on data furnished by this office; such printed records are simply historical, and it is suggested for careful consideration whether similar records printed for this office could properly be accepted by the auditing officers as the "official" basis for action.

All complex systems of necessity involve division of duties and responsibilities. It is a correct rule of our administrative systems that the auditing officers of the Government are dependent on other officers for the official information needed to enable them to pass on the validity of claims, and, therefore, even if absolutely complete military histories were now compiled in this office, the printing of such records and distribution to other Bureaus of the Government would present a grave question, as in this case. For instance, for volunteers, the military records of this office would virtually be transferred to the Pension Office, and the Adjutant-General, instead of an active executive officer, would simply become the mere custodian of the original rolls. For these reasons the further recommendation for the printing and distribution of the cards of the One hundred and sixty-fourth New York Volunteers, just completed, is not concurred in.

The next recommendation of the board is that all the cards for a regiment should be arranged in one alphabetical series instead of by companies, and the reason assigned is that such an arrangement would facilitate the search for the record of a member of a regiment whose rank and company is not remembered by him, or known to his friends; cases which, the board adds, must increase in frequency with the lapse of time.

The existing system of military records, National and State, affords such facilities for locating individual soldiers by companies that the reason given for the change to a regimental arrangement of names loses much of its force, and it is not therefore deemed advisable to change the present method of arrangement by companies, which preserves intact the unit of military organization throughout the service.

The suggestion that when the rolls of a State have been printed it will be practicable to arrange the cards in alphabetical series for the States, simply tends further to obliterate all military organizations, converting military records into a vast agglomeration of individual records without relation or co-ordination, and its supposed advantages are not commensurate with the utter impossibility, without reference to the original rolls—a reference which the card system renders unnecessary—to determine the personnel of a given command.

To facilitate the work of the copyists in the preparation of the cards the board suggests the adoption of cylinders on which the rolls may be mounted while being copied.

While no special objection is seen to giving this decision a practical test, and the size and condition of the roll (repaired, when needed, before being given to the copyist) not considered a serious drawback to the copyist, it is thought that to place a roll on the cylinder, clamp it, the continuous changing and clamping would necessarily consume more time than at present with the use of long steel rulers, readily moved from line to line as needed.

The fourth recommendation of the board is that hereafter when a call is received for the full military history of soldiers from the rolls of a regiment which has not yet been carded, that the searchers fill up cards similar to those prepared in the card-index record division, adding, of course, result of search made of any other record to answer the call. These cards to be printed in copying ink and press-copied. The press-copy to be furnished the officer making the call, while the original cards should be filed alphabetically by regiments, thus furnishing ready information for any subsequent calls in those cases.

It is not possible, in this brief paper, to do more than indicate some of the many practical reasons which should prevent the adoption of this purely theoretical recommendation.

A card-record slip is a full record of entries found opposite the name of a man on the muster-in, muster-out, and each and every intermediary muster roll; while, in a report to the Pension Office, after noting date of commencement of service, the clerk's examination of subsequent rolls is limited to observing whether the soldier is reported "present," without making a record of each entry, until he reaches a roll indicating a change of status.

One is a complete record of entries made on the original rolls, the other is a brief résumé of service, and it is hardly necessary to add that an attempt to combine them would entail great loss of time in the preparation of reports.

The card-record slip is carefully verified. The report is simply examined before being sent out. The first can be accepted as an official permanent record; the second, for obvious reasons, can not and should not.

Twelve thousand reports are made monthly. To press-copy them would divert much time from more important work, not to speak of additional time required to properly assort the originals. Another consideration is that the crowded condition of the rooms affords not an inch of space for the filing of these numerous papers.

The statement that in view of the approaching completion of the work in the pension and record division of the Surgeon-General's Office, one hundred clerks can probably, a year hence, be transferred to the record slip division of this office, is one, when the time arrives, for the action of the Secretary of War. It is unnecessary to add that such a large addition to the force would very materially increase results, and if suitable accommodations be provided, such a transfer will be highly desirable. The regular force of the record slip division is increased as rapidly as consistent with the volume of business in other divisions. The reduction of business connected with answers to calls for information from the rolls depends necessarily on the number of such calls received, and this number can not be anticipated. For instance, while the monthly average of calls received since July, 1887, has been 11,921, the number received in February, March, April, May, and October of this year has ranged from 13,174 to 17,205.

The alternative is suggested by the board that all hospital records, by retransfer to the Surgeon-General's Office, would relieve a number of clerks in this office and that such a transfer would enable the office to answer many more calls.

Prior to 1884 hospital records of every description were found in the Adjutant-General's and Surgeon-General's Offices, and with a view to a proper division of this class of records, an arrangement was carried out, with the sanction of the Secretary of War, whereby all records of *regimental* hospitals then with the Surgeon-General were transferred to this office, while to his office were transferred all medical records *not strictly regimental*, viz, records of medical directors of departments, general, corps, division, and brigade hospitals, etc.

The proper division brought together, in this office, all military records of soldiers while under *regimental* control, and has resulted, as anticipated, in greatly facilitating the rendition of reports and simplifying the business between the two offices and the Pension Bureau.

The alternative proposition should not therefore be entertained, as its direct effect would be to recreate the confusion of records existing prior to 1884.

The last recommendation of the board is to discontinue the pension record division. Unless it is formally assumed that the numerous calls, verbal and written, from Senators, Members, and others, for information, should be disregarded and left unanswered, the pension record division is a necessity and its existence very materially lessens the time needed to answer such calls. and assures to the office a concise record of all cases received and answered.

Respectfully submitted.

R. C. DRUM,
Adjutant-General.

[Received, War Department, January 2, 1889.]

WAR DEPARTMENT, *January* 18, 1889.

Having carefully considered the report of the board on the "card-index records of the rolls of the late volunteer force" and the remarks of the Adjutant-General thereon, I am of opinion that a practical test of the value of the system, which has been commenced, can only be made by printing and distributing to the proper officers the card-index of the muster-rolls of one regiment.

It is therefore ordered that the card-index of the rolls of the One hundred and sixty-fourth New York Volunteers be printed and, to facilitate search, that the cards of said regiment be arranged in one alphabetical list. Requisition will accordingly be made upon the Public Printer for not less than three hundred copies of the work, the printed volume to contain a statement on the title-page that it is a transcript of the muster-rolls only.

When printed the book will at once be distributed to all officers of the Government who need a copy in the performance of their duties. Each officer to whom one or more copies may be sent will be requested to report as early as possible whether the book is of value in the dispatch of public business.

This will enable the Department to report to Congress definite information as to the cost and value of the work.

WILLIAM C. ENDICOTT,
Secretary of War.

APPENDIX No. 6.

CREDIT REQUISITIONS.

WAR DEPARTMENT,
BOARD ON BUSINESS METHODS,
August 6, 1888.

The following letter from the Secretary of the Treasury conveying recommendations of the Treasury Commission that the War Department prepare credit requisitions from lists of deposits furnished by the book-keepers division of the Third Auditor's office, was referred to this board by the Secretary of War:

TREASURY DEPARTMENT, OFFICE OF THE SECRETARY,
Washington, D. C., July 21, 1888.

SIR: I have the honor to invite your attention to the following recommendations of the Treasury commission, being certain changes in the present business methods in the book-keepers division of the Third Auditor's office, viz:

(1) That certificates of deposit issued by national banks and by the Treasurer and assistant treasurers, to the order of the various United States disbursing officers, be listed on one and the same list, the heading of said list to read "U. S. Treasury and National Banks."

(2) That, at option, more than one certificate of deposit be listed on each of the lists sent to the Commissioner of Pensions for requisition to issue.

(3) That the War Department and the Interior Department be requested hereafter to make out their own credit requisitions from the lists sent to them from the book-keepers division of the Third Auditor's office.

As the recommendations include a request that your Department hereafter make out your own credit requisitions which appear to have been heretofore made out in the book-keepers division of the Third Auditor's office, I have the honor to submit the matter for your consideration, and, if approved by you, to request that you issue the necessary instructions to carry into effect the changes recommended by the commission so far as they relate to your Department.

If the proposed change meets with your approval, please so advise me, and any blank requisitions now on hand in the Third Auditor's office, or further details concerning the work desired by you, will be furnished.

Respectfully, yours,

C. S. FAIRCHILD,
Secretary.

The SECRETARY OF WAR.

Upon investigation it is found that deposit requisitions are prepared in the office of the Second and Third Auditors, for the signature of the Secretary of War, from deposit lists made up from the certificates of deposit passing through those offices; that the unsigned deposit requisitions are forwarded to the Secretary of War for signature, together with the deposit lists upon which they are based; that while it is not known under what order or understanding the practice of preparing these requisitions in the Treasury Department arose, it has been found to be a convenient arrangement, so far as the War Department is concerned, as this Department is saved that much clerical labor, the number of credit requisitions received per month averaging one hundred and fifty.

The Treasury commission recommends that the War Department be requested hereafter to make out its own credit (deposit) requisitions from the lists sent to it from the book-keepers division of the Third Auditor's office.

Considering the two Departments together, the change if adopted, would neither increase nor diminish the amount of clerical labor now bestowed upon these requisitions, and therefore no reason can be assigned why the War Department should not prepare its own requisitions.

The board is of opinion, however, that a great amount of clerical labor can be saved in the two Departments, and the multiplication of papers avoided by the adoption of a form upon a single sheet of paper, which would answer all the purposes of the three papers by which War Department deposits are now covered into the Treasury, and known respectively as "a deposit list," a "deposit requisition," and a "repay covering warrant."

This consolidated form, or "deposit list-requisition-warrant," is appended to this report as exhibit A.

It will be found to differ from the present form of deposit lists (see Exhibits B, E, H, L, O, and R) in that it contains six separate columns for appropriations, thus allowing of the entry on one line of a deposit of moneys pertaining to different appropriations; the present form requires a separate line for each appropriation to which a deposit pertains.

A separate column for such moneys of the deposit as pertain to "miscellaneous receipts" dispenses with the necessity of making a separate explanatory note, which is now made on the deposit lists. (See Exhibits B and E.)

The introduction of separate columns for different appropriations permits of the entry of many more deposits on a list of the usual size, and in order to illustrate this graphically six actual deposit lists (Exhibits B, E, H, L, O, and R) which accompanied six requisitions prepared for the signature of the Secretary of War in the book-keepers division of the Third Auditor's office, have been entered on the one consolidated form (Exhibit A). Copies of the six requisitions referred to are also appended to this report as Exhibits C, F, I, M, P, and S. It will be observed that the order of the entries as they appear on deposit lists must be rearranged on the requisitions now in use in order that all the deposits relating to any one appropriation may appear together, and the amount deposited to the credit of each appropriation be clearly represented.

The proposed form meets this requirement fully as each appropriation has a separate column. Should the list embrace moneys deposited to the credit of appropriations having the same title, but pertaining to two different years, this distinction can readily be made by footing the total for each year separately, and indicating the years opposite the respective totals.

On the reverse side of the form, will be found a complete requisition, and a complete warrant, each so worded that it will not be necessary to repeat any of the items noted on the list of deposits except the number of the deposit list, and the total amount to be "covered in."

The requisition and warrant so appearing on this form, answer the purposes of the six requisitions appended to this report as Exhibits C, F, I, M, P, and S, and the six warrants appended as Exhibits D, G, K, N, Q, and T.

The board is informed that the deposit lists, requisitions, and warrants are filed in separate offices in the Treasury Department; should this not prove to be an insuperable objection to the consolidation of the three documents into one, it is evident that a large amount of clerical labor would be saved, for after a list is prepared it will no longer be necessary to—

(1) Re-arrange the items on the list according to appropriation.
(2) Make new computation of totals in accordance with such arrangement.
(3) Copy the re-arranged list on the requisition.
(4) Examine the requisition to see that it is a correct copy.
(5) Copy the requisition on the warrant, and
(6) Examine the warrant to see that it is correctly copied.

But this is not all that the proposed blank will accomplish. While it may require eight signatures, the number affixed to the list, requisition, and warrant now in use, so much space is gained by the introduction of columns for separate appropriations that the blank will ordinarily take the place of six or more sets of deposit lists, requisitions and warrants. The six sets of lists, requisitions, and warrants appended to this report require forty-eight official signatures, viz, each of the six lists is signed by the chief of the warrant division, Treasury Department; each of the six requisitions is signed by the Secretary of War, the Second Comptroller, and the Third Auditor; each of the six warrants is signed by the Secretary of the Treasury, the First Comptroller, the Register, and the Treasurer. Thus one paper is substituted for eighteen, and eight signatures for forty-eight. This reduction in bulk of papers is alone an important consideration in view of the large number of deposit lists, deposit requisitions and repay warrants that are made out during the year, from all of which would be eliminated the chance of error likely to arise in copying from one paper to another, and from a second to a third, and rendering entirely unnecessary the work of comparing these copies.

Should such form be adopted the book-keepers division of the Third Auditor's office would be at once relieved from the task of preparing deposit requisitions, as recommended by the Treasury commission.

The board also deems it proper to express its opinion that a great saving of time and labor can be effected and possibility of error due to copying avoided by the consolidation upon one sheet of the following papers: (1) The letter of request of the head of a Bureau that the Secretary of War issue an accountable requisition; (2) the accountable requisition based upon such request; and (3) the accountable warrant based upon such requisition.

When it is necessary to place public moneys pertaining to one or more appropriations to the credit of a disbursing officer, the proper head of Bureau forwards a letter (Exhibit U) to the Secretary of War, requesting that a certain sum be placed in a designated depository to the credit of the officer named, for which he is to be held accountable, and to be charged to the several appropriations in specified amounts. This request is then copied on a blank form of "accountable requisition" (Exhibit V) in the division of requisitions and accounts, Office of the Secretary of War, signed by the Secretary, and forwarded to the Secretary of the Treasury, when the requisition is copied on a blank form of accountable warrant (Exhibit W) in the warrant division, Office of the Secretary of the Treasury.

The consolidated form to take the place of these three documents is appended to this report as Exhibit X.

With the approval of the Secretary of War so much of this suggestion as looks to the consolidation of the letter of request and the requisition has been carried into effect.

The letter of request is thus reduced to one line on the margin of the requisition, containing the words "Requested by ———," and a space for the signature of the head of the Bureau. The body of the requisition is filled out in the Bureau, thus saving the labor of copying from a letter on a requisition as is now done in the division of requisitions and accounts. In the proposed blank the lower half is a complete warrant so worded that it will not be necessary to repeat any of the items noted on the requisition, except the number of the requisition and the total amount to be placed to the credit of the officer.

While the proposed consolidated form (Exhibit X) will require as many signatures as now appear on the request, requisition, and warrant, it reduces those three papers to one, saves two copyings, diminishes the possibility of error, and prevents the accumulation of duplicate or triplicate files practically containing identical information.

The board therefore suggests that the question of the adoption of these consolidated forms (Exhibits A and X) be submitted to the Secretary of the Treasury for his consideration.

Respectfully submitted.

JOHN TWEEDALE,
L. W. TOLMAN,
JACOB FRECH,
Members of Board.

Hon. WILLIAM C. ENDICOTT,
Secretary of War.

EXHIBIT A.

DEPOSIT REQUISITION. WAR DEPARTMENT.

No. 5435.

To the Secretary of the Treasury:

SIR: Please issue a warrant on the persons named in within deposit list No. 89 | 1068, in favor of the Treasurer of the United States for eighteen hundred and fifty-two dollars and twenty-one cents, to go to the credit of the specified appropriations.

Given under my hand this 1st day of August, 1888.

$1,852.21.

WILLIAM C. ENDICOTT,
Secretary of War.

Countersigned August 2, 1888.

S. BUTLER,
Second Comptroller.

Registered August 3, 1888.

JNO. S. WILLIAMS,
Third Auditor.

WAR REPAY COVERING WARRANT. TREASURY DEPARTMENT.

No. 1021.
$1,852.21.

To the persons named within:

Pay to the Treasurer of the United States, to be credited to the appropriations named within, eighteen hundred and fifty-two dollars and twenty-one cents, amount of deposits to his credit, pursuant to foregoing requisition duly countersigned and registered. And for so doing this shall be your warrant.

Given under my hand and seal of the Treasury Department this fifth day of August, 1888.

I. H. MAYNARD,
Assistant Secretary.

Countersigned.

M. J. DURHAM,
First Comptroller.

Registered.

W. S. ROSECRANS,
Register.

Office of the Treasurer of the United States.

JAMES W. HYATT,
Treasurer.

Received August 7, 1888.

Deposits to the credit of the Treasurer of the United States in the undermentioned depositories during the first quarter of 1889, on account of appropriations, under the direction of the War Department.

Office of the Third Auditor of the Treasury.
List No. 80 | 1068.   Form ——.

Deposits.			Appropriations.								
Date.	Place.	For whose credit.	Year.	Regular supplies.	Clothing, C. & G. E.	Incidental expenses.	Army transportation.	Construction and repair of hospitals.	Quarters for hospital stewards.	Total.	Miscellaneous receipts.
1888. July 2	A. Tr., San Francisco, Cal.	Lt. Wm. H. Smith.	1888	$9.34	$11.55	......	......	23.48	405.60	449.97	......
" 6	...do.........	Lt. D. E. Holley.	"	5.15	......	......	......	......	......	5.15	......
" 9	...do.........	Lt. L. H. Strother.	"	10.51	16.25	......	......	......	......	26.76	......
" 18	Tr., Washington, D. C.	Lt. W. M. Williams.	"	475.31	241.22	$4.17	......	......	......	720.70	$34.00
" 14	1st N. B., Denver, Colo.	Lt. R. N. Getty..	"	57.81	32.87	......	......	......	......	90.68	116.30
" 13	1st N. B., Portland, Oreg.	Lt. W. W. McCammon.	"	11.12	28.56	......	......	......	......	39.68	......
" 16	1st N. B., Rock Island, Ills.	Capt. Jas. Rockwell, jr.	"	17.39	......	1.89	$44.73	......	......	64.01	......
" 11	Los Angeles N. B., Cal.	Lt. Jno. A. Baldwin.	"	1.44	11.18	......	......	.81	......	13.43	......
" 13	...do.........	Lt. Robt. D. Read, jr.	"	12.95	12.90	......	......	......	......	25.85	......
" 16	...do.........	Lt. Geo. Palmer.	"	16.53	28.32	......	......	......	......	44.85	......
" 17	1st N. B., Helena, Mont.	Lt. H. E. Tutherly.	"	......	7.95	......	......	......	......	7.95	......
" 18	San Antonio N. B., Tex.	Maj. A. J. McGonnigle.	"	......	......	......	......	51.05	......	51.05	......
" 5	1st N. B., St. Paul, Minn.	Lt. Guy Howard.	"	8.75	2.00	......	......	......	......	10.75	......
" 9	Omaha N. B., Neb.	Lt. J. W. Summerhayes.	"	42.26	124.05	......	......	......	......	166.33	......
" 10	1st N. B., Portland, Oreg.	Capt. W. S. Patten.	"	36.66	2.26	......	......	......	......	38.92	......
" 12	A. Tr., New York, N. Y.	Lt. A. F. Curtis.	"	......	......	33.33	7.95	......	......	41.28	......
" 17	Tr., Washington, D. C.	Lt. Col. G. B. Dandy.	"	......	......	......	54.85	......	......	54.85	......
Total....				705.24	519.11	39.39	107.53	75.34	405.60	1,852.21	......

Correct:

W. F. MacLennan,
Chief Warrant Div.

17958——4

Exhibit B.

[Form No. 7.]

U. S. TREASURY.

List No. ——, F Y 89 | 1075.] [Covered by requisition No. ——.

Deposits to the credit of the Treasurer of the United States in the undernamed depositories during the first quarter of 1889, on account of appropriations under the direction of the War Department.

Deposit.		For whose credit.	Appropriation.	Amount of each appropriation.	Total amount of each deposit.
Date.	Place.				
1888. July 7	2 A. Tr., San Francisco, Cal.	Lieut. Wm. H. Smith..	Regular supplies...1888.. Clothing, &c........ " .. Const. and rep. of hospitals, 1888. Qrs. for hosp. stewards, 1888.	$0.34 11.55 23.48 405.60	$449.97
"	6 ....do	Lieut. D. E. Holley....	Regular supplies...1888..		5.15
"	9 ....do	Lieut. L. H. Strother ..	Regular supplies...1888.. Clothing, &c........ " ..	10.51 16.25	26.76
"	18 Tr., Washington, D. C.	Lieut. W. M. Williams.	Regular supplies...1888.. Inc'd't'l expenses.. " .. Clothing, &c........ " ..	475.31 4.17 241.22	720.70
					1,202.58
	Total deposit........... $754.70 Miscl. receipts .... 34.00 Listed by 3d Aud'r. 720.70 = 754.70				

Indorsed on back:

| Third Auditor's Office, |
| July 23, 1888. |
| Book-keeper's Division. |

| Treasurer's Office, |
| Jul. 23, 1888. |
| Division of Accounts. |

Correct:

W. F. MacLennan,
Ch'f Warrant Division.

Exhibit C.

[Office of the Third Auditor of the Treasury. Form 11. Deposit requisition.]

WAR DEPARTMENT.

No. ———

To the Secretary of the Treasury:

SIR: Please issue a warrant on the persons named below in favor of the Treasurer of the United States for one thousand two hundred and two dollars and fifty-eight cents, being amount deposited to the credit of the Treasurer of the United States, as per list of deposits No. 89–1075, herewith, to go to the credit of the under-mentioned appropriations.

Given under my hand this 1st day of August, 1888.

$1,202.58.

               WM. C. ENDICOTT,
                 Secretary of War.

Countersigned August 2, 1888. .

               S. BUTLER,
                Second Comptroller.

Registered August 3d, 1888.

               JNO. S. WILLIAMS,
                Third Auditor.

Name and rank.	Appropriation.	Period.	Amount.	Total.
Lieut. Wm. H. Smith	Regular supplies	1888	$9.34	
" D. E. Holley	......do......	"	5.15	
" L. H. Strother	......do......	"	10.51	
" W. M. Williams	......do......	"	475.31	
				$500.31
Do	Incid'tl expenses	"	....	4.17
Lieut. Wm. H. Smith	Clothing, &c	"	11.55	
" L. H. Strother	......do......	"	16.25	
" W. M. Williams	......do......	"	241.22	
				269.02
Lieut. Wm. H. Smith	Const. and rep. of hospitals	"	....	23.48
Do	Qrs. for hosp. stewards	"	....	405.60
				$1,202.58

War Department,
Jul. 26, '88.
13171
Division of Requisitions and Accounts.

Exhibit D.

[Office of the Secretary of the Treasury division of warrants, estimates, and appropriations. Form 61. Repay covering warrants.]

TRASURY DEPARTMENT.

No. ——.

To Lieut. Wm. H. Smith and three others:

Pay to the Treasurer of the United States, to be credited to the appropriations named in the margin of this warrant, one thousand two hundred and two dollars and fifty-eight cents. Amount of deposits to credit of the Treasurer, as per list No. 89-1075 herewith, pursuant to a requisition, No. 5441, of the Secretary of War, dated August 1, 1888, countersigned by the Second Comptroller of the Treasury and registered by the Third Auditor. And for so doing this shall be your warrant.

Given under my hand and the seal of the Treasury Department this 5th day of August, in the year of our Lord one thousand eight hundred and eighty-eight, and of Independence the one hundred and thirteenth.
$1,202.58.

I. H. MAYNARD,
Assistant Secretary.

Countersigned:

M. J. DURHAM,
First Comptroller.

Registered: /

W. S. ROSECRANS,
Register.

Appropriations.

	$					$	
188 . Pay, &c., of the Army				1888. Incidental expenses of the Quartermaster's Department		4	17
188 .				188 . Horses for cavalary and artillery			
188 .							
188 .							
188 . Ordnance, ordnance stores, and suplies				188 . Barracks and quarters			
188 . Ordnance service				188 . Transportation of the Army and its supplies			
188 . Repairs of arsenals				1888. Clothing, camp and garrison equipage		269	02
Permanent—Arming and equip'ng the militia				188 . Subsistence of the Army			
188 . Expenses of recruiting				1888. Cons. and repair of hospitals		23	48
188 . Medical and hospital department				1888. Qrs. for hosp. stewards		405	60
1888. Regular supplies of the Quartermaster's Department	$	500	31		1	202	58

OFFICE OF THE TREASURER OF THE UNITED STATES.

Received August 7th, 1888.

JAMES W. HYATT,
Treasurer.

Exhibit E.

[Form No. 7.]

U. S. TREASURY.

List No. 1108.   F. Y. 1889.   Covered by requisition No. 5447.

Deposits to the credit of the Treasurer of the United States in the under-named depositories during the first quarter of 1889, on account of appropriations under the direction of the War Department.

Deposits.		For whose credit.	Appropriation.	Amount of each appropriation.	Total amount of each deposit.
Date.	Place.				
1888. July 14	1st N. B., Denver, Colo.	Lt. R. N. Getty............	Regular supplies, 1888 .	$57.81	
			Clothing, &c............	32.87	$90.68
		Total deposit.$206.98			
		Misc'l. receipts.... 116.30			
		Listed by 3d Aud'r 90.68			
		206.98			
" 13	1st N. B., Portland, Oreg.	Lt. W. W. McCammon....	Regular supplies, 1888 .	11.12	
			Clothing, &c............	28.56	39.68
" 21	1st N. B., Rock Island, Ill.	Capt. Jas. Rockwell, jr....	Regular supplies, 1888 .	17.39	
			Inc'd t'l expenses......	1.89	
			Army trans.............	44.73	64.01
					194.37

Third Auditor's Office,
Jul. 28, 1888,
Book-keeper's Division.

Correct.

7-28-88. Q.

W. F. MACLENNAN,
Ch'f Warrant Div.

Exhibit F.

[Office of the Third Auditor of the Treasury. Form 11. Deposit requisition.]

WAR DEPARTMENT.

No. ——.

To the Secretary of the Treasury:

SIR: Please issue a warrant on the persons named below, in favor of the Treasurer of the United States, for one hundred and ninety-four dollars and thirty-seven cents, being amount deposited to the credit of the Treasurer of the United States as per List of Deposits No. 89 | 1108, herewith, to go to the credit of the under-mentioned appropriations.

Given under my hand this 1st day of August, 1888.
$194 37/100.

                                                               WM. C. ENDICOTT,
                                                                   Secretary of War.

Countersigned August 2d, 1888.

                                                               S. BUTLER,
                                                                 Second Comptroller.

Registered August 3d, 1888.

                                                              JNO. S. WILLIAMS,
                                                                   Third Auditor.

Name and rank.	Appropriation.	Period.	Amount.		Total.	
Lt. R. N. Getty	Regular supplies	1888	$57	81		
" W. W. McCammon	......do	"	11	12		
Capt. Jas. Rockwell, jr	......do	"	17	39		
					$86	32
Do	Inc'd t'l expenses	"			1	89
Do	Army transp'n	"			44	73
Lt. R. N. Getty	Clothing, etc	1888	32	87		
" W. W. McCammon	......do	"	28	56		
					61	43
					194	37

War Department.

Jul. 31, 1888.

13415.

Division of Requisions and Accounts.

Exhibit G.

[Office of the Secretary of the Treasury, division of warrants, estimates, and appropriations. Form 61. Repay covering warrant.]

TREASURY DEPARTMENT.

No. ——.

To Lieut. R. N. Getty and two others:

Pay to the Treasurer of the United States, to be credited to the appropriations named in the margin of this warrant, one hundred and ninety-four dollars and thirty-seven cents, amount of deposits to credit of the Treasurer, as per list No. 89 | 1108 herewith, pursuant to requisition No. 5447, of the Secretary of War, dated August 1, 1888, countersigned by the Second Comptroller of the Treasury and registered by the Third Auditor. And for so doing this shall be your warrant.
$194.37.

Given under my hand and the seal of the Treasury Department this 5th day of August, in the year of our Lord one thousand eight hundred and eighty-eight, and of Independence the one hundred and thirteenth.

I. H. MAYNARD,
Assistant Secretary.

Countersigned:

M. J. DURHAM,
First Comptroller.

Registered:

W. S. ROSECRANS,
Register.

Appropriations.

188 . Pay, etc., of the Army				1888. Incidental expenses of the Quartermaster's Department	$1	89
188 .						
188 .						
188 .				188 . Horses for cavalry and artillery		
188 . Ordnance, ordnance stores, and supplies				188 . Barracks and quarters		
188 . Ordnance service				1888. Transportation of the Army and its supplies	44	73
188 . Repairs of arsenals				1888. Clothing, camp and garrison equipage	61	43
Permanent — arming and equip'ng the militia				188 . Subsistence of the Army		
188 . Expenses of recruiting						
188 . Medical and hospital department					194	37
1888. Regular supplies of the Quartermaster's Department	$	86	32			

OFFICE OF THE TREASURER OF THE UNITED STATES.

Received August 7, 1888.

JAMES W. HYATT,
Treasurer.

Exhibit H.

[Form No. 7.]

U. S. TREASURY.

List No. 1106. Feb., 1889.   Covered by requisition No. 5445.

Deposits to the credit of the Treasurer of the United States in the under-named depositories during the first quarter of 1889, on account of appropriations under the direction of the War Department.

Deposits.		For whose credit.	Appropriations.	Amount of each appropriation.	Total amount of each deposit.
Date.	Place.				
1888. July 11	Los Angeles N. B., Cal.	Lt. Jno. A. Baldwin	Reg. supplies, 1888	$1.44	
			Clothing, &c., "	11.18	
			Const. and Rep. hospitals, 1888.	.81	$13.43
" 13	....do	Lt. Robt. D. Read, jr	Reg. supplies, 1888	12.95	
			Clothing, &c., "	12.90	25.85
" 16	....do	Lt. Geo. Palmer	Reg. supplies, "	16.53	
			Clothing, &c., "	28.32	44.85
" 17	1st N. B., Helena, Mont.	Lt. H. E. Tutherly	Clothing, &c., "	....	7.95
" 18	San Antonio N. B., Tex.	Maj. A. J. McGonnigle	Const. and Rep. hospitals, 1888.	....	51.05
					143.13

Correct.

JULY 28, '88. Q.

W. F. MacLennan,
Chf., Warrant Div.

Indorsed on back:

Third Auditor's Office.
Jul. 27, 1888.
Book-keeper's Division.

Treasurer's Office.
Jul. 27, 1888.
Division of Accounts.

Exhibit I.

[Office of the Third Auditor of the Treasury. Form 11. Deposit requisition.]

WAR DEPARTMENT.

No. 5445.

To the Secretary of the Treasury:

SIR: Please issue a warrant on the persons named below, in favor of the Treasurer of the United States for one hundred and forty-three dollars and thirteen cents, being amount deposited to the credit of the Treasurer of the United States, as per list of deposits No. 89–1106, herewith, to go to the credit of the under-mentioned appropriations.

Given under my hand this 1st day of August, 1888.

$143 13/100.

WM. C. ENDICOTT,
Secretary of War.

Countersigned August 2d, 1888.

S. BUTLER,
Second Comptroller.

Registered August 3d, 1888.

JNO. S. WILLIAMS,
Third Auditor.

Name and rank.	Appropriation.	Period.	Amount.		Total.	
Lt. Jno. A. Baldwin	Regular supplies	1888	1	44		
" Robt. D. Reed, jr	....do	"	12	95		
" Geo. Palmer	....do	"	16	53		
					30	92
Lt. Jno. A. Baldwin	Clothing, etc	1888	11	18		
" Robt. D. Reed, jr	....do	"	12	90		
" Geo. Palmer	....do	"	28	32		
" H. E. Tutherly	....do	"	7	95		
					60	35
Lt. Jno. A. Baldwin	Const. and rep. of hospitals	1888		81		
Maj. A. J. McGonnigle	....do	"	51	05		
					51	86
					143	13

War Department,
Jul. 31, '88.
13412.
Division of Requisition and Accounts.

EXHIBIT K.

[Office of the Secretary of the Treasury, division of warrants, estimates, and appropriations. Form 61. Repay covering warrant.]

No. ——.

TREASURY DEPARTMENT.

To Lieut. Jno. A. Baldwin and four others :

Pay to the Treasurer of the United States, to be credited to the appropriations named in the margin of this warrant, one hundred and forty-three dollars and thirteen cents, amount of deposits to credit of the Treasurer, as per list No. 89-1106, herewith, pursuant to a requisition, No. 5445, of the Secretary of War, dated August 1st, 1888, countersigned by the Second Comptroller of the Treasury and registered by the Third Auditor. And for so doing this shall be your warrant.
$143.13.

Given under my hand and the seal of the Treasury Department this 5th day of August, in the year of our Lord one thousand eight hundred and eighty-eight, and of Independence the one hundred and thirteenth.

I. H. MAYNARD,
Assistant Secretary.

Countersigned :

M. J. DURHAM,
First Comptroller.

Registered :

W. S. ROSECRANS,
Register.

Appropriations.

				Appropriation	$	cts
188 . Pay, etc., of the Army				1888. Regular supplies of the Quartermaster's Department	$ 30	92
188 .				188 . Incidental expenses of the Quartermaster's Department		
188 .				188 . Horses for cavalry and artillery		
188 .				188 . Barracks and quarters		
188 . Ordnance, ordnance stores, and supplies				188 . Transportation of the Army and its supplies		
188 . Ordnance service				1888. Clothing, camp and garrison equipage	60	35
188 . Repairs of arsenals				1888. Const. and repair of hospitals	51	86
Permanent—Arming and equip'ng the militia						
188 . Expenses of recruiting						
188 . Medical and hospital department					143	13

OFFICE OF THE TREASURER OF THE UNITED STATES.

Received August 7th, 1888.

JAMES W. HYATT,
Treasurer.

EXHIBIT L.

[Form No. 7.]

U. S. TREASURY.

List No. ——, F.Y. 89–1070.   Covered by requisition No. ——.

Deposits to the credit of the Treasurer of the United States in the under-named depositories during the first quarter of 1889 on account of appropriations under the direction of the War Department.

Deposits.		For whose credit.	Appropriation.	Amount of each appropriation.	Total amount of each deposit.
Date.	Place.				
1888. July 5	1st N. B., St. Paul, Minn.	Lieut. Guy Howard...	Regular supplies, 1888.	$8.75	
			Clothing, etc., "..	2.00	$10.75
" 9	Omaha, N. B., Neb....	Lieut. J. W. Summerhayes.	Regular supplies, 1888.	42.28	
			Clothing, etc., "..	124.05	
					166.33
					177.08

Third Auditor's Office,
Jul. 23, 1888.
Book-keeper's Division.

Correct.

JULY 23, 1888.

W. F. MACLENNAN,
Ch'f Warrant Div.

Q.

EXHIBIT M.

[Office of the Third Auditor of the Treasury. Form 11. Deposit Requisition.]

WAR DEPARTMENT.

No. 5436.

To the Secretary of the Treasury:

SIR: Please issue a warrant on the persons named below, in favor of the Treasurer of the United States for one hundred and seventy-seven dollars and eight cents, being amount deposited to the credit of the Treasurer of the United States as per list of deposits No. 89 | 1070, herewith, to go to the credit of the undermentioned appropriations.

Given under my hand this 1st day of August, 1888.
$177.08.

WM. C. ENDICOTT,
Secretary of War.

Countersigned August 2d, 1888.

S. BUTLER,
Second Comptroller.

Registered August 3d, 1888.

JNO. S. WILLIAMS,
Third Auditor.

Name and rank.	Appropriation.	Period.	Amount.		Total.	
Lieut. Guy Howard	Regular supplies	1888	8	75		
Lieut. J. W. Summerhayes	......do............	"	42	28		
					51	03
Lieut. Guy Howard	Clothing, etc	1888	2	00		
Lieut. J. W. Summerhayes	......do............	"	124	05		
					126	05
					$ 177	08

War Department.
Jul. 20, '88.
13100.
Division of requisitions
and accounts.

EXHIBIT N.

[Office of the Secretary of the Treasury, division of warrants, estimates, and appropriations. Form 61. Repay covering warrant.]

TREASURY DEPARTMENT.

No. ——

$177.08.

To Lieut. Guy Howard and one other:

Pay to the Treasurer of the United States, to be credited to the appropriations named in the margin of this warrant, one hundred and seventy-seven dollars and eight cents, amount of deposits to credit of the Treasurer, as per List No. 89 | 1070, herewith, pursuant to a requisition No. 5436, of the Secretary of War, dated August 1, 1888, countersigned by the Second Comptroller of the Treasury and registered by the Third Auditor. And for so doing this shall be your warrant.

Given under my hand and the seal of the Treasury Department this 5th day of August, in the year of our Lord one thousand eight hundred and eighty-eight, and of Independence the one hundred and thirteenth.

I. H. MAYNARD,
Assistant Secretary.

Countersigned:

M. J. DURHAM,
First Comptroller.

Registered:

W. S. ROSECRANS,
Register.

Appropriations.

188 . Pay, &c., of the Army...				1888. Regular supplies of the Quartermaster's Department.	$ 51	03
188				188 . Incidental expenses of the Quartermaster's Department..........		
188						
188				188 . Horses for cavalry and artillery..........		
188 . Ordnance, ordnance stores, and supplies..........						
188 . Ordnance service........				188 . Barracks and quarters..		
188 . Repair of arsenals......				188 . Transportation of the Army and its supplies......		
Permanent—Arming and equip'ng the militia........				1888. Clothing, camp, and garrison equipage..........	126	05
188 . Expenses of recruiting...				188 . Subsistence of the Army.		
188 . Medical and hospital department..........						
					177	08

OFFICE OF THE TREASURER OF THE UNITED STATES.

Received Aug. 7th, 1888.

JAMES W. HYATT,
Treasurer.

EXHIBIT O.

[Form No. 7.]

U. S. TREASURY.

List No. ——, F. Y. 89 | 1068.　　　　　　　　　　　Covered by requisition No. 5435.

Deposits to the credit of the Treasurer of the United States in the undernamed depositories during the first quarter of 1889, *on account of appropriations under the direction of the War Department.*

Deposits.		For whose credit.	Appropriation.	Amount of each appropriation.	Total amount of each deposit.
Date.	Place.				
1888. July 10	1st N. B., Portland, Oreg.	Capt. W. S. Patten....	Regular supplies, 1888. Clothing, etc., " .	$36.06 2.26	.... $38.92

Third Auditor's Office.
Jul. 21, 1888.
Book-keeper's Division.

·

Treasurer's Office.
Jul. 21, 1888.
Division of Accounts.

Correct.

July 21, '88.　Q.

W. F. MACLENNAN,
Ch'f Warrant Div.

Exhibit P.

[Office of the Third Auditor of the Treasury. Form 11. Deposit requisition.]

WAR DEPARTMENT.

No. 5435.

To the Secretary of the Treasury:

SIR: Please issue a warrant on the persons named below, in favor of the Treasurer of the United States, for $38.92, being amount deposited to the credit of the Treasurer of the United States as per list of deposits No. 89 | 1068 herewith, to go to the credit of the undermentioned appropriations.

Given under my hand this 1st day of August, 1888.

$38.92.

Countersigned August 2, 1888.

Registered August 3, 1888.

WM. C. ENDICOTT,
Secretary of War.

S. BUTLER,
Second Comptroller.

JNO. S. WILLIAMS,
Third Auditor.

Name and rank.	Appropriation.	Period.	Amount.	Total.
Capt. W. S. Patten	Regular supplies	1888	....	$36.66
Do	Clothing, etc	1888	....	2.26
				38.92

War Department.
July 28, 1888.
13168.
Division of requisitions
and accounts.

Exhibit Q.

No. ——.

[Office of the Secretary of the Treasury, division of warrants, estimates, and appropriations. Form 61. No. ——. Repay covering warrant.]

TREASURY DEPARTMENT.

To Capt. W. S. Patten:

Pay to the Treasurer of the United States, to be credited to the appropriations named in the margin of this warrant, thirty-eight dollars and ninety-two cents, amount of deposits to credit of the Treasurer, as per list No. 89 | 1068 herewith, pursuant to a requisition, No. 5435, of the Secretary of War, dated August 1, 1888, countersigned by the Second Comptroller of the Treasury and registered by the Third Auditor. And for so doing this shall be your warrant.

Given under my hand and the seal of the Treasury Department this 5th day of August, in the year of our Lord one thousand eight hundred and eighty-eight, and of Independence the one hundred and thirteenth.

$38.92.

I. H. MAYNARD,
Assistant Secretary.

Countersigned.

M. J. DURHAM,
First Comptroller.

Registered.

W. S. ROSECRANS,
Register.

Appropriations.

188 . Pay, &c., of the Army				188 . Incidental expenses of the Quartermaster's Department			
188 .							
188 .							
188 .				188 . Horses for cavalry and artillery			
188 . Ordnance, ordnance stores, and supplies				188 . Barracks and quarters			
188 . Ordnance service				188 . Transportation of the Army and its supplies			
188 . Repairs of arsenals				1888. Clothing, camp and garrison equipage		2	26
Permanent—arming and equip'ng the militia							
188 . Expenses of recruiting				188 . Subsistence of the Army			
188 . Medical and hospital department						38	92
1888. Regular supplies of the Quartermaster's Department	$	36	66				

OFFICE OF THE TREASURER OF THE UNITED STATES.

Received August 7, 1888.

JAMES W. HYATT,
Treasurer.

Exhibit R.

[Form No. 7.]

U. S. TREASURY.

List No. ——.   F. Y. 89 | 1073.   Covered by requisition No. 5439.

Deposits to the credit of the Treasurer of the United States in the undernamed depositories during the first quarter of 1889, on account of appropriations under the direction of the War Department.

Deposits.		For whose credit.	Appropriation.	Amount of each appropriation.	Total amount of each deposit.
Date.	Place.				
1888. July 12	A. Tr., New York, N. Y.	Lieut. A. F. Curtis	Inc'd't'l expenses, 1888.	$33.33	
			Army transp'n, "	7.95	$41.28
" 17	Tr., Washington, D. C.	Lt. Col. G. B. Dandy..	Army transp'n, 1888...	....	54.85
					96.13

Correct:

7, 21, '88.   B.

W. F. MacLennan,
 Ch'f Warrant Div.

Third Auditor's Office,
Jul. 21, 1888.
Book-keeper's division.

Treasurer's Office,
Jul. 21, 1888.
Division of accounts.

Exhibit S.

[Office of the Third Auditor of the Treasury. Form 11. Deposit requisition.]

WAR DEPARTMENT.

No. 5439.

To the Secretary of the Treasury:

SIR: Please issue a warrant on the persons named below, in favor of the Treasurer of the United States for ninety-six dollars and thirteen cents, being amount deposited to the credit of the Treasurer of the United States as per list of deposits No. 89 | 1073 herewith, to go to the credit of the undermentioned appropriations.

Given under my hand this 1st day of August, 1888.

$96 13/100.

WM. C. ENDICOTT,
Secretary of War.

Countersigned August 2d, 1888.

S. BUTLER,
Second Comptroller.

Registered August 3d, 1888.

JNO. S. WILLIAMS,
Third Auditor.

Name and rank.	Appropriation.	Period.	Amount.		Total.	
Lieut. A. F. Curtis	Inc'd't'l expenses	1888			33	33
Lieut. A. F. Curtis	Army transp'n	"	7	95		
Lt. Col. G. B. Daudy	......do	"	54	85		
					62	80
					$96	13

War Department,

Jul. 26, '88.

13169.

Division of requisitions and accounts.

Exhibit T.

[Office of the Secretary of the Treasury, division of warrants, estimates, and appropriations. Form 61. Repay covering warrant.]

TREASURY DEPARTMENT.

No. ———.

To Lieut. A. F. Curtis and one other:

Pay to the Treasurer of the United States, to be credited to the appropriations named in the margin of this warrant, ninety-eight dollars and thirteen cents, amount of deposits to credit of the Treasurer, as per list No. 89 | 1073 herewith, pursuant to a requisition, No. 5439, of the Secretary of War, dated August 1st, 1888, countersigned by the Second Comptroller of the Treasury and registered by the Third Auditor. And for so doing this shall be your warrant.

$98.13.

Given under my hand and the seal of the Treasury Department this 5th day of August, in the year of our Lord one thousand eight hundred and eighty-eight, and of Independence the one hundred and thirteenth.

I. H. MAYNARD,
Assistant Secretary.

Countersigned.

M. J. DURHAM,
First Comptroller.

Registered.

W. S. ROSECRANS,
Register.

Appropriations.

188 . Pay, etc., of the Army				188 . Regular supplies of the Quartermaster's Department			
188 .				1888. Incidental expenses of the Quartermaster's Department	$	33	33
188 .				188 . Horses for cavalry and artillery			
188 . Ordnance, ordnance stores, and supplies				188 . Barracks and quarters			
188 . Ordnance service				1888. Transportation of the Army and its supplies		62	80
188 . Repairs of arsenals				188 . Clothing, camp and garrison equipage			
Permanent—arming and equip'ng the militia				188 . Subsistence of the Army			
188 . Expenses of recruiting							
188 . Medical and hospital department						96	13

OFFICE OF THE TREASURER OF THE UNITED STATES.

Received August 7, 1888.

JAMES W. HYATT,
Treasurer.

EXHIBIT U.

WAR DEPARTMENT.

$2,002.05.   No. 1840.

OFFICE OF THE QUARTERMASTER-GENERAL,
Washington City, July 27, 1883.

To the Secretary of War :

SIR : Please cause the sum of two thousand and two $\frac{05}{100}$ dollars to be placed in the following-named depositories, viz:

	Dollars.	Cts.
Asst. treasurer U. S., New York	2,002	05
Total	2,002	05

Officer's bond, dated April 1, 1881.

to the credit of Col. Chas. H. Tompkins, Assist. Qr. Mr. Gen'l U. S. Army, Governor's Island, N. Y. Harbor, who is to be held accountable therefor, and charged to the appropriations for—

					Dollars.	Cts.
Regular supplies, Quartermaster's Dept., for fiscal year ending June 30,				188		
Incidental expenses, Quartermaster's Dept.,	"	"	"	188		
Barracks and quarters	"	"	"	188		
Transportation of the Army and its supplies	"	"	"	1888	2,001	40
Horses for cavalry and artillery	"	"	"	188		
Clothing, camp and garrison equipage	"	"	"	1888		15
Construction and repairs of hospitals	"	"	"	1888		50
National cemeteries	"	"	"	188		
Pay of supts. of national cemeteries	"	"	"	188		
Total					2,002	05

Respectfully,

S. B. HOLABIRD,
Quartermaster-General, U. S. Army.

EXHIBIT V.

WAR DEPARTMENT.

Accountable requisition No. 541.

To the Secretary of the Treasury:

SIR: Please cause a warrant for two thousand and two dollars and five cents to be issued in favor of asst. treasurer U. S., New York, to be placed to the credit of Col. Chas. H. Tompkins, asst. qr. mr. genl. U. S. Army, Governor's Island, N. Y. Harbor, for which sum he is to be held accountable. To be charged to the undermentioned appropriations.

Given under my hand this 1st day of August, 1888.

$2,002 05/100.

WM. C. ENDICOTT,
Secretary of War.

Countersigned:

S. BUTLER,
Second Comptroller.

Registered:

JOHN S. WILLIAMS,
Third Auditor.

Appropriations.

Regular supplies of the Quartermaster's Department		
Incidental expenses of the Quartermaster's Department		
Horses for cavalry and artillery		
Barracks and quarters		
Transportation of the Army and its supplies, 1888	$2,001	40
National cemeteries		
Construction and repairs of hospitals, 1888		15
Clothing, camp and garrison equipage, 1888		50
Subsistence of the Army		
	2,002	05

EXHIBIT W.

TREASURY DEPARTMENT.

[Office of the Secretary of the Treasury, division of warrants, estimates, and appropriations. Form 57
Accountable warrant.]

No. ——.
$2,002.05.

To the Treasurer of the United States, greeting:

Pay to asst. treasurer U. S., New York, to be placed to the credit of Col. Chas. H. Tompkins, asst. qr'm'r-genl. U. S. Army, Governor's Island, N. Y. Harbor, or order, to be charged to the appropriations named in the margin, two thousand and two dollars and five cents; for which sum he, Chas. H. Tompkins, is to be held accountable, pursuant to a requisition, No. 541, of the Secretary of War, dated August 1, 1888, countersigned by the Second Comptroller of the Treasury and registered by the Third Auditor. And for so doing this shall be your warrant.

Given under my hand and the seal of the Treasury Department this fifth day of August, in the year of our Lord one thousand eight hundred and eighty-eight, and of Independence the one hundred and thirteenth.

C. S. FAIRCHILD,
Secretary.

Countersigned:

M. J. DURHAM,
First Comptroller.

Registered:

W. S. ROSECRANS,
Register.

Appropriations.

Subsistence of the Army.............				1888. Clothing, camp and garrison equipage..........................	50
Medical and hospital department..				1888. Construction and repairs of hospitals.........................	15
Regular supplies Quartermaster's Department.......................				Pay, &c., of the Army..............	
Incidental expenses Quartermaster's Dep't.......................				Ordnance, ordnance stores, and supplies..........................	
Barracks and quarters..............				Ordnance service...................	
1888. Transportation of the Army and its supplies...................	2	001	40	Repairs of arsenals................	
National cemeteries.................				Arming and equipping the militia.	
Pay of superintendents of national cemeteries.......................					

OFFICE OF THE TREASURER OF THE UNITED STATES.

Received for this warrant the following draft: No. —— on ——; No. —— on ——. Mailed ——.

EXHIBIT X.

WAR DEPARTMENT.

Accountable requisition No. 541.

To the Secretary of the Treasury:

SIR: Please cause a warrant for two thousand and two dollars and five cents to be issued in favor of asst. treasurer U. S., New York, to be placed to the credit of Col. Chas. H. Tompkins, asst. qr. mr. genl. U. S. Army, Governor's Island, New York Harbor, or order, for which sum he, Chas. H. Tompkins, is to be held accountable. To be charged to the undermentioned appropriations.

Given under my hand this 1st day of August, 1888.
$2,002.05.

WM. C. ENDICOTT,
Secretary of War.

Countersigned:

S. BUTLER,
Second Comptroller.

Registered:

JNO. S. WILLIAMS,
Third Auditor.

Appropriations.

	Appropriation	Amount	
Requested by ———	Regular supplies of the Quartermaster's Department		
	Incidental expenses of the Quartermaster's Department		
	Horses for cavalry and artillery................................		
	Barracks and quarters................................	$2,001	40
	Transportation of the Army and its supplies, 1888		50
	National cemeteries		15
	Construction and repairs of hospitals, 1888		
	Clothing, camp and garrison equipage "		
	Subsistence of the Army................................	2,002	.05

TREASURY DEPARTMENT.

Accountable warrant No. 1001.

To the Treasurer of the United States, greeting:

Pay two thousand and two dollars and five cents, pursuant to the foregoing requisition, duly countersigned and registered, and for so doing this shall be your warrant.

Given under my hand and the seal of the Treasury Department this fifth day of August, 1888.
$2,002.05.

C. S. FAIRCHILD,
Secretary.

Countersigned:

M. J. DURHAM,
First Comptroller.

Registered:

W. S. ROSECRANS,
Register.

OFFICE OF THE TREASURER OF THE UNITED STATES.

Received for this warrant the following draft; No. —— on ——; No. —— on ——, mailed, ——.

WAR DEPARTMENT,
Washington City, August 9, 1888.

SIR: I have the honor to acknowledge the receipt of your letter of the 21st of July embodying a recommendation of the Treasury commission that the War Department be requested hereafter to make out its own credit requisitions from the lists sent here from the book-keepers division of the Third Auditor's office.

In reply thereto I inclose herewith a report of the War Department board on business methods upon the subject.

The board has prepared a consolidated form embracing a deposit list, a credit requisition, and a repay warrant, all in one, which, should it meet with your approval, will relieve the book-keepers division of the Third Auditor's office from the work of this Department which it is now doing, and at the same time impose no additional work upon this Department, save the Treasury Department from the labor of filling out the repay warrants, and make a large reduction in the number of papers which now must be signed by many officials and then occupy valuable filing space.

The board has also prepared a consolidated form embracing in one sheet a letter of request for accountable requisition, the accountable requisition based upon such request, and the accountable warrant based upon such requisition.

The adoption of this form, if it should also meet with your favorable consideration would, it is believed, save the Treasury Department considerable labor in the preparation of such warrants, and also diminish the quantity of papers to be filed.

If it is deemed advisable by the Treasury Department that the credit requisition, now prepared in the Third Auditor's office, should be prepared in this Department, before action shall have been had upon the recommendation of the War Department board, I will thank you to forward the blank requisitions now on hand in that office and the necessary instructions will be given to carry into effect the change recommended by the commission.

Very respectfully,

WILLIAM C. ENDICOTT,
Secretary of War.

The SECRETARY OF THE TREASURY.

Inclosures: Copy of report of board of August 6, 1888, and Exhibits A to X inclusive.

Pending the action of the Treasury Department upon the proposed consolidated forms (Exhibit A and X) the recommendation of the board for the consolidation of a number of deposit lists upon one deposit requisition was carried into effect by printing upon the back of the existing form (Exhibit C) of requisitions the following form, which permitted the consolidation of a number of deposit lists upon one requisition, thus greatly reducing the number of credit requisitions:

Appropriations.

Name and rank.	Year.	Regular supplies, Q. M. D.	Clothing, camp and garrison equipage.	Incidental expenses, Q. M. D.	Army transportation.			Total.	Miscellaneous receipts.
Total									

At the same time a circular was issued by the Secretary of War consolidating upon one form the letter of request (Exhibit U) for accountable requisition and the accountable requisition itself (Exhibit V), in order to carry into effect so much of the suggested reform as lay in the power of the War Department to accomplish.

The circular and the consolidated form are given below:

[Circular.]

WAR DEPARTMENT, *August 9*, 1888.

In order to simplify the business of this Department, reduce the possibility of error nd avoid the duplication of papers containing practically the same information, the ecretary of War directs that the practice in the different Bureaus of writing a separate "request" upon which to base an accountable requisition be discontinued, and hat in place thereof the accountable requisition heretofore made in the division of requisitions and accounts, Secretary's office, upon such request, be hereafter prepared in the proper Bureau for the signature of the Secretary of War, and that a note, viz, "requested by —— ——," signed by the head of the Bureau, be written on the margin of such requisition as indicated on the accompanying form.

By order of the Secretary of War.

SAM'L HODGKINS,
Acting Chief Clerk.

WAR DEPARTMENT.

Accountable requisition No. ——.

To the Secretary of the Treasury:

Sir: Please cause a warrant for —— —— dollars and —— cents to be issued in favor of ——, for which sum he is to be held accountable. To be charged to the under-mentioned appropriations.

Given under my hand this —— day of ——, 18—

$——.

——— ———,
Secretary of War.

Requested by

Countersigned:

——— ———,
Second Comptroller.

Registered:

——— ———,
Auditor.

Appropriations.

Regular supplies of the Quartermaster's Department	....
Incidental expenses of the Quartermaster's Department	....
Horses for cavalry and artillery	....
Barracks and quarters	....
Transportation of the Army and its supplies	....
National cemeteries	....
Construction and repairs of hospitals	....
Clothing, camp and garrison equipage	....
Subsistence of the Army	....

APPENDIX No. 7.

REQUISITIONS ON PUBLIC PRINTER.

WAR DEPARTMENT,
BOARD ON BUSINESS METHODS,
September 10, 1888.

A communication from the Chief Signal Officer, dated April 12, 1888, inviting attention to the increase of work involved in preparing requisitions in duplicate for printing and binding upon the Public Printer having been referred by the Secretary of War to the board, it was found that said duplicate requisitions were required by War Department order of March 28, 1864. At that time and until February, 1-88, the Bureaus of the Department were located in buildings remote from the main office, and the numerous inquiries in regard to requisitions rendered it necessary to have the duplicates at hand, in the Secretary's office, for ready reference.

The location of the Bureaus of the Department (with one exception) being now in the War Department Building, the board is of opinion that the duplication of such requisitions is no longer necessary, and it is recommended that the practice be discontinued.

Respectfully submitted.

JOHN TWEEDALE,
L. W. TOLMAN,
JACOB FRECH,
Members of Board.

Hon. WILLIAM C. ENDICOTT,
    Secretary of War.

The following order was issued upon the recommendation of the board:

[Circular.]

WAR DEPARTMENT,
Washington City, September 11, 1888.

All the Bureaus of the War Department, with one exception, being now located in the War Department Building it is no longer necessary that duplicates of requisitions on the Public Printer for printing and binding be prepared, and hereafter only one copy of such requisitions need be sent to the office of the Secretary of War, division of requisitions and accounts, a press-copy of the requisition to be retained in the office or bureau in which it was made, for reference therein.

By order of the Acting Secretary of War.

SAM'L HODGKINS,
Acting Chief Clerk.

APPENDIX NO. 8.

ADMINISTRATION.

WAR DEPARTMENT,
BOARD ON BUSINESS METHODS,
December 29, 1888.

The following proposed circular was referred to the board for consideration:

[Circular.]

WAR DEPARTMENT, *October* —, 1885.

Letters and other papers received at the War Department or any of its Bureaus will, unless otherwise directed, be at once sent to the offices to which they pertain without instructions, each chief of a bureau being responsible that the mail sent to him is promptly acted upon, and report made to the Secretary of War in cases requiring his action, or to which he should reply. When acted upon by the Secretary the proper notation will be made and the papers sent to the office to which the subject-matter pertains, unless instructions to the contrary are given, and generally only such papers will be filed in the office of the Secretary of War as do not pertain to the business of any of the subordinate Bureaus. This rule will also apply to the filing of papers in the Bureaus and offices of the Department. Only such papers will be filed in a given Bureau or office as clearly belong to its business and are within the jurisdiction of the chief thereof.

A paper submitted for the action of the Secretary of War will be so prepared as that the last indorsement or report shall contain in the fewest possible words a summary of the case, unless this appears in some report on the same or an accompanying paper to which reference is made; it should also show the question to be decided, and conclude with an opinion or recommendation. When necessary, the law, orders, or customs of the service governing in like cases will be stated, and each case made complete in itself, so that reference to previous papers will only be necessary to afford more definite information upon matters already summarized in the report.

Where it is evident that it will be necessary to send the report of the Bureau officer with the reply of the Secretary of War, the report should be separate from the papers or a copy of it submitted.

The Secretary of War requests chiefs of Bureaus to see that the requirements of this circular are fully complied with.

By direction of the Secretary of War.

——— ———,
Chief Clerk.

The consideration of this circular was deferred until the subject of correspondence was taken up. That subject has now been considered, and with the information thus obtained the board has the honor to report that the proposed circular will undoubtedly simplify and hasten the transaction of business. It requires papers to be filed where they properly belong and where they would naturally be looked for, and gives instructions how to prepare papers for the action of the Secretary so that the time necessary for their consideration will be reduced to the minimum.

These objects are of great importance, but as valuable suggestions may occur to chiefs of Bureaus which would tend to make the circular more complete and more certainly accomplish the object desired, it is respectfully recommended that a copy be referred to each chief of Bureau for his views and for such amendments as in his opinion should be made to it in order to simplify and hasten the work of the Department, and do away with unnecessary routine, and also that he be requested to transmit therewith a detailed statement of the classes of work falling within the jurisdiction of his office; the statements from the several Bureaus, when received, to be classified and arranged for ready reference, then printed and distributed, so that the clerks need not be in doubt where to send a paper as soon as its subject is ascertained.

The board would further recommend that the subject of correspondence be indicated by the writer in the upper left-hand corner of the first page of the letter or report. This can readily be done in three or four words, and would materially assist the speedy disposition of a large correspondence. The word "subject" should be printed on letter-heads at the place suggested, and a sufficient space left for the insertion of the necessary words.

This recommendation is based upon a similar system in use by the legal profession, by large corporations and commercial establishments, and is found to work well.

As a precedent in the line of action proposed in the circular under consideration, attention is invited to the letter of Quartermaster-General Meigs, dated August 22, 1873, and the decision of the Secretary of War thereon, as follows:

WAR DEPARTMENT,
QUARTERMASTER-GENERAL'S OFFICE,
Washington, D. C., August 22, 1873.

MY DEAR SIR: I have thought for a long time that a very unnecessary burden is imposed upon the War Department and upon the Secretary personally in the reviewing of papers transmitted from this office which might quite as well be disposed of here.

I send nothing to the Secretary which under present regulations and customs does not require his decision; but of this the daily mass is very great.

Ninety-nine out of the hundred are returned with the "recommendation of the Quartermaster-General approved," signed either by the Secretary himself, or by some officer, or by the chief clerk, as by his order. In every one of these cases a report must be written here, entered, and copied. This report and the papers go to the War Department, where they are entered, and the approval of the Secretary is noted and entered. They then are returned to this office and entered again, and the decision is transmitted or made known to the persons interested.

Now the cases in which the Secretary does not concur with the Quartermaster-General and simply approve are, I think, always of exceptional character, and are such as would be anticipated here—cases in which there is room for a difference of opinion, or in which there is doubt as to facts or as to law or regulations.

If the Quartermaster-General were authorized to dispose of such cases as he believes to be properly within the scope of his own authority by deciding them as Quartermaster-General, and if in the cases in which he is convinced that the decision of the Secretary can be distinctly foreseen by him, he was authorized to decide them and sign the decision by order of the Secretary, this would leave only the cases of delicacy or of doubt to be forwarded to the War Department; and while no great error, I think, would be likely to occur, it would very much relieve the Secretary's desk of mere routine which takes up his time and attention, and it would also diminish the clerical labor of record.

I am obliged to draught a formal report setting forth reasons for action, in order that the facts may be distinctly before you, whereas, were I authorized to decide in your name and "by order," no written report would be needed—the case would be decided upon personal knowledge and experience.

In cases in which the Quartermaster General may fall into error, appeal to the Secretary will generally prevent any great evil arising from his erroneous decision, and such appeal will generally be made by the parties to whom any injustice or injury is done through such mistake.

I make these suggestions, you will do me the justice to believe, from no desire to increase the powers of the Quartermaster-General, but simply from a desire to simplify the business and to diminish the volume of routine business and of record required in a routine or custom which has gradually grown up, I think, without any real necessity.

I think a change would leave both to the Secretary of War and to the Quartermaster-General more time and opportunity for thought and study of the higher and more responsible portion of their duties. Both are now too much buried under the weight of accumulating papers.

I am, very respectfully, your obedient servant,
M. C. MEIGS,
Quartermaster-General.

Hon. WILLIAM W. BELKNAP,
Secretary of War.

WAR DEPARTMENT, *September* 9, 1873.

Respectfully returned to the Quartermaster-General, who is hereby authorized to dispose of such cases as he may believe to be properly within the scope of his authority by deciding them as *Quartermaster-General;* and in cases in which the Quartermaster-General is convinced that the decision of the War Department can be distinctly foreseen by him, he is authorized to decide such cases and sign the decision " *By order of the Secretary of War.*"

WM. W. BELKNAP,
Secretary of War.

The present-Quartermaster-General, in a letter expressing his views as to the possibility of simplifying and improving the present method of conducting the correspondence of his office, says:

"In communicating with citizens not connected with the military service, upon matters which they may bring before the office, the correspondence is, as a rule, direct with the interested parties, and I can suggest no improvement in this respect. But the volume of papers which are placed upon my desk for signature consists largely of correspondence forward and backward between army officers, passing through this office as a channel from and to the Secretary of War and the Adjutant-General.

"To illustrate: A lieutenant and acting assistant quartermaster stationed at a military post, and 'reporting to an officer commanding troops,' receives a quantity of freight hauled from the nearest railroad station to the quartermaster's store-house, with a bill of perhaps fifty cents or a dollar, presented by the driver of the vehicle. The acting assistant quartermaster, in view of the law of July 5, 1884, 'that all transportation of stores by private parties shall be done by contract after due legal advertisement, except in cases of emergency, which must be at once reported to the Secretary of War,' prepares a report to his immediate commanding officer, through the adjutant of the post, setting forth in full the circumstances of the case, which report is forwarded, through the assistant adjutant-general of the department, to the department commander; referred to the department quartermaster for report; returned by the department quartermaster to the assistant adjutant-general of the department with report; forwarded by the department commander, through the assistant adjutant-general of the division, to the division commander; referred by the assistant adjutant-general of the division to the division commander; referred by the assistant adjutant-general of the division to the division quartermaster for notation or report; returned by the division quartermaster to the assistant adjutant-general of the division; forwarded by the division commander, through the Adjutant-General, to the Lieutenant-General of the Army; referred by the Adjutant-General to the Quartermaster-General for remark, 'to be returned;' returned by the Quartermaster-General to the Adjutant-General; submitted by the Lieutenant-General to the Secretary of War for approval; approved by the Secretary of War, and returned to the Lieutenant-General, who, through the Adjutant-General, advises the division commander of the decision of the Secretary of War, sending a copy of the letter to the Quartermaster-General, but as a rule retaining the papers upon the files of the Adjutant-General's Office, necessitating further research and correspondence, if they are needed for reference in similar cases which may arise, or in revision of officers' accounts of money or property expended. The division commander thereupon, it is presumed, communicates the decision of the Secretary of War, through the same channels, backward till it eventually reaches the lieutenant and acting assistant quartermaster, with whom the case originated, who thereupon prepares formal vouchers for the service.

"In like manner purchases of supplies made 'in cases of emergency without legal public notice and formal contract' are reported and acted upon through the same channels, and generally all matters requiring the action of the War Department.

"It is far from the purpose of the Quartermaster-General to interfere with or even to criticise the methods of correspondence which regulations prescribe and which in the wisdom of officers commanding troops may be necessary for proper military discipline; but it is submitted that in cases where such officers are not interested (where the laws specifically prescribe, as in section 1134, U. S. Revised Statutes), that the Quartermaster's Department alone, under the direction of the Secretary of War, shall act, irrespective of commanders of troops, and in all cases affecting merely the fiscal relations and responsibilities of officers of the Quartermaster's Department, all this circumlocutory routine, involving a waste of time, of high-priced clerical labor, and unnecessary work, should be abolished."

The Quartermaster-General concludes with the remark that—

"If the Secretary of War can be relieved of the work of reviewing cases, the principles of which have been previously determined (by intrusting and delegating to the Quartermaster-General the power of acting in his name), it is my opinion that it would result in a better and more economical dispatch of public business."

With reference to the views above expressed, it may be remarked that the order above quoted, of September 9, 1873, has not been revoked by the Secretary of War, and therefore it is believed that the proposed circular, in addition to this order, will accomplish the object desired by the Quartermaster-General, as far as it is possible to do so consistently with the duties of the Secretary of War.

If the order of September 9, 1873, is to be continued in force it should now be extended to all of the Bureaus of the Department, and the circular amended so as to authorize chiefs of Bureaus to dispose of such cases as they may believe to be properly within the scope of their authority, by deciding them in their own name; and when existing regulations or orders require certain cases to be submitted to the Secretary of War for his action, but in which there is no difference of opinion, no doubt as to the facts, law, or regulations, where the amount involved does not exceed $——, when the action of the Secretary in person is not required by law, in which the decision of the Secretary can be distinctly foreseen, or the principles of which have been previously determined, chiefs of Bureaus are authorized to decide such cases and sign the decision "By authority of the Secretary of War."

If all cases acted on under delegated authority are signed "By authority of the Secretary of War" and the signature "By order of the Secretary of War" is only used in cases where the Secretary has seen the papers and given orders, then the records will show with certainty just what cases have received the personal action of the Secretary of War. All of the cases signed by the Secretary or "By order of the Secretary of War" should be recorded or noted in the Secretary's office, in order that he may have under his immediate control the record of his own acts.

To further complete the circular, a clause should be added authorizing chiefs of Bureaus to correspond with any military commander or staff officer upon the business of their respective Bureaus, forwarding the same, or a copy, through or to any commander who should be informed of the contents thereof. This, it is thought, will secure rapidity and correctness of execution as well as of action, and save not only clerical labor but the time of officials who now have to deal with the matters under consideration.

Views in accord with the foregoing were expressed by several of the chiefs of Bureaus in their reports to the Secretary of War in April, 1885. These views are here quoted.

The Adjutant-General says:

"A large number of papers of an almost exclusively administrative character are sent to this office which, it seems to me, should be sent direct to the chiefs of administrative Bureaus having charge of the matters to which they relate. This would not only reduce considerably the clerical work of at least one of the branches of my office, but would greatly facilitate the transaction of business. To illustrate the present system of dealing with papers of this class I will cite an instance: An application is made by a post commander, through his post quartermaster, for an amount of lumber to make certain repairs; this is forwarded, approved, to department headquarters; from there it is sent to the division headquarters, and thence to the Adjutant-General. On its receipt here it is referred to the Quartermaster-General, and by him returned to the Adjutant-General, when the latter submits it to the Lieutenant-General, who returns it to the Adjutant-General to be laid before the Secretary of War. To simplify this, I beg to suggest that the Regulations be so modified that papers of the class mentioned shall be sent by the department commander direct to the chief of the Bureau who must take action upon them, and by him submitted to the Secretary of War for consideration. If the application involves a military question upon which the Secretary of War would like to have the opinion of the highest military authority before finally acting upon it, the paper, by his direction, can be submitted to the General commanding the Army for his views. I am quite satisfied that some such course would save labor in this office, not increase it in others, and be more likely to secure prompt and intelligent action than the circumlocutory one now pursued."

The Quartermaster-General says:

"The work of the office will be more efficient, provided:

"(1) The Quartermaster-General shall be permitted to act upon the papers pertaining to the fiscal matters of his own department, and, when necessary, to give the orders of the honorable the Secretary of War in regard thereto, being responsible to the honorable Secretary of War alone for his action. The officers of the Quartermaster's Department should correspond upon fiscal matters directly with the Quartermaster-General and receive his instructions directly thereon. (Copies of instructions received by any officer of the Quartermaster's Department affecting the distribution of supplies, public property, or a redistribution, should be shown to the military commander interested by the officer serving under him who receives them.)

"(2) The Quartermaster-General, under the Secretary of War, should give to any and all officers of the Quartermaster's Department all the necessary instructions about the transportation 'of military property and stores' throughout the United States under section 220, Revised Statutes. This applies to ordnance stores, to and from arsenals, to medical supplies, subsistence and quartermaster's stores, and to all transportation for the civil bureaus of the Government across the continent, under the statutes for land-grant roads.

"(3) The Quartermaster-General ought to give the honorable Secretary of War's instructions in regard to purchase of supplies out of the appropriation for his department, designating the place, time, and amounts authorized, the usual information about the same being given by them to the commanders under whom they are serving.

"To transact fiscal business through the medium of many different agents causes infinite confusion and confounds all principles of the division of labor, and renders it impossible to define and establish a just responsibility in the expenditures of public funds. The officers of the Quartermaster's Department, wherever stationed, when doing duty under their bonds, should be subject to the orders of the Quartermaster-General, under sections 1133 and 1139, in so far as they are fiscal officers, or in what relates to the expenditure of the appropriation for their Department, and no military commander should interfere with that part of their duties, unless in an emergency or to prevent a plain case of fraud on the Government. A gradual modification of the regulations will be necessary to fix these practices upon their proper legal footing, which prevailed in the military establishment until the late war.

"It is important that the Quartermaster-General keep the papers relating to his own Department in regard to fiscal matters and the supply of troops at military posts with fuel, forage, straw, stationery, water, and general supplies; and also in the construction of barracks and quarters; for, without the data and the proper knowledge of the changes and business of his Department going on at the several posts and stations he can form no correct opinions nor hold the officers of his Department to any such accountability as is contemplated by statute."

The Commissary-General of Subsistence says:

"In my opinion not only the work of this Bureau of the War Department, but that of others, has been considerably increased in recent years by the practice that has grown up, under the requirement of military commanders, whereby very much of the correspondence of the staff and supply departments of the Army has to be conducted by or through the Adjutant-General's Department of the Army, instead of being conducted directly with the chiefs of those departments, as formerly."

The Chief of Ordnance says:

"(1) The Ordnance Bureau is a branch of the War Department, and its records are a portion of the War Department records. All Ordnance Bureau papers, no matter where referred for action within the War Department, should therefore be finally returned to this office for file; a note of such disposition by other offices through which it passes being sufficient for the completion of their records. The same rule should apply to the papers belonging to other Bureaus passing through and acted on in like manner.

"(2) Army Regulations 2520 requires that requisitions, after approval by the *department* commander, shall be sent direct to the Chief of Ordnance, but it is of frequent occurrence to receive requisitions which, instead of being mailed direct by the department commander, have been by him forwarded to the division commander, and by him to the Adjutant-General, and by the latter sent to this office. A compliance with regulations would in such cases, and they are very numerous, save the Government much needless labor. It seems to me that so simple a rule should govern even without special regulations, and that is, that a paper that on its face clearly calls for the action of the Chief of Ordnance, and can not be acted on by any other official, ought to be sent *direct* to him. Should action be required by higher authority, it then goes properly indorsed by the only official whose duty is to advise, and the completed papers are in condition for final action."

In conclusion, if the recommendations of the board are approved, it is suggested that as this circular will authorize chiefs of Bureaus, as such, to dispose of cases which are within the scope of their authority, they should be requested to report hereafter, and as soon as business will permit, a list of general orders and paragraphs of Army Regulations which should be amended or revoked so as to conform to the letter and spirit of the circular, accompanied with a draught of an order to accomplish the purpose.

The circular, therefore, if amended in accordance with the foregoing suggestions, will read as follows:

[Circular.]

WAR DEPARTMENT,
—— ——, 1889.

Letters and other papers received at the War Department or any of its Bureaus will, unless otherwise directed, be at once sent to the offices to which they pertain without instructions, each chief of a Bureau being responsible that the mail sent to him is promptly acted upon and report made to the Secretary of War in cases requiring his action, or to which he should reply. When acted upon by the Secretary the proper notation will be made and the papers sent to the office to which the subject-matter pertains, unless instructions to the contrary are given; and generally only such papers will be filed in the office of the Secretary of War as do not pertain to the business of any of the subordinate Bureaus. This rule will also apply to the filing of papers in the Bureaus and offices of the Department. Only such papers will be filed in a given bureau or office as clearly belong to its business and are within the jurisdiction of the chief thereof.

A paper submitted for the action of the Secretary of War will be so prepared as that the last indorsement or report shall contain, in the fewest possible words, a summary of the case, unless this appears in some report on the same or an accompanying paper to which reference is made; it should also show the question to be decided, and conclude with an opinion or recommendation. When necessary the law, orders, or customs of the service governing in like cases will be stated, and the case made complete in itself, so that reference to previous papers will only be necessary to afford more definite information upon matters already summarized in the report.

Where it is evident that it will be necessary to send the report of the Bureau officer with the reply of the Secretary of War, the report should be separate from the papers or a copy of it submitted.

The subject of correspondence will be indicated by the writer in the upper left-hand corner of the first page of the letter or report, the "subject" not to exceed three or four words.

Chiefs of Bureaus are authorized to decide cases properly within the scope of their authority in their own name. When existing regulations or orders require certain cases to be submitted to the Secretary of War for his action, but in which there is no difference of opinion, no doubt as to the facts, law, or regulations, where the amount involved does not exceed $——, when the decision of the Secretary of War can be distinctly foreseen, or the principles of which have been previously determined, chiefs of Bureaus are authorized to decide such cases and sign the decision "By authority of the Secretary of War," provided, any case so decided pertains to the particular class of business over which the chief of the Bureau who decides the case has jurisdiction.

All cases decided by the Secretary of War, or in which he has given orders, will be signed either by the Secretary or "By *order* of the Secretary of War," and all such cases must be noted or recorded in the office of the Secretary.

Chiefs of Bureaus are authorized to correspond with any military commander or staff officer upon the business of their respective Bureaus, forwarding the same, or a copy, through or to any commander who should be informed of the contents thereof.

The Secretary of War requests chiefs of Bureaus to see that the requirements of this circular are fully complied with.

By order of the Secretary of War.

———— ————,
Chief Clerk.

Respectfully submitted.

JOHN TWEEDALE,
L. W. TOLMAN,
JACOB FRECH,
Members of Board.

Hon. WILLIAM C. ENDICOTT,
Secretary of War.

[Indorsement.]

WAR DEPARTMENT,
January 15, 1889.

Respectfully referred to* for his views and for such amendments as in his opinion should be made to the circular in order to simplify and hasten the work of the Department and do away with unnecessary routine; also for a detailed statement of the classes of work falling within the jurisdiction of his office. This report is desired by the 22d instant. It is the intention when the statements from the several chiefs of Bureaus are received to have them classified and arranged for ready reference; then to be printed and distributed, so that there need be no doubt where to send a paper when its subject is ascertained.

When report shall have been made upon this circular, you are requested to transmit as soon as possible thereafter a list of general orders and paragraphs of Army Regulations which should be amended or revoked, so as to conform to the letter and spirit of this circular, accompanied with a draught of an order to accomplish the purpose.

WILLIAM C. ENDICOTT,
Secretary of War.

---

* To the chiefs of the several Bureaus of the War Department.

APPENDIX No. 9.

MESSENGER SERVICE.

WAR DEPARTMENT,
BOARD ON BUSINESS METHODS,
January 17, 1889.

The board having taken into consideration the subject of transfer of official papers between bureaus, divisions, sections, and desks, has the honor to submit the following report and recommendation:

MEANS OF FREQUENT COMMUNICATION BETWEEN BUREAUS, DIVISIONS, SECTIONS, AND DESKS BY MESSENGER SERVICE.

A letter, paper, or case necessarily passes through many hands from the time of its receipt in the Department until it is finally acted upon and disposed of. Hence the necessity for frequent communication in person or by messenger between officials or clerks who have in any manner to deal with one and the same item of business.

In theory, cases not routine are transferred as soon as ready for action by another person; but new business follows close on the completed, and the mind occupied with it instantly leaves the finished work, which may not be at once transferred by reason of the messenger being otherwise engaged. In practice, therefore, it happens that delays do occur, and the mail is consequently moved at irregular intervals. This delay principally affects the merely routine cases, which constitute a large part of the work, and which are not liable to have attention called to them. It becomes of great importance, therefore, to adopt a system which shall be automatic, and move all cases with the rapidity of special cases.

The amount of delay resulting from infrequent communication becomes apparent in timing the transfer of a paper which for the sake of brevity and simplicity will be presumed in the following illustration to require but slight action at each of the six stages through which it is traced, and that papers of that class are transferred as often as twice a day.

(1) A receives a paper on Monday morning, acts on it without delay, and places it with similar papers in a basket or box for delivery by messenger to B.

(2) B receives it on the same day by afternoon delivery, acts on it, and places it in a basket for delivery by messenger to C.

(3) C receives it on Tuesday morning, acts on it, and it goes in a similar manner to D.

(4) D receives it on Tuesday afternoon, acts on it, and sends it to E.

(5) E receives it on Wednesday morning, acts on it, and sends it to F.

(6) F receives it on Wednesday afternoon, acts on it, and sends it to G, who receives it on Thursday morning.

Thus there may be three whole days consumed in simply passing a paper through six hands; and this on a supposition that it is acted on by each person as soon as received, or at least is not delayed by arrearage of similar papers not yet acted on at any of the stages of its progress. It is evident that much of this delay can be obviated by providing for the more frequent transfer of papers from one branch of work to another.

Half-hourly office mail delivery.

It is therefore recommended that round-trip collections and deliveries be punctually made at the different delivery baskets or boxes in a Bureau, at least once every half hour, thus bringing all the rooms, sections, and divisions of a Bureau in frequent and regular communication with each other; so that a paper that has received appropriate action at any stage of its progress, goes from the desk at which it has just been acted on to the desk at which it is to receive its next action within thirty minutes.

It is also recommended that similar half-hourly collections and deliveries be adopted for the transfer of papers between the several Bureaus and the office of the Secretary.

In order that the fullest benefit may be derived from this frequent means of communication—

(1) All papers should be immediately taken up on receipt and placed in the hands of one or more of the clerks engaged upon the class or classes of work pertaining thereto.

(2) If such clerks have an arrearage of work on hand, every possible exertion should be made to dispose of such arrearage, so that a paper will not have to lie hours or days simply awaiting its turn.

(3) Every paper that has received suitable action should be placed in the delivery-box before or at the time of the next collection.

(4) In other words, if two or more cases are acted on by any clerk in any half hour, let them all be transferred by the next delivery; but if only one case has been acted on by him in any half hour, let it be transferred by the next delivery, and not lie on a desk simply because other similar cases have not yet been acted on.

Under this method of frequent and regular delivery of papers, every case will be moved with practically the same expedition as special cases. The necessity for replying to urgent inquiries about delayed cases, entertaining requests to make such cases special, looking them up in the office, taking them out of their regular routine, and watching them closely at each stage of their progress to prevent their relapse into the routine, would be practically reduced to the minimum.

Cases requiring immediate action should, of course, be delivered at once from hand to hand by clerks or messengers, as the frequent regular delivery is intended only to expedite cases which are now moved at longer intervals of time.

Office mail-cards.

In order that a paper or number of papers may be readily dispatched to their destination, appropriate reversible cards or jackets, plainly addressed, should be provided for the transmission of such papers wherever practicable.

Such card or jacket can be placed on top of a thick package of papers or folded about a few papers, and held fast by means of a rubber band, so that it may be readily unfastened.

The cards should have the address in red ink of the room or division from which sent on the inside of both folds, and that of the room or division to which sent in black ink on the outside of both folds, so that when the card is folded the address may be readily seen with either side up. The folds should be of stiff card-board, hinged with muslin.

As the addresses on the card accompanying the papers will always clearly indicate to whom they are to go, and from whom they came, addressing of envelopes or slips will be obviated.

Where A usually sends papers to B, the cards used by A may be addressed to B in black, and contain the address of A on the reverse side in red, with remark: "Return to A." This will insure the return of the cards to A for use by the next delivery.

So, where B has occasion to send papers to A, B should be provided with a similar set of cards, with A's address in black and B's in red, with remark: "Return to B." This will prevent all the cards being at one end of the line when some are wanted at the other.

While a difference in color of addresses is not indispensable, it will be found convenient where many cards from different sources are handled, as when a card is received having a black address on the outside it is at once known that it belongs to the division indicated in red on the reverse side, so it need simply be reversed, after taking out the papers, and dropped into the outgoing basket, while one received with a red address outside is retained, it having arrived at the division where it belongs.

To accomplish the half-hourly mail delivery it will be necessary in most of the Bureaus to have one or more messengers exclusively engaged upon this work. They can, no doubt, be readily designated, as the other messengers will have more time to attend to other work.

Respectfully submitted.

JOHN TWEEDALE,
L. W. TOLMAN,
JACOB FRENCH,
Members of Board.

Hon. WM. C. ENDICOTT,
Secretary of War.

[Orders.]

WAR DEPARTMENT,
Washington City, January 18, 1889.

In order to secure frequent and prompt delivery of official papers between the rooms or sections of a Bureau, the chief of each Bureau in which the business transacted will warrant such action, is hereby directed to assign an assistant messenger or laborer to the duty of regularly collecting and delivering official papers.

Collections and deliveries to be punctually made by the designated carrier at all the delivery baskets or boxes in a Bureau every half hour, viz, 8.45, 9.15, 9.45, 10.15, 10.45, 11.15, 11.45 a. m.; 12.30, 1.00, 1.30, 2.00, 2.30, 3.00 and 3.30 p. m.; the carrier calling at each mail-basket twice each trip, once going and once returning, so as to insure the transmission of completed papers in either direction throughout the Bureau each half hour.

Similar half-hourly collections and delivery of papers will be made between the several Bureaus and the office of the Secretary by an assistant messenger or laborer, to be designated by the chief clerk of the Department; the hours of delivery being 9.00, 9.30, 10.00, 10.30, 11.00, and 11.30 a. m.; 12.00 m.; 12.45, 1.15, 1.45, 2.15, 2.45, 3.15, and 3.45 p. m.

In order that the fullest benefit may be derived from this method of communication, chiefs of Bureaus will require that all papers delivered be immediately taken up and placed in the hands of clerks engaged upon the work pertaining thereto; and that every paper that has been acted upon in one room, and which requires action in another, be placed in the delivery box before or at the time of the next collection. Cases which require immediate action will, of course, be delivered at once. The half-hour delivery applies to cases which have been moved at longer intervals.

Reversible mail-cards or jackets, plainly addressed, will be used for the protection and safe transmission of papers, wherever their shape or size will permit; the address of the room or division from which sent to be in red ink on the inside of both folds, and of the room or division to which sent in black ink on the outside of both folds.

In order to allow time for the preparation of the necessary mail-cards, this order will be carried into effect on the 1st of February next.

In the meantime estimates of the number and sizes of cards will be made by each Bureau.

As explanatory of this system, the report of the board on business methods is hereto appended.

WM. C. ENDICOTT,
Secretary of War.

APPENDIX No. 10.

SUPPLY DIVISION.

WAR DEPARTMENT,
BOARD ON BUSINESS METHODS,
January 18, 1889.

The board has the honor to submit the following report upon the subject of the procurement of supplies for the Department and its Bureaus:

For many years prior to 1882 the contract for supplying stationery was awarded to the bidder whose total bid for all the items on the schedule was the lowest, and each Bureau purchased directly from the contractor. The form of the advertisement inviting proposals for stationery was changed by the Secretary of War in his advertisement of May 22, 1882, the following clause being inserted: "Bids will be considered on each item separately." Bidders were required to submit samples of the goods proposed to be furnished, and a board of experienced clerks was appointed to pass upon the samples received, with instructions to "consider each item separately and determine their recommendation for an award on each article before passing to the next." Upon the approval of the recommendation of the board by the Secretary of War, a contract was entered into with the lowest bidder who proposed to furnish a particular item of stationery equal to the sample selected.

Prior to 1883 each Bureau had a separate appropriation for office contingencies, out of which articles of stationery and miscellaneous supplies were purchased, and until that year miscellaneous supplies were purchased as needed by each Bureau without advertisement. In the act approved March 3, 1883 (22 Statutes, 552), the fourteen separate appropriations for office contingencies, were merged into two appropriations, one for stationery, the other for contingent expenses, which includes miscellaneous supplies, and these two appropriations were placed under the direct control of the Secretary of War. The method adopted in 1882 for the purchase of stationery, as described above, has since 1883 been applied as far as possible to the purchase of miscellaneous supplies.

The following table shows the result for each year from 1882 to 1888:

Statement of expenditures.

FOR MISCELLANEOUS SUPPLIES.

Office or Bureau.	Fiscal year ending—						
	June 30, 1882.*	June 30, 1883.*	June 30, 1884.	June 30, 1885.	June 30, 1886.	June 30, 1887.	June 30, 1888.
Secretary's			$5,188.60	$7,774.03	$5,050.90	$6,552.83	$7,449.38
Adjutant-General			11,494.98	11,003.08	10,400.21	10,643.93	10,467.28
Surgeon-General			11,452.55	10,716.45	9,854.19	10,055.59	12,644.18
Quartermaster-General			7,791.86	7,816.21	7,971.90	6,581.41	7,135.41
Paymaster-General			3,091.65	2,398.12	2,783.79	2,525.02	2,142.30
Chief of Engineers			2,036.66	2,017.57	1,423.29	1,447.29	2,527.96
Chief of Ordnance			1,418.27	2,106.66	1,369.54	1,941.56	1,766.94
Commissary-General			1,801.45	2,313.39	2,115.30	1,560.54	2,200.58
Winder Building			4,291.70	4,144.21	8,777.46	5,880.71	3,748.87
Inspector-General			284.82	430.46	162.28	144.20	404.04
War Records			1,717.88	1,785.53	1,920.14	1,944.69	1,241.57
Judge-Advocate-General			1,207.90	1,979.01	1,519.89	1,476.09	704.56
Signal			1,906.95	7,036.15	7,304.22	7,090.03	7,012.74
Total			53,745.45	61,610.87	60,653.11	57,849.89	59,535.81

* No separate record.

FOR STATIONERY.

Secretary's	$8,502.26	$1,449.58	1,983.48	3,025.68	2,700.03	2,668.48	1,846.91
Adjutant-General	5,635.24	3,627.71	3,965.28	4,613.80	5,356.10	3,368.71	0,714.71
Surgeon-General	5,758.18	4,920.15	4,489.31	5,011.17	4,645.62	3,811.74	4,087.87
Quartermaster-General	3,594.84	2,078.61	2,985.52	2,914.16	2,987.30	3,235.25	2,945.53
Paymaster-General	1,127.49	773.04	384.97	441.82	658.48	504.01	651.76
Chief of Engineers	1,184.42	1,074.05	1,053.77	858.02	988.03	1,159.83	772.02
Chief of Ordnance	864.92	629.70	858.64	703.27	531.89	939.95	840.21
Commissary-General	562.06	402.13	292.18	344.37	400.05	457.58	232.53
Winder Building							
Inspector-General	241.00	36.45	57.43	194.55	254.80	139.68	130.86
War Records	1,081.43	578.91	360.75	538.80	464.87	404.28	411.29
Judge-Advocate-General	217.80	222.89	222.88	285.22	305.00	243.12	260.41
Signal	4,249.48	2,655.69	4,519.68	3,489.63	4,182.85	3,710.61	4,060.34
Total	33,919.12	18,448.91	21,173.89	22,420.49	23,474.62	20,643.24	22,954.44

The first column (1882) of the table of expenditures for stationery shows the amount expended under the old system when the contract was awarded in bulk to one person, and is about the average amount expended in previous years. The other columns show the result of the new system, under which the saving in the Secretary's office was over 80 per cent. in 1883, and over 75 per cent. in 1884, and over 40 per cent. in the whole Department, and yet early in 1883 over six hundred new clerks were added to the force of the Department. The expenditures have been substantially uniform in amount since the adoption of the new system. It is to be regretted that, as no separate account was kept of the expenditures for miscellaneous supplies prior to July 1, 1883, it is not possible to make a comparison of the expenditures for those supplies.

Up to July 21, 1884, the chief clerk of the Department, under the Secretary, had charge of the purchase and issue of stationery and miscellaneous supplies, with the proper assistants in immediate charge. The system worked well and economically, but neither the Secretary nor the chief clerk could exercise careful personal supervision of the work, their time being so fully occupied with more important official matters. The Secretary, therefore, to relieve himself of direct responsibility for the purchase and issue of supplies for which he was contracting officer, decided to place the business in charge of a bonded officer of the Quartermaster's Department of the Army. Accordingly the following circular was issued:

[Circular.]

WAR DEPARTMENT,
Washington City, July 21, 1884.

The following is published for the information and guidance of the chiefs of Bureaus and officers on duty in the War Department:

(1) The stationery and miscellaneous supply divisions of the War Department will be consolidated, and known as the "supply division of the War Department."

(2) The officer assigned to duty in charge of the supply division will purchase, issue, and account for all supplies for the War Department and its Bureaus, in accordance with the regulations prescribed for the Quartermaster's Department of the Army. Exclusive of the libraries, he will take up and account for all public property belonging to the War Department and its Bureaus. Chiefs of Bureaus will cause their chief clerks, superintendents of buildings, or other persons in charge to furnish the officer accountable with memorandum receipts for all property in their respective Bureaus or divisions.

(3) For all indebtedness incurred by the officer in charge of the supply division on account of the War Department and its Bureaus he will prepare and certify proper vouchers for payment by the disbursing clerk of the War Department. He will have charge of and properly keep the books referred to in section 197, Revised Statutes of the United States, and will keep such other books and records as may be necessary to make, at all times, a clear and correct exhibit of all purchases, issues, stock on hand, and expenses incurred on account of the War Department and its Bureaus.

(4) Notice of the allotment to the several Bureaus and offices from the amount appropriated for contingent expenses will be given from this office, and the sum allotted to each will not be exceeded without special authority from the Secretary of War.

(5) When property or supplies are required for the service of any Bureau of the War Department, requisition therefor, signed or approved by the chief of Bureau, will be made by the officer in charge of the supply division of the War Department.

Bills for gas, telegraphing, freight, and express charges will be rendered as heretofore, verified by the respective chiefs of Bureaus, and forwarded to the Secretary of War for payment.

Repairs of buildings and furniture, which require immediate attention, may be made under the supervision of the chief of the Bureau in which the repairs are needed, and the bills for the same, after having received his approval, will be forwarded to this office for payment.

ROBERT T. LINCOLN,
Secretary of War.

The officer detailed (Capt. C. H. Hoyt) has since continued in charge. He makes all the contracts and issues the supplies. It was the intention, as will be seen from the circular, to have the officer account for the supplies "in accordance with the regulations prescribed for the Quartermaster's Department;" that is, his accounts, vouchers, etc., should be audited by the Third Auditor of the Treasury, that officer having charge of the accounts of quartermasters. But the quartermaster in charge of the War Department supply division makes no disbursements. All of his accounts are paid by the disbursing clerk of the War Department, from the proper appropriation, which is contained in the legislative, executive, and judicial appropriation act. The expenditures from this appropriation are audited by the First Auditor of the Treasury, and the accounts and vouchers of the officer in charge of the supply division must go there for audit if anywhere. But that officer does not audit the accounts of quartermasters, and consequently has no clerks skilled in the requirements of the Army Regulations. To overcome the difficulty a circular was issued, providing that after passing the scrutiny of the Quartermaster-General the accounts should be filed in the office of the Secretary.

The following is the circular:

[Circular.]

WAR DEPARTMENT,
WASHINGTON CITY, *February 19, 1885.*

Referring to the circular of July 21, 1884, from this Department, establishing the "supply division of the War Department," the following regulations will be observed in accounting for the supplies furnished said division:

The officer assigned to duty in charge of the supply division will purchase, issue, and account for all supplies for the War Department and its Bureaus, in accordance with the regulations prescribed for the Quartermaster's Department of the Army. His property returns will be examined in the office of the Quartermaster-General, and if not satisfactory, he will furnish such additional information as will satisfy the Quartermaster-General that the property has been properly purchased, issued, and accounted for; except that the propriety of the purchase of any article will not be raised by the Quartermaster-General.

The officer in charge of the supply division—when in doubt as to the propriety of filling any requisition made upon him under Paragraph V of War Department circular of July 21, 1884, will submit the question to the Secretary of War for decision.

When the returns have passed the scrutiny of the Quartermaster-General, and are satisfactory to him, they will be forwarded to the Secretary of War for file in the War Department.

When supplies are issued from the supply division to the War Department and its Bureaus, they will be receipted for in each Bureau by an officer of the Army on duty in the Bureau designated for the purpose, with the approval of the Secretary of War, and in the office of the Secretary of War by the chief clerk or the officer acting for him, which receipts will be a sufficient discharge of the officer in charge of the supply division of his accountability for the articles covered by the receipts.

Fuel and articles of stationery and the minor items of miscellaneous supplies will be dropped from further accountability when issued and properly receipted for; the larger and more important articles of miscellaneous supplies will be accounted for by the officer in charge of the supply division, under section 197 of the Revised Statutes.

ROBERT T. LINCOLN,
Secretary of War.

From the foregoing it will be seen that an officer of the Army was assigned to the charge of the supply division for two reasons; first, that he might be the contracting officer, and as such contract in his own name for supplies for the Department and be directly responsible for their purchase and issue; and, second, that he should account for all such supplies purchased and issued in accordance with the regulations prescribed for the Quartermaster's Department of the Army.

The second reason for the assignment has not been fully accomplished, because, as stated above, it was not practicable to have his accounts audited where those of other quartermasters were audited. It may also be said that he has no accounts to audit, as he makes no disbursements, all of the accounts for supplies purchased being paid by the disbursing clerk of the War Department, whose accounts are audited by the First Auditor.

The second reason failing, the first may readily be met by requiring one of the clerks to give bond for the faithful performance of his duties and authorizing him to contract for supplies.

It is believed the security afforded by an officer of the Army being in charge of the division is not any greater than it would be if a bonded clerk was placed in charge. All of the Bureaus of the Department (except the Signal Office) are now in one building, and the records and stores of the supply division may be inspected at any time. As the officer in charge of the division will go upon the retired list this year, the board has no hesitation in recommending that the supply division be placed in charge of a clerk in the Secretary's Office, who shall be required to give bond. From consultation with chiefs of Bureaus it is believed this will give general satisfaction. The system of purchasing and issuing supplies in this Department is practically the same as that adopted in the Department of the Interior, the Treasury, and in other Departments.

In concluding this report attention is called to the fact that the salaries of like positions in other Departments are as follows: The chief of the division of stationery, printing, and blanks, Treasury Department, $2,500; the chief of the miscellaneous division, Treasury Department, $2,500; the chief of the stationery and printing division, Interior Department, $2,000, and the custodian in charge of miscellaneous supplies, same Department, $1,600. The custodian gives bond in the sum of $5,000. The supply division of the War Department purchases and issues both stationery and miscellaneous supplies. The salary of the chief of that division should therefore equal that of the chief of the stationery division of the Treasury. In the annual estimates the salaries of all chiefs of division in this Department are recommended to be $2,400.

Respectfully submitted.

JOHN TWEEDALE,
L. W. TOLMAN,
JACOB FRECH,
Members of Board.

Hon. WILLIAM C. ENDICOTT,
Secretary of War.

[Orders.]

WAR DEPARTMENT,
Washington City, January 19, 1889.

Capt. Charles H. Hoyt, assistant quartermaster, U. S. Army, is hereby relieved from duty in charge of the supply division of this Department, and will report to the Quartermaster-General.

Mr. M. R. Thorp, chief clerk of the supply division, is assigned to the charge of the supply division. He will give bond in the sum of $10,000 for the faithful performance of his duties; and will enter upon his duties after his bond is approved by the Secretary of War.

He will purchase, issue, and account for all supplies and property in accordance with the regulations contained in the circulars of July 21, 1884, and February 19, 1885, except that portion of the regulations mentioned which requires supplies to be purchased, issued, and accounted for in accordance with the regulations prescribed for the Quartermaster's Department of the Army and the property returns of the officer in charge to be examined in the office of the Quartermaster-General, in lieu of which requirements the books and accounts of the supply division will be hereafter inspected and reported upon by an officer of the Inspector-General's Department, in accordance with the regulations governing that Department.

WILLIAM C. ENDICOTT,
Secretary of War.

APPENDIX No. 11.

DAILY REPORTS OF WORK.

WAR DEPARTMENT,
BOARD ON BUSINESS METHODS,
January 19, 1889.

The attention of the board having been called to the matter of daily reports of the amount and character of work performed by clerks, after careful examination the following report is respectfully submitted:

The act approved August 26, 1842 (section 13, now section 173, Revised Statutes), provides that "each chief clerk in the several Departments and bureaus, and other officers connected with the Departments, shall supervise, under the direction of his immediate superior, the duties of the other clerks therein, and see that they are faithfully performed."

In the same section (now section 174, Revised Statutes) it is also provided that he "shall take care, from time to time, that the duties of the other clerks are distributed with equality and uniformity according to the nature of the case. He shall revise such distribution, from time to time, for the purpose of correcting any tendency to undue accumulation or reduction of duties, whether arising from individual negligence or incapacity, or from increase or diminution of particular kinds of business; and he shall report monthly to his superior officer any existing defect that he may be aware of in the arrangement or dispatch of business."

And in the same section (now section 175, Revised Statutes) it is further provided that "each head of a Department, chief of a bureau, or other superior officer, shall, upon receiving each monthly report of his chief clerk, rendered pursuant to the preceding section, examine the facts stated therein, and take such measures in the exercise of the powers conferred upon him by law, as may be necessary and proper to amend any existing defects in the arrangement or dispatch of business disclosed by such report."

On the 11th of April, 1845, the President addressed the following letter to the Secretary of War upon the subject:

WASHINGTON CITY, *April* 11, 1845.

SIR: In executing the laws there is no duty which appears to me more imperative than to take care that officers who receive the public money shall promptly and fully perform the duties for which the law appropriates their respective salaries. Justice to the public and a proper regard for the clearly expressed will of Congress require that this shall be done. Those who come to the seat of Government on public business should not be unnecessarily delayed by the negligence or inattention of the heads of bureaus or clerks connected with the Executive Departments. I therefore invite your attention to the thirteenth section of the act of Congress approved on the 26th August, 1842, entitled "An act legalizing and making appropriations for such necessary objects as have been usually included in the general appropriation bills without authority of law, and to fix and provide for certain incidental expenses of the departments and officers of Government, and for other purposes;" and to the twelfth section of the "Act to reorganize the General Land Office," approved on the 4th of July, 1836.

I desire that you will cause the monthly reports required by the act of 1842 to be regularly made and that you will transmit them to me.

The law contemplates that the distribution of labor amongst the clerks shall bear a fair proportion to their compensation, and it is unjust that the meritorious and faithful should have to perform the duties of such as may be found to be negligent, idle, or incompetent. To prevent this injustice, it is essential that each clerk shall attend regularly in his office, and discharge his own appropriate duties. It is desired that each head of a bureau shall cause to be kept a daily statement showing the absence of each clerk from his duty, during office hours—the causes of such absence as far as he may be able to ascertain them, and that this statement accompany the monthly reports.

I also desire that you will accompany the monthly reports with a statement of any complaints which may be made to you of any clerk in your office who may have contracted debts since his appointment, and does not pay them agreeably to his contract. Disclaiming any right to interfere with the private affairs of officers of Government, I am yet unwilling that they shall be embarrassed in the performance of their public duties by the just importunities of disappointed creditors, who trusted them on the faith of their compensation from the Treasury.

Believing that the duties required of the officers and clerks employed in the several Executive Departments are by no means unreasonable, and impressed with the importance of a prompt and efficient dispatch of the public business, I desire that you will take measures for the due execution of the laws to which I have called your attention.

Respectfully, yours,

JAMES K. POLK.

Hon. WILLIAM L. MARCY,
    Secretary of War.

Thereupon the following circular was issued by the Secretary of War

[Circular to the bureaus of the War Department.]

WAR DEPARTMENT, *April* 25, 1845.

Particular attention is directed to be paid to the reports required by the thirteenth section of the act of August 26, 1842, relative to clerks, etc., and a strict compliance with all its provisions is required; and it is further required that all absences from office between the hours of half past eight a. m. and half past three p. m., for which permission has not been given, be embraced in the monthly reports. "It is unjust that the meritorious and faithful should have to perform the duties of such as may be found negligent, idle, or incompetent."

W. L. MARCY,
    Secretary of War.

The monthly reports of chief clerks required by section 174, Revised Statutes, do not seem to have been made in writing from December, 1851, until April, 1887, when the following circular was issued by the Secretary of War:

[Circular.]

WASHINGTON CITY, *April* 23, 1887.

The attention of heads of bureaus of the War Department is invited to sections 173, 174, and 175, of the Revised Statutes, and a strict compliance therewith is enjoined.

Heads of bureaus will require each clerk in their respective offices to make a daily report of his (or her) attendance, and of the amount and character of work performed, and will require the respective chief clerks to submit to them a monthly report, compiled from the daily reports, showing the attendance of the clerks, the business transacted in the office during the month, and the amount remaining on hand to be disposed of. These reports should be made on blank forms, and should not contain statements of work which can not be verified by reference to the records, such as oral inquiries and replies, a remark on the blank form being sufficient to cover all that need be said in regard to work that can not be tabulated.

By order of the Secretary of War:

JOHN TWEEDALE,
    Chief Clerk.

This circular provides that the daily report of work performed by each clerk "should not contain statements of work which can not be verified by reference to the records, such as oral inquiries and replies."

From the fact that only statements of oral inquiries and replies were specifically excepted from the requirements of the circular, it was generally understood that a detailed report was required of all work not falling under the head of oral inquiries or replies. As a consequence, at the end of each month the chief clerks of some of the Bureaus receive a voluminous mass of figures to consolidate, indicating minute classification of clerical business, from much of which no useful deduction can be made as to the relative or actual amount of work performed by individual clerks or by the divisions in the Bureau.

The blank form for the monthly report of the chief clerk of the Signal Office has two hundred and twelve columns, with a printed heading for each, indicating the various kinds of work performed. The footings of the columns on the November re-report vary from 2 to 40,144.

The Chief Signal Officer, in his annual report for 1888, invites attention "to the great and apparently profitless consumption of time at Government expense entailed by the daily reports of work, made by each person performing clerical duty, to the chief clerk of this office as prescribed by existing orders. It is within bounds to estimate that the cost of such work to the Government consumes the time of four clerks, at an expense of about $4,000 annually. The outcome of such daily reports is a summary, which, indeed, tells how many letters have been read and distributed, how many briefed, recorded, and numbered, how many noted, and other items of like character, but it is impossible that data of this character shall give any adequate idea of the amount of work annually performed by the clerk. Many letters are of such a character that fifty such letters daily would not be an arduous task for a type-writer or copyist, while others are of such length, and are written under such disadvantages that ten of them would entail a hard day's work.

"The chiefs of divisions should be, and are believed to be, men of such character and standing that they can be relied upon to see that the clerks under their charge do a fair day's work for the Government, and in case any division chief is inclined to favor any person under his charge, he is enabled, under the present system, to so arrange matters that the poorest clerk in the division can have the largest record on paper. It is urgently recommended that the report be discontinued."

The chief clerk of the Surgeon-General's office says:

"Experience in this office has developed some features probably not so clear at the date of the circular. These features are all of an unfavorable character. The smallest apparent objection is that it consumes time. The last monthly report showed 357 clerks present for duty the whole or part of the time, making approximately 9,000 days' work, the details of which are to be compiled and tabulated. These details for the month aggregate 611,867, or for the year, 7,342,404. I compute that the time occupied in making and tabulating these reports is equal to that of three clerks the year round. As the average pay of clerks in this Bureau is $1,259.47 the annual expense to the country is $3,778.41.

"What the above enormous figures represent is not easy to say, as they have no common measure, and there is not the slightest resemblance in the things counted. I shall for the nonce call the items of work, of whatever kind—'somethings'—and we soon find that one man does a good many more 'somethings' than another, who may be just as fully employed. The clerks in the museum average 169 'somethings,' while those in the library, under the same supervision, make 1,600. 'A' is credited with doing 28,101 'somethings' in the month, and on the same page, opposite the name of 'B,' is the figure 2. Even things of the same name are not necessarily equivalent. What I now write may be called a letter and so may a sheet that requires only three lines of writing, and it is so throughout.

"Again the figures, whatever they may mean, have not the character of evidence. They are written solely by the men whose real or supposed interest is to make the best showing they can. I do not say that any one makes a false report; but I do say that if in a body of three hundred and fifty men not one will deviate a unit from verity to favor himself, then they are honest enough to do without this contrivance. If they be not honest it will do no good. It may be said that the clerk's report should be verified and certified by the chief of the division. To that the simple answer is that it can't be done. Suppose a clerk claims to have made two hundred entries and cross references, here and there in several books. To verify them would take nearly as much time as to make them—that is, the whole of it; and during the verification the clerk and his books would be idle. The process would be self-destructive.

"When a clerk is employed upon work presenting no result that can be counted or measured he is allowed to be let off with a marginal remark. I find, in consequence, seventy-nine men employed wholly, and seventy-one partly, on work that can not be counted. To count a part and omit the rest gives no better measure than to omit the whole. 'B,' named above, did two 'somethings' in March and an indeterminate quantity of something else; and the total would be as intelligible if the first element were left out. Thus for one hundred and fifty clerks the reports fail on their face; and those who handle them best know that for the remainder they afford nothing either significant or reliable.

"It has been found impossible to substitute these reports for any of the records or memoranda already kept by the office for its own information. Hence they are wholly superadded. When a clerk works six days under an intelligent superior, a pretty fair estimate can be made of his capabilities, and his assignment to any particular duty is based upon such estimate."

In view of the foregoing and upon examination of the forms used, the board is of opinion that the order of April 23, 1887, has been too literally construed, and that in consequence labor and time have been consumed in reporting details of work without corresponding beneficial results.

It is therefore recommended that the circular of April 23, 1887, be rescinded, and that chiefs of Bureaus be authorized to exercise their discretion in the matter of reports of work performed in their respective Bureaus, having in view the duties required to be performed by chief clerks under sections 173 and 174 of the Revised Statutes.

Respectfully submitted.

JOHN TWEEDALE,
L. W. TOLMAN,
JACOB FRECH,
Members of Board.

Hon. WILLIAM C. ENDICOTT,
Secretary of War.

The following order was issued upon the recommendation of the board:

[Circular.]

WAR DEPARTMENT, *January* 21, 1889.

The circular of April 23, 1887, which requires reports to be made of work performed in the several Bureaus of the Department is hereby rescinded.

Chiefs of Bureaus are authorized to exercise their discretion in the matter of reports of work performed in their respective Bureaus, having in view the duties required to be performed by chief clerks under sections 173 and 174 of the Revised Statutes.

By order of the Secretary of War.

SAM'L HODGKINS,
Acting Chief Clerk.

CORRESPONDENCE.

WAR DEPARTMENT,
Washington City, February 15, 1889.

SIR: In connection with my letter of January 23, ultimo, transmitting the report of the Board on Business Methods and appendices, I have the honor now to transmit herewith the report of the board on the subject of "correspondence," with my orders of this date upon the subject; also copy of the circular of the 9th instant, directing that cases be traced in the several divisions of the Department.

I also inclose a copy of my order of the 13th instant on the subject of administration, a copy of a list showing the assignment of work in the offices and bureaus of the Department; also a copy of the circular of the 9th instant, requiring similar lists to be prepared of the work pertaining to each bureau and giving the names of officials to whom it is sent after its receipt and entry.

It is important that the reports of the board be printed for distribution in the Department, and it is estimated that about 3,000 copies will be needed for this purpose. The adoption of the recommendations upon the subject of correspondence will make it necessary to purchase a number of cabinet letter-files, and about 500,000 blanks will have to be printed for the card-index system. There are some forty record divisions at present in existence in the Department. If each division requires two letter-files, eighty will be required, at an average cost of $50, $4,000. An appropriation of $5,000 should therefore be made in the deficiency bill for the Department. A deficiency estimate of $10,000 has already been submitted (page 12, House Ex. Doc. 71, Fiftieth Congress, second session) for printing and binding, and that amount should be appropriated.

The difficulty of overcoming bias in favor of existing systems is great, and while reports and rules may point the way to improvements and orders enforce them for a time, persistent effort closely followed up is the only hope of enduring results. If, therefore, it is desired that this work shall be done by a board, and this seems best to secure uniformity, the investigation must go into minute particulars, which will take a long time. The members for a board to investigate thoroughly all matters involving clerical labor in the Department can not well be spared from the force now allowed by law, for, as stated by the Board in its report of the 21st ultimo, the members of a board necessarily on duty at the place where their regular duties are performed are frequently consulted upon matters pertaining to their regular official duties, and thus the investigation is interrupted and delayed; so for a board to conduct an extended investigation there should be an appropriation to provide for the payment of the members of the board and expenses, and this would enable the Secretary to fill the places of those members of the board selected from the employés of the Department.

Very respectfully,

WM. C. ENDICOTT,
Secretary of War.

Hon. F. M. COCKRELL,
Chairman of the Senate Select Committee to Examine the Methods of Conducting Business in the Executive Departments.

(INCLOSURES.)

Report of Board and exhibits, No. 1.
Circular of February 9, 1889, No. 2.
Circular of February 13, 1889, No. 3.
Assignment of business, No. 4.
Circular of February 9, 1889, No. 5.

APPENDIX No. 12.

[Inclosure No. 1.]

CORRESPONDENCE.

WAR DEPARTMENT, BOARD ON BUSINESS METHODS,
February 14, 1889.

The board has the honor to report upon the subject of departmental correspondence.

DEFINITIONS.

To avoid repetition, certain words and phrases used in this paper, when not otherwise explained, are to be understood as meaning as follows:

By "action on papers" is meant whatever is done with a paper up to and including the final decision thereon, except the carrying of it around by messengers or passing it from one to another, which can not of course be reckoned among any of the successive steps in its progress to a final decision, and except also the processes of briefing, entering, indexing, noting, and recording, which are occasionally mentioned collectively herein under the term "recording."

"Clerks" include all persons in the civil service of the Department not appointed by the President.

"Department" includes all offices or bureaus connected with the War Department in the city of Washington.

"Important papers" include all papers emanating from or received at the Department which contain, either in themselves or by reference thereto, information of value for future reference.

"Information of value" includes facts, decisions, laws. This is not to be understood as including all facts, for instance, the mere re-statement of facts which appear on the records, where they will be searched for in any event, is in the nature of an extract from the records and need not be again recorded, the original being sufficient. If, however, the search has consumed time the result of which may be useful in the future, it should be preserved in some way, provided it will not take as much time to find the result of the search as to again search the original record.

The word "mail" or "letters" or "papers" includes all correspondence upon official business received at or sent from the several bureaus or offices of the Department, as defined in the instructions of October 1, 1870. The personal or semi-official correspondence of an official is not included, and does not become a part of the official correspondence until the person addressed so decides. With such a letter, therefore, an interval may elapse before its apparent receipt at the Department, as shown by the date-stamp, during which it has been in the personal possession of the official addressed.

"Recorded" or "recording" includes all the work therewith connected, viz, briefing, recording, numbering, indexing, or notating.

INSTRUCTIONS AT PRESENT IN FORCE.

The existing "instructions for keeping the records and transacting the clerical business of the War Department" were published October 1, 1870, in a pamphlet, a copy of which is herewith submitted, marked Exhibit A. This book defines "letters received" and "letters sent," provides rules for the receipt and distribution of the mail, gives instructions how to brief and record letters received, to prepare communications for executive action, to record letters sent, to index communications and precedents; it directs that handwriting in books and on papers shall be plain and of good size, and forbids flourishes or ornamental writing. The rules are clear and concise; they have been in use in the present form eighteen years, and rules very similar have been in use for a much longer period. The result of this long use is largely in their favor, papers or precedents are quickly found, and when it is desired to collect all correspondence on a given subject extending over a series of years it can be done in a short time, provided the first search is supplemented by one or two special searches on lines suggested by the papers found on the first search, and it may reasonably be assumed that the papers thus collected comprise all that have been filed on the subject, except those which have not remained on the files, and in lieu of such papers the books afford information as to their contents and the action thereon. The system by which this is accomplished is of great value, but it may be carried so far as to unnecessarily delay the public business; thus if important papers are recorded and trifling matters noted, the time of clerks will be taken up with work not really necessary, and the record-books and files incumbered with useless entries and papers.

It then becomes important to consider what the present instructions for keeping the records require. They classify official business, and define "letters received" and "letters sent" as follows:

"All the clerical business of an executive bureau or military office is comprehended within the terms 'letters received' and 'letters sent;' and all action upon official papers is either of a record or executive character.

"'Letters received' consist of written or printed communications coming into the bureau, whether in the guise of a formal letter, an indorsement upon a letter, a memorandum, a numbered or unnumbered circular, general or special order in any way relating to the business of the bureau, an *unofficial* or *informal* communication upon official matters, if it be necessary or proper to be recorded, a memorandum made in the office of any verbal communication of which a record should exist, and generally of any communication reaching the bureau to which future reference *may* become necessary or desirable.

"'Letters sent' consist of all communications of foregoing character issued from the bureau."

The instructions also contain provisions as follows: "Papers requiring immediate action should be briefed and recorded at the first opportunity." * * * "A brief of every official communication received should be indorsed upon its first or upper fold, exhibiting the place where the letter was written, the date of the communication, the name or official designation of the writer, or the title of the Department, bureau, office, court, etc., whence the communication proceeds, and a synopsis of the contents or subject of the letter. Everything of importance should appear in the brief, but prolixity should be avoided." The clerk should note in the book of letters received the action taken upon the papers entered (see p. 8), but on page 11 it is provided that "simple reference of papers by indorsement, as well as reference for 'report' or 'remark' only, should be made according to a set form of phraseology, to save the necessity of recording them at length in the book of letters sent." (Such indorsements may, therefore, under the rules, either be noted in "letters received" or recorded in "letters sent." "No communication properly briefed should be again briefed in the same or any other office." "When a letter received has been briefed, it should be entered in a record book kept for the purpose." "No communication should be recorded in more than one record book in the same bureau, unless more than one class of record business is involved in it, in which case entries of so much of its subjects and the action upon it as relate to other record divisions may be made in the books of those divisions and proper notations thereof placed on the paper." "A record book of letters sent" "should be kept in connection with the record book of letters received, in which should be recorded in full all communications issued from the bureau, except simple indorsements of reference for action, report, or remark, and regular series of orders of which sets are separately kept on file." "Such letters sent as are of a purely routine character and of frequent recurrence should be prepared upon printed forms, designated by numbers or otherwise, in which case only the manuscript portion of the letter, with the designation of the form affixed, need be recorded. Brief descriptive headings should precede the entry of such indorsements as do not within themselves set forth the names of persons and things or the subjects concerned sufficiently for indexing purposes."

These instructions require the briefing, entering, numbering, and indexing of all letters received "to which future reference may become necessary or desirable," and the recording and indexing of all letters sent and indorsements, with the following exceptions:

(1) An unofficial or informal communication upon official matters, if it is not necessary or proper to be recorded.

(2) The report upon any case by an assistant in a bureau, when the superior officer prefers that the report should appear over his own name or signature; in such case the report of the assistant should not be recorded.

(3) Simple indorsements of reference for action, report, or remark, and regular series of orders of which sets are regularly kept on file.

(4) Letters sent of a purely routine character prepared upon printed forms; in such case only the manuscript portion of the letter with designation of the form need be recorded.

EXCEPTIONS IN PRACTICE.

The result of practice and experience, however, has been to make many additional exceptions to these rules, as shown by the following table. This table also shows, in some instances, the classes of papers which are now recorded, and where not stated it is presumed all other papers are recorded:

Letters received.

Office.	Subject.	Briefed.	Entered.	Remarks.
Secy. War. Record division..	Requisitions for funds	No	No	To reqn. div.
	Requisitions on Public Printer	No	No	Do.
	Estimates from Public Printer	No	No	Do.
	Memorandum bills from Public Printer.	No	No	Do.
	Advice of drafts from Treasury Department.	No	No	Do.
	Letters relative to advertising	No	No	To cor. div.
	Accounts for advertising	No	No	Do.
	Requisitions for supplies	No	No	To supply div.
	Acknowledging receipt of Rebellion Records.	No	No	To library.
	Applications for duplicate discharge.	No	No	To A. G. O.
	Applications for removal charge of desertion.	No	No	Do.
	Application for re-muster	No	No	Do.
	Applications for address of officers or soldiers.	No	No	Do.
	Applications for Army Register.	No	No	Do.
	Applications for Army Regulations.	No	No	Do.
	Applications for appointment in Army.	No	No	Do.
	Applications for discharge from Army.	No	No	Do.
	Applications for remission of sentence.	No	No	Do.
	All papers in regard to appointment in Military Academy.	No	No	Do.
	Application for supt. national cemetery.	No	No	To Q. M. G.
	Application for headstones	No	No	Do.
	Inquiries about burial place of soldiers.	No	No	Do.
	Application for commutation of rations.	No	No	To C. G. S.
	To be examined for assistant surgeon.	No	No	To S. G. O.
	For appointment as assistant surgeon.	No	No	Do.

93

Letters received—Continued.

Office.	Subject.	Briefed.	Entered.	Remarks.
Secy. War. Record division..	For pensions...............	No............	No............	To Comr. Pensions.
	About pensions...............	No............	No............	Do.
	About pay and bounty...............	No............	No............	To 2d Audr.
	(The last three are merely put in envelopes and sent to proper address.)			
	All other letters...............	Yes............	Yes............	
A. G. O. Enl. Brch., Reg. Army.	All cases...............	Yes, if not already briefed.	Yes............	
A. C. P. branch ...	Letters: Except such as in judgment of clerk in charge "contain nothing of any value for future reference;" judgment based on experience; a fixed rule not wise. L. R. not entered are not briefed; usually returned by indorsement or letter (some times printed). Such letters include—	Yes............	Yes............	
	Inquiry for address of officers or ex-officers.	No............	No............	
	Inquiries about appointments, vacancies, etc.	No............	No............	
Miscls. branch ...	All received from Army thro' military channels which exclusively pertain to another bureau or staff. Marked in red ink or blue pencil "Q. M. G.," "C. G. S.," etc., entered in memoranda book, name, date, very brief purport, and when sent to bureau.	No............	No............	
	Inquiries for address of officers and enlisted men.	No............	No............	
	Requests for orders, regulations or publications.	No............	No............	
	Letters from members of Congress or others urging speedy action on cases.	No............	No............	
	Inquiries relating to matters not requiring a permanent record. These filed with press-copy of answer, and after 2 years such as no use destroyed.	No............	No............	
	All other letters...............	Yes............	Yes............	
Vol. service branch.	Requests for routine information	No............	No............	
	Requests urging speedy reports on calls. (Returned by indorsement with information.)	No............	No............	
	Other letters...............	Yes............	Yes............	
Vol. enl. branch.	For certificate in lieu of lost discharge unaccompanied by testimony.	No............	No............	
	For address of officers and enlisted men of vol. service.	No............	No............	
	For information concerning claims for vols. of Revolutionary war and war of 1812.	No............	No............	
	Requests from attorneys, members of Congress, and claimants that reports be furnished Second Auditor and Commissioner of Pensions.	No............	No............	
	For information about bounty and pension claims, horse claims, and claims for commutation of rations while prisoners of war.	No............	No............	
	For information about claims for commutation for artificial limbs.	No............	No............	
	For information about claims of men in Navy or Marine Corps.	No............	No............	

Letters received—Continued.

Office.	Subject.	Briefed.	Entered.	Remarks.
A. G. O. Vol. enl. branch.	For record of soldiers for G. A. R. and Sons of Veterans purposes.	No	No	
	For settlement of accounts of deceased soldiers.	No	No	
	From supt. military homes for military history of disabled vols.	No	No	
	From adjutant-general of States for military histories.	No	No	
	Calls from Pension Office, Land Office, and heads of bureaus for statements of military service, etc.	No	No	
	Only letters of importance or containing information of value are briefed and entered.			
Ins. Gen	All letters received	Yes	Yes	
	Except acknowledgment of blanks.	No	No	Filed with application.
J. A. G	Court-martial records: (Register kept of date received, No., name, rank, regiment of party tried, president of court, judge advocate, and when and where convened.)			
	Letters transmitting record. Numbered.	No	No	Filed with record.
	Application for abstract of trials. (Note in book—date received, name, rank, company, and regiment of party tried and name or office of applicant.)			
	All other letters received	Yes	Yes	
Q. M. G	Settlement letters from Second and Third Auditor. Noted on Register of Accounts.	No	No	Forwarded to officer.
	All other letters received	Yes	Yes	
C. G. S	Printed matter including G. and S. O. and circulars	No	No	Properly noted.
	Requisitions for blanks	No	No	Do.
	Acknowledgments of orders, annual reports, etc.	No	No	Do.
	Accounts current	No	No	Do.
	Returns of subsistence stores	No	No	Do.
	Returns of subsistence property	No	No	Do.
	Letters of transmittal of above	No	No	Do.
	Weekly and monthly statements of funds.	No	No	Do.
	Treasury settlements	No	No	Do.
	Certificates of deposit	No	No	Do.
	Inventory and inspection reports.	No	No	Do.
	Claims of prisoners of war	No	No	Do.
	Claims of enlisted men on furlough during the war.	No	No	Do.
	Claims of miscellaneous character.	No	No	Do.
	Inquiries as to claims	No	No	Do.
	Inquiries from Pension Office and Second Auditor in connection with pending claims.	No	No	Do.
	Replies from Adjutant-General, Depot Commissary of Subsistence, Second Auditor, Surgeon General, or Commissioner of Pensions in connection with pending claims.	No	No	Do.
	Printed slips of advertisements from Secretary's Office.	No	No	Do.
	Printed monthly price-list subsistence stores, Washington depot.	No	No	Do.
	Other letters received	Yes	Yes	
Sur. Gen.: Disbg. and truss division.	Relate to claims	Name of claimant only.	No	Filed with claim alphabetically.
Administrative division.	Those that belong to division	Yes	Yes	
	Others sent to destination	No	No	

Letters received—Continued.

Office.	Subject.	Briefed.	Entered.	Remarks.
Sur. Gen.:				
Property division.	Letters of transmittal forwarding returns or vouchers	No	No	Filed with returns or vouchers.
Record and pension division.	Relating to employés of the division.	Yes	No	Filed in envelope alphabetically.
	Calls for medical history from Commissioner of Pensions, Adjutant-General, Second Auditor, etc.	Detached brief made.	Name, regiment, and office No. of call on alphabetical index only.	Call returned with report in the case; detached brief with result of search filed.
Museum and Library division.	All letters received	Yes	Yes	
P. M. G	Second Auditor and Second Comptroller inquiries as to payment to officers and soldiers. Date received stamped.	No	No	Returned with reply indorsed.
	Back-pay and bounty inquiries for private persons.	No	No	Referred to proper officer.
	Notification from Second Auditor of allowance of a claim and that certificate will be sent when Congress makes appropriation.	No	No	Filed awaiting certificate.
	All other letters received	Yes	Yes	
Engineers	Requests from officers on official blank forms.	Yes	No	Filed in division.
	Applications on official blank forms.	Yes	No	Do.
	Returns on official blanks	Yes	No	Do.
	Acknowledgments on official blanks.	Yes	No	Do.
	All other letters received	Yes	Yes	
Ordnance	Errors in property returns	No	No	Filed with returns.
	Asking for blanks	No	No	Retained till receipt of blanks and publications have been ack'g'd, and then destroyed.
	Asking for publications	No	No	
	Letters of transmittal, not explanatory.	No	No	Destroyed when account is settled.
	Other letters received	Yes	Yes	
Signal:				
Corresp. div., sig. series.	Important letters	Yes	Yes	Name and purport indexed.
Corresp. div., obs. series.	From paid observers are briefed at station; date received, No., and station recorded, and filed by station.			
Enlstmt. series	Applications for enlistment. Applications listed by name, No., date received, and filed in envelopes alphabetically.	No	No	
Miscl. series	Unimportant letters generally from private persons on routine matters. Listed by surname, No., date received, initialed, and filed alphabetically.	No	No	
"V" series	From voluntary observers	No	No	
"D" series	For meteorological data	No	No	
	V and D same as "miscellaneous," except V series has volunteer station noted on brief fold and filed by stations.			
Property and disbg. division.	Money and property accounts, name and subject indexed.	Subject	On not more than one line.	Filed numerically.
	Letters transmitting bills	No	No	Filed.
Publication office.	Requesting publications (not indexed).	Writers' initial.	No	Filed alphabetically.
Examiners' division.	Letters, name, and purport indexed.	Yes	Yes	Filed numerically.
	These included—			
	Letters transmitting property returns, etc.	Yes	No	Entry discontinued Oct. 5, '88.
	Statements of public funds, reports of other line funds.	Yes	No	Do.

Letters sent.

Office.	Written.	Printed.	Press-copied.	Recorded.	Remarks.
Sec. of War: Record div....		To Civil Service Commission:			
		To certify name............	Yes....	Yes....	
		Name selected............	Yes....	Yes....	
		Advice that appointee has taken oath and entered on duty.	Yes....	Yes....	
		Advice of permanent appointment.	Yes....	Yes....	⎫ Press copies filed with papers.
		Advice of changes.......	Yes....	Yes....	
		Letter of appointment..	Yes....	No......	
		Letter of promotion.....	Yes....	No......	
		Letter of transfer..........	Yes....	No......	
		Letter of reduction in grade.	Yes....	No......	
		Letter accepting resignation.	Yes....	No......	
		Letter of discharge	Yes....	No......	
Requisitions and accounts division.		Notification that letters of transmittal not required with certificates of deposit.	Yes....	No.....	Press copy kept in book and indexed.
Supply division.		Disbursing clerk notified of accounts sent out.	Yes....	No......	Press copy kept in book and indexed.
		Orders for supplies under contract.	Yes....	No......	Press copy kept and properly noted.
		Orders for supplies not under contract, miscellaneous.	Yes....	No......	Do.
		Orders for supplies not under contract, stationery.	Yes....	No......	Do.
		Orders for repairs.........	Yes....	No......	Do.
		Request to execute contract.	Yes....	No......	Do.
		Notification of awards..	Yes....	No......	Do.
		Inclosing copy of contract.	Yes....	No......	Do.
		Notice to report for work.	Yes....	No......	Do.
		Action on requisitions..	Yes....	No. ...	Do.
		Request for signature to receipts.	Yes....	No......	Do.
		Transmitting accounts for signature.	Yes....	No......	Do.
Correspondence div'n.		For special passport	Yes....	Yes....	Press copy filed with papers.
		For admission free of duty.	Yes....	No......	Do.
		Sending papers to House Committee on War Claims.	Yes....	Yes....	Do.
		Inclosing report on bill to House Committee on Military Affairs.	Yes....	Yes....	Do.
		Evidence to Attorney-General for Court of Claims.	Yes....	Yes....	First letter of this kind in book recorded, and thereafter written portions only.
		To Attorney-General, evidence of loyalty or disloyalty in Court of Claims case.	Yes....	Yes....	Press copy filed with papers.
		To Court of Claims transmitting papers.	Yes....	Yes....	First letter of this kind in book recorded, and thereafter written portions only.
		To Court of Claims, no record found of claim.	Yes....	Yes....	Press copy filed with papers.
		Notification of transmittal.	Yes....	Yes....	Do.

Letters sent—Continued.

Office.	Written.	Printed.	Press-copied.	Re-corded.	Remarks.
Sec. of War: Correspondence div'n—Cont'd.		Requests to make designations for "Official Records War of Rebellion."	Yes.....	Yes.....	Press copy filed with papers.
		Request for present post-office address of person designated.	Yes.....	Yes.....	Do.
		Request to make another designation if organization does not exist.	Yes.....	Yes.....	Do.
		Transfer of books.	Yes.....	Yes.....	Do.
Library division.		Inclosing receipt for signature.	Yes.....	Yes.....	Do.
		Sending "Official Records War of Rebellion" to Bureaus.	Yes.....	Yes.....	Do.
		For binding Records War of Rebellion for subscribers.	Yes.....	Yes.....	First of this kind in book recorded, and thereafter written portions only.
		Subscribers notified that order given for binding work.	No.....	No.....	Noted.
		Duplication of designations.	Yes.....	Yes.....	Press copy filed with papers.
		Response to requests for annual reports.	No.....	No.....	Noted.
		Acknowledgment of receipt of money.	Yes.....	No.....	Do.
		When party designated has died.	No.....	No.....	Do.
		To return book to Library.	No.....	No.....	Do.
A. G. O.: A.C.P.branch	Letters which will ever be needed for reference.		No.....	Yes.....	
	Letters in reply to such letters received as are not entered, as a rule.		No.....	No.....	
Miscl. brch...	Answers to letters not entered.		Yes.....	No.....	
Vol. service branch.	Such as do not embrace decisions.		Yes*.....	No.....	Filed with papers.
Vol. enlst. branch.	List of letters noted under letters received, as not recorded. Many are answered by printed and manuscript answers.		Some.	Some.	Press copies kept for awhile and then destroyed.
Inspr. Gen......		Letters transmitting blanks.	No.....	No.....	Noted opposite application on letters received.
J. A. G...........	All other letters sent.		Yes.....	Yes.....	
	Answers to applications for abstract of trials.			No.....	Noted on application book.
Q. M. G...........	All other letters sent.		Yes.....	Yes.....	Indexed.
	All letters sent and endorsements.		Yes.....	Only important.	Others noted on L. R. and press-copy filed with papers.
C. G. S...........	Letters sent.		Yes.....	Yes.....	Noted in record books.
	Some letters sent.		Yes.....	No.....	
	Answers to inquiries as to status of claim.		No.....	No.....	
	Replies to requests for blanks to make out claim.		No.....	No.....	
S. G.: Administration div.	All—indexed by subject and author.		Yes.....	Yes.....	

* Or draft preserved.

Letters sent—Continued.

Office.	Written.	Printed.	Press-copied.	Recorded.	Remarks.
S. G.: Disbg. and trust div.		Replies by circular.	No	No	Noted on claims.
Property division.	Written.		Yes	No	Filed with claim.
	Letters of notification of action of office.		Yes	No	Press-copy books indexed, numbered, and preserved.
		Notification of settlement of accounts.	No		Noted on record books.
Record and pension div.	Relating to employés.		No	No	Copy filed alphabetically.
	Reports to Comr. of Pensions, Adjt. General, Second Auditor, and others from records on file.		No	No	Searchers' slips filed with detached brief.
Museum and library div.	All letters sent.			Yes	
		Letters of acknowledgment.		Yes	Name, address, and article nckg'd. and blanks indicated.
P. M. G.		For statement of service from Adjt. Gen.	No	No	Filed with reply.
		Statement of suspensions in accounts.	No	No	Filed with P. M.'s reply, which is entered as a letter received.
		For list of outstanding checks.	No	No	Noted on record of outstanding checks.
		Requesting report of change of station and address.	No	No	Response recorded in letters received.
		Removal of suspensions (in duplicate).	(Original only) Yes.	No	Checked on record.
		Soldiers' deposit.	No	No	Properly noted.
		Paymaster notified; account sent to Second Auditor.	No	No	Noted on register of paymasters' accounts.
		Letters of advice about funds.	No	No	
	All other letters sent.		Yes	Yes	
Engineers.		Written on regular printed forms.	Yes	No	Press books indexed.
	Routine unimportant letters.		Yes		Noted in L. R. and press-copy filed with papers.
Ordnance.	Other letters sent.		Yes	Yes	
	Indorsement on letters which are eventually returned to office for file.		Yes	No	Press books retained. Accounts show date.
	Errors in returns or accounts.		Yes	No	
	Notification of examination of property or cash accounts.		Yes	No	
	Other letters sent.		Yes	Yes	
Signal.	All letters.		Yes	No	
	Press-copied into books corresponding in general to series of letters received. Name of person written to. Series indicates subject, so that is not indexed except "Miscellaneous" and "Signal." Two press-copies of important letters taken, one of which is filed with papers.				

This list of papers, which experience has shown to be unnecessary to record, is here condensed, and to make the practice uniform throughout the Department it is recommended that all papers of the classes here enumerated be not recorded hereafter:

(1) All papers that do not pertain to the business of the office where received, and which, under the circular of 13th instant, will be at once sent to the proper office for action. Where necessary to keep a list, see recommendation as to card-index briefs.

(2) Official calls for information from records on file, when necessary to keep more than a mere list, see recommendation as to card-index brief, on which can be noted the date when such a paper is referred elsewhere for information, when received back and finally disposed of. These cards to be filed alphabetically and destroyed when no longer needed.

(3) Letters inquiring as to status of claims, or requesting action thereon, which contain no information of value, to be answered by indorsement whenever practicable; if answered by letter they should be destroyed when no longer needed. Should they, however, contain material information additional to that which is already filed they should be placed with the papers in the case.

(4) Weekly and monthly statements of funds, accounts current, vouchers, returns of stores and property, inventories, inspection reports, or both, and generally any regular reports or returns that are in the ordinary course of business necessarily noted or listed elsewhere than on letters-received books, and filed systematically for ready reference. The fact of being listed or noted should be stamped thereon, with date and name of office, so they may not be again noted or listed.

(5) Letters of transmittal containing no material information additional to the matter transmitted need not be preserved; such letters should only be written when the matter transmitted does not show by whom it was sent.

(6) Requests for and acknowledgments of receipts of publications and blanks. Where they are numerous requests should be listed, and acknowledgments noted on such lists.

(7) Circulars, orders, etc., should be preserved in separate files.

(8) Letters from persons evidently insane.

Papers not recorded, listed, noted, or filed away in such manner as to be easily referred to, if worth keeping, may be filed in cabinet-letter files as suggested under head of "General remarks."

With these classes excluded, it is probable there may still remain many papers which need not be recorded. To ascertain this it is important that the experience of the clerks be utilized to ascertain, if possible, what classes of papers are rarely if ever referred to, and also whether any of the classes named above should be recorded, and why. In order that this information may be exact, and not depend on the memory of searchers, it is recommended that searchers be required to keep a memorandum book, showing the subject of papers searched for, the office-mark of the papers, or name if not entered, and for whom searched. From these books they can compile the information needed in the reports suggested, and it will take no longer for a searcher to keep this book than to make a memorandum on a loose slip of paper. It is also recommended that this information be compiled once a year, say on the first Monday in October, and that the reports from the several bureaus be collated. If it shall thereupon appear that the opinion on a given class of papers is almost unanimous, this expert testimony will be of the greatest value in determining with safety what classes of papers need not be recorded, and also whether any of the excepted classes should be recorded.

The searcher can not make a record that will show what papers are not called for; that will depend on the memory of those who enter the papers. The searcher's book will only show the papers called for. If there has been but one call during the year for papers of a class of which many are entered, it will be possible to say of that class that it is rarely referred to, while if many calls are made for papers of another class, that will be evidence of the value of recording such papers.

The searcher's book above recommended will also serve as a charge-book for papers taken from the files temporarily. Papers are often so withdrawn and returned the same day, thus canceling the charge. If a charge remains on the searcher's book for a few days it should be ascertained if the papers are likely to remain off the files for an indefinite period, and, if so, the charge should be noted on the card-index number book suggested under the title "Card-index." If the card-index is not adopted the charge should then be made on the book of letters received. By keeping the charges on the searcher's book a compact record is kept of papers off the files temporarily, and it should be the duty of the searcher to keep track of them with a view to their early return to the files. Under the present system papers temporarily withdrawn from the files are at once charged in the book of letters received, and it is not the particular duty of any one to look after the paper to see that it is returned. If returned, the charge may be removed; if not, the charge remains, and the paper is supposed to be somewhere about the office. It may have been acted upon and the charge overlooked.

The method proposed is simple. Charges now are scattered through large volumes of about one thousand pages. Back and forth the clerk goes making charges and removing them. On the searcher's book many charges are canceled and need not be posted to the permanent record. It also expedites business because it provides for calling up papers on which action might otherwise be delayed.

While a record should only be made of such papers as are important, it is to be borne in mind that there is no limit of time within which claims must be presented, with a very few exceptions not necessary to name here, and the necessity of care in selecting classes of papers is therefore apparent.

METHOD OF ENTERING AND ACTING ON PAPERS.

Having disposed of the classes of work that need not be recorded, it is proper now to illustrate the method of entering a letter received at the Department. To show clearly the several steps of its progress from the time of its receipt until the action thereon is completed, an actual case has been traced and is here given:

Transfer of steamer Success from Quincy, Illinois, to Plum Point Reach, Mississippi River.

On December 14, 1888, Capt. Smith S. Leach (1), Corps of Engineers U. S. Army, stationed at Memphis, Tenn., addressed a letter to the Chief of Engineers U. S. Army, Washington, D. C., requesting approval of the employment of a pilot for the transfer of the steamer *Success* with tow from Quincy, Ill., to Saint Louis, Mo., $25, and of another pilot from Saint Louis to Fletcher's Point, Ark., at rate of $150 per month; to be paid from allotment for improving Plum Point Reach. The letter, with the other mail matter re-received at the same time, was on December 17, 1888, brought from the Washington City post-office in the War Department mail-wagon (2), contained in the locked mail-pouch belonging to the office of the Chief of Engineers, which pouch was taken from the wagon to said office by Mr. F. C. Hartman (3), an assistant messenger of that office (salary $720 per annum), who unlocked the pouch, took therefrom its contents, and placed the same upon the desk of Mr. Wm. J. Warren, chief clerk of the office (salary $2,000 per annum). Mr. Warren (4), after examining it and separating the personal from the official mail, turned the latter over to Mr. Hartman (5), who cut open the envelopes, and, without removing their contents, placed them again upon the desk of Mr. Warren (6), who removed and read the papers in each case for the purpose of acquainting himself with the contents and to give the papers proper disposition for action. Finding that this case pertained to "third division" of the office, he placed upon the letter a slip of paper upon which was printed in bold type "third division" first stamping the slip with office stamp showing date of receipt of the letter, placed a rubber band around the papers, and sent them to General T. L. Casey, Chief of Engineers. General Casey (7) looked the case over and placed it in a basket upon his desk labeled "Major Post," from which it was taken by messenger (8) and carried to Maj. J. C. Post, Corps of Engineers, who has supervision of the class of business to which the case related. Major Post (9), after reading the case, sent it to Mr. P. J. Dempsey (10), a clerk of class 4, chief clerk of third division, who stamped "III" in lower left-hand corner of first fold, and sent it by messenger (11) to Mr. S. Duryee (12), a clerk of class 4, chief of the record division, for record. Upon its receipt by Mr. Duryee, he handed it to Mr. John B. Nichols (13), a clerk of class 1, in charge of "B" book of letters received, who stamped it with office stamp showing date of receipt, numbered it (5402), placed a brief upon the first fold, showing date, name, and rank of writer and summary of the subject-matter, and entered it in letters-received book (B), the entry, including the headings and notations of action taken in the case, being as follows:

1888.

Letters received (B) Engineer Department.

Date of receipt and file No.	Name of writer.	Date and subject of letter.	Action.
*	*	*	*
Dec. 17........ 5102	Leach, Capt. S. S. 5591 A. W. D. 1888.	Memphis, Tenn. Dec. 14 .... In connection with transfer of Str. *Success* and tow from Quincy, Ill., to Plum Point Reach, reqs. approval of employment of a pilot from Quincy to St. Louis, $25, and of another pilot from St. Louis to Fletcher's Pt., Ark., at rate of $150 pr. mo.: to be paid from allotment for impg. Plum Point Reach.	III Dec. 17. To Sec'y War Dec. 21, '88, recomd. Back Dec. 24,'88, approved Dec. 22. III Dec. 26. To Capt. Leach Dec. 27,'88, for guidance by foregoing endt.; to be ret'd. Back Jan. 3, '89. Filed Jan. 3, '89.
*	*	*	*

Mr. Nichols then placed a perpendicular mark in the upper left-hand corner to signify that the case had been entered in the book of letters received.

The case was then passed to Mr. M. W. Saxton (14), a clerk of class 3, who indexed it in the index-book both by name and subject, the book being alphabetically tagged, and containing on the right-hand pages a marginal cut index, giving, by combinations, the first three letters of any name or subject, and giving, also, the subject in full, in such cases as form the subject of frequent correspondence, thus enabling immediate reference to be made to any particular subject upon which information may be desired. The pages, at the top of which the year is printed, are divided by blue lines into spaces of about one inch long and three-quarters of an inch wide, into one of which is written the subject and file-number of the paper indexed. The subject and file-number are written in red ink, except in the cases of papers coming into the office from the War Department or cases of an extraordinary character, which are indexed in black ink. This case was indexed under six separate headings or key-words, as follows:

1888.

L	Leach, Captain	Smith S.		Employ pilot in taking tow Success from Quincy to Plum Pt., 5402-B.	
P	Pilots.		Leach employ —to take dredge Success to Plum Pt., 5402-B.		
S	Success, Tow B	Dredge oat.		Leach employ pilots to take— from Quincy to Plum Pt., 5402-B.	
P	Plum Point Re	ach, Miss. River.		Leach employ pilot to take str. Success from Quincy, Ills., to —, 5402-B.	
B	Boats, Tow.		Success P. 951.		
(Tug) War Dept.	War Dept.*	*Mississippi Ri	ver Commission	Approves Leach's hire of pilot, trans. str. Success, 5402-B.	

NOTE—The dash, thus —, is used in indexing to obviate the repetition of, and is in substitution for, the index word.
* Heading at top of page.

Mr. Saxton then made a mark across the perpendicular mark in upper left-hand corner, to signify that the case had been indexed, and returned the case to Mr. Nichols (15), who charged it to third division by a notation in red ink in the column headed "Action," opposite the entry of the case in the book of letters received, and sent it by messenger (16) to Mr. Dempsey (17), who in turn sent it by messenger (18) to Major Post (19). After reading it over Major Post sent it to Mr. R. W. Burgess (20), civil engineer (salary $3,600), who drafted an indorsement on a slip of paper and returned the case therewith to Major Post (21), who looked it over and signified his approval of the proposed indorsement by placing his initials (J. C. P.) upon the slip. He then sent the case by messenger (22) to General Casey (23), who, approving the indorsement, so signified by writing upon the slip the word "Yes," and affixing his initials, "T. L. C." He then returned the case to Major Post (24), who again sent it to Mr. Dempsey (25). By Mr. Dempsey it was handed to Mr. S. R. Kiner (class 1) (26), who placed upon the paper the indorsement, as per draft, and returned the case to Mr. Dempsey (27), who again sent it to Major Post (28), who, after examining the indorsement, placed his initials in the upper left-hand corner and sent it by messenger (29) to General Casey (30) for signature. After signing the indorsement General Casey returned the case to Major Post (31), who again sent it to Mr. Dempsey (32). The latter then handed it to Mr. W. Jansen (class 3) (33), who press-copied the indorsement on a loose sheet, entered the case in a "dispatch" book (memorandum receipt book), and sent it by messenger (34) to the record division of the War Department in a sealed envelope addressed, in print, to the "Secretary of War—Room 65." The following shows the entry:

Name.	When sent.	Nature of communication.	Signature of receiver.
Secretary of War..................	Dec. 22, '88	Leach for pilot, $\frac{5402\ '88}{B}$	H. D. Burwell. (35)

Mr. Jansen then folded the press copy of the indorsement into three equal folds, wrote in pencil upon the back of the first fold the date, file number of the paper upon which the indorsement was based, name of person to whom sent, and sent it by messenger (36) to Mr. Duryee (37), who passed it to Mr. Nichols (38), class 1, who made therefrom a notation in red ink in the book of letters received, showing the action as per the indorsement, as follows: "To Secy. War, Dec. 21, '88, recom'd." He then handed the press copy to Mr. Johnson (39) (skilled laborer, salary $720), who placed it in a temporary wrapper to await final disposition of the case. The indorsement was as follows:

[1st indorsement.]

J. C. P.
            OFFICE CHIEF OF ENGINEERS U. S. ARMY.
                         Dec. 21, 1888.
Respectfully submitted to the Secretary of War with recommendation for approval.
                     THOS. LINCOLN CASEY,
                       Brig. Gen., Chief of Engineers.

$\frac{5402}{B}$ 1888.

Upon receipt of the case in the record division of the War Department the envelope in which it was contained was (in the absence of the chief of the division, who at the time was acting chief clerk of the Department) opened by Mr. C. H. Carrington (40), a clerk of class 4, and at the time acting chief of the division, who, after removing the paper and reading its subject-matter, marked upon it in pencil "Maj. Adams," to signify to the clerk in charge of the letters-received book, in which the case was to be entered, that it was to be sent to Major Adams, the subject being of a class usually acted upon by that officer. Mr. Carrington then handed it to one of the office messengers (41), who stamped it with office stamp upon the first fold, showing the date of its receipt December 22, 1888, and handed it to Mr. A. L. Robinson (42), class 2, who indexed it both by name and subject, and placed upon it the file number (5591) and letter of the book (A) in which it was to be entered. The index book is alphabetically tagged on left-hand pages, and on right-hand pages is an alphabetical cut index, which constitutes an index by the *second* letter of the name or subject concerning which information may be desired, and facilitates reference thereto. Each page is ruled with a marginal line on the left, and at the top of the page are printed the first three letters of the name or subjects beginning, and the names or subjects ending, the entries on the page. To illustrate: A page having printed at the top GLE GLY would show it to be the proper page on which to index any name or subject the first two letters of which are Gl and the third letter of which is any letter from E to Y, inclusive.

The case was indexed under six separate headings or key-words, as follows:

E Engineers, Chief of..........Plum Point Reach, Miss. River. Pilots for str. *Success.* 5591a.
L Leach, Capt. S. S.................Pilots for str. *Success.* 5591a.
P Pilots...............................Str. *Success.* Plum Point Reach. 5591a.
P Plum Point Reach ....(See Miss. River.)
Q Quincy, Ill.......................Str. *Success* to Plum Point Reach. Pilots, 5591a.
M Mississippi River..............Plum Point Reach. Pilots for str. *Success.* 5591a.

The case was then taken from Mr. Robinson's desk by Mr. J. T. Smith (43), class 1, in charge of Book A of letters received, who entered it in said book, made a notation thereon in red ink charging the case to Major Adams (Maj. M. H. Adams, Corps of Engineers), and placed it in the mail-box on his desk, from which it was carried by messenger (44) to that officer.

The entry in the book of letters received, including notations of actions taken, is as follows:

1888. Dec. 22. 5591	CHIEF OF ENGINEERS, *Dec.* 21, '88 Submits, recommending approval, comn. of Capt. S. S. Leach, Memphis, Tenn., in connection with transfer of str. *Success* and tow from Quincy, Ill., to Plum Point Reach, requesting approval of employment of a pilot from Quincy to St. Louis, $25, and another pilot from St. Louis to Fletcher's Point, Ark., at a rate of $150 per mo., to be paid from allotment for improving Plum Point Reach.	Maj. Adams, Dec. 22. Rec'd back 22. Approved. By order of the Secretary of War: SAML. HODGKINS, *Acting Chief Cl rk.* WAR DEPT., *Dec.* 22, '88. Engrs., Dec. 24.

Upon receipt of the case by Major Adams (45) he submitted it to the Secretary of War (46), who, having expressed his approval of the recommendation of the Chief of Engineers, Major Adams drafted an indorsement and sent the case therewith to Mr. J. B. Randolph (47), class 4, assistant to the chief clerk of the Department. Mr. Randolph read the case, placed the indorsement, as per draft, thereon, checked the letter "a" in the word WAR in the indorsement with a red-ink mark, to signify that the indorsement was drafted by Major Adams, and placed the case in a basket on his desk in which are regularly placed such papers as are to be signed by the chief clerk. He then filed the draft of the indorsement in a pigeon-hole in one of the office book-cases in which such drafts are usually kept for a reasonable time for reference, should it become necessary or desirable. The acting chief clerk, Mr. Samuel Hodgkins (48), upon taking up the case, examined it with reference to its subject-matter and the recommendation submitted by the Chief of Engineers, and, thus satisfying himself that it was clerically correct, he signed his name to the indorsement and returned the case to Mr. Randolph (49), who placed it in the mail-box upon his desk belonging to the record division, whence it was taken by messenger (50) of that division.

The indorsement was as follows:

Approved.

By order of the Secretary of War:

SAML. HODGKINS,
Acting Chief Clerk.

WAR DEPT.,
Dec. 22, '88.

The case when taken by the messenger of the record division from the office of the chief clerk was handed to Mr. Carrington (51), acting chief, who read the indorsement and sent the case by messenger (52) to Mr. Smith (53), who entered the indorsement in red ink opposite the entry of the case in "A" book of letters received, charged it to the Engineer Bureau by a notation in red ink in said book, placed a red-ink check-mark in upper left-hand corner of the indorsement, to signify its entry, and sent it to the Engineer Bureau by messenger (54).

Upon its receipt back by Mr. Warren (55), chief clerk of the office of the Chief of Engineers, he put upon it a third division slip, and sent it to General Casey (56), the slip being stamped with office stamp, showing date of receipt back, and having written upon it by Mr. Warren, in blue pencil, the words, "From the War Department," so that the general might see that the case was one which had been acted upon by the Secretary of War, and that immediate attention might thus be drawn to the case. It was then placed by General Casey in Major Post's mail basket, taken by messenger (57) to that officer (58), and by him sent by messenger (59) to Mr. Dempsey (60). Mr. Dempsey then sent it by messenger (61) to Mr. Duryee (62), by whom it was handed to Mr. Nichols (63), who stamped it on first fold with office stamp, showing its receipt back December 24, approved, and on second fold showing only its receipt back, December 24, 1888, and handed to Mr. Saxton (64), who indexed the indorsement of the Secretary of War, placing a check mark in blue pencil on the lower left-hand corner thereof, to signify its having been indexed, and returned the case to Mr. Nichols (65). The latter then charged the case to third division by a notation opposite its entry in the book of letters received, and sent it to Mr. Duryee (66), who returned it to Mr. Dempsey (67). Mr. Dempsey then sent it to Major Post (68), who examined it and handed it to Mr. Burgess (69), who drafted an indorsement and returned the case therewith to Major Post (70), who then placed his initials in the upper left-hand corner of the draft and sent the case to General

Casey (71), who wrote upon the draft the word "Yes," affixed his initials thereunder, signifying his approval, and returned the case to Major Post (72), who again sent it to Mr. Dempsey (73). The latter then handed it to Mr. Jansen (74), who placed upon the paper the indorsement as per draft and returned it to Mr. Dempsey (75), who sent it to Major Post (76) for signature. After being signed by Major Post it was returned to Mr. Dempsey (77), who again handed it to Mr. Jansen (78), who made a press copy of the indorsement on a loose sheet, and placed the original paper in an envelope properly addressed for the mail. He then folded the press copy into three equal folds, upon the first of which he wrote in pencil the date, file number of the paper on which it was based, and name of person to whom sent, and sent it to Mr. Duryee (79), who handed it to Mr. Nichols (80), who made therefrom a notation opposite the entry of the case in the book of letters received, showing the action as per the indorsement, and handed it to Mr. Johnson (81), who placed, with the previous press copy, in a temporary wrapper to await final disposition of the case.

The indorsement was as follows:

[3d indorsement.]

OFFICE CHIEF OF ENGINEERS U. S. ARMY,
Dec. 27, 1888.

Respectfully returned to Capt. S. S. Leach, Corps of Engineers, inviting attention to the foregoing indorsement, by which he will be guided.
After such record as may be necessary has been made, this paper will be returned to this office. By command of Brig. Gen. Casey:

JAS. C. POST,
Major of Engineers.

$\frac{5402}{B}$ 1888.

Upon the receipt of the case at the office of Captain Leach (82) it was stamped on the first fold with office stamp, showing date, and was returned to the Chief of Engineers U. S. Army, by indorsement as follows:

[4th indorsement.]

U. S. ENGINEER OFFICE,
Memphis, Tenn., Dec. 31, 1888.

Respectfully returned to the Chief of Engineers U. S. Army, as required in 3d indorsement, record having been made for the files of this office.

SMITH S. LEACH,
Captain of Engineers.

The case was received back at the office of the Chief of Engineers January 3, 1889, having been brought from the Washington City post-office in the War Department mail-wagon (83), contained, with other mail matter, in the locked mail-pouch of the office of the Chief of Engineers, which was taken from the wagon to that office by Mr. F. C. Hartman (84), an assistant messenger of said office, who unlocked the pouch, took therefrom its contents and placed the same upon the desk of the chief clerk, Mr. William J. Warren (85). After separating the personal from the official mail, Mr. Warren turned the latter over to Mr. Hartman (86), who cut open the envelope and covers and, without removing the contents, replaced the same upon Mr. Warren's (87) desk. Mr. Warren then glanced at the subject-matter of each case, and finding that this one pertained to third division, he placed upon it a slip with "third division" printed upon it, first stamping the slip with office stamp to show the date of receipt, placed a rubber band around the papers and sent them to General Casey (88), who, after looking over the case, placed it in a basket upon his desk labeled "Maj. Post," from which it was taken by messenger (89) and carried to that officer (90). Major Post, after examining the case and finding that no further action thereon was required, wrote in pencil upon the first fold the word "File," under which he affixed his initials, and sent the case by messenger (91) to Mr. Dempsey (92). By Mr. Dempsey it was sent to Mr. Duryee (93), by whom it was handed to Mr. Nichols (94), who stamped it both on the first and third folds with office stamp, showing the date of its receipt back, made a notation of its receipt back, in red ink, opposite the entry of the case in the book of letters received; also made a similar notation of the case being filed, checked the notation "File, J. C. P." with blue pencil, to signify that said notation had been made, and handed the case to Mr. Johnson (skilled laborer, salary $720) (95), who filed it in a file-box, filing also therewith the press copies of indorsements which had previously been filed in a temporary wrapper to await final disposition of the case.

The *division slips* which are placed upon cases by Mr. Warren, the chief clerk, remain with them until they reach the record division (Mr. Duryee), where, after proper record of the cases, the slips are filed for a reasonable period for reference should it be desirable. When a large number of them has accumulated, and it is certain that no occasion for reference to them will arise, they are disposed of as waste paper, they not being regarded as a record, but simply as office memoranda.

The following is a copy of the slip that was used in this case, and others which accompanied it, when it left Mr. Warren's desk:

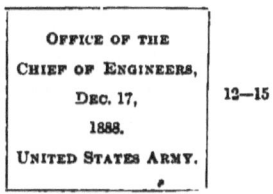

III DIVISION.

J. C. P.

5393—5402
B   17, 3.30

5404—5411   18, 10.15

The office stamp being placed *above* the word "division" signifies that the case was received by Mr. Warren *before* 12 o'clock m. Had the case been received by him *after* the hour the stamp would have been placed *below* the word "division."

The figures 12—15 in pencil to the right of the office stamp indicate the time (12.15 o'clock) at which the papers were received at the record division.

The initials J. C. P. in pencil are those of Maj. J. C. Post, and signify that he examined all the cases which accompanied the slip.

The figures 5393—5402, 5404—5411, signify that cases which were numbered from 5393 to 5402, inclusive, and from 5404 to 5411, inclusive, accompanied the slip. The figures 17,—3.30 indicate the day (17) and the hour at which the cases from 5393 to 5402, inclusive, were sent from the record division for action. The figures 18,—10.15 indicate the day (December 18) and the hour at which the cases from 5404 to 5411 were similarly sent.

Case No. 5403, which, it will be observed, is an intermediate number to the above, was a telegram which, having been immediately disposed of upon its receipt, was not noted upon the slip.

NOTE.—It will be observed that in the transfer of the papers from one to another the mode of transfer is not specified in each case, it being impossible, by reason of the lapse of time since the case was disposed of, to determine whether the transfer was by messenger or by the clerk from whom transferred. Where it could be determined with reasonable certainty that the transfer was made by messenger it is so stated.

Following is a transcript of Captain Leach's letter:

529

IMPROVING MISSISSIPPI RIVER,
1ST AND 2D DISTRICTS,
U. S. Engineer Office, Memphis, Tenn., December 14, 1888.

CAPT. SMITH S. LEACH,
Corps of Engineers U. S. A.,
In charge.

To the CHIEF OF ENGINEERS U. S. ARMY,
Washington, D. C.:

SIR: I have the honor to ask for the approval of the employment of one pilot for the trip from Quincy, Ill., to St. Louis, Mo., at $25.00 for the trip; and of another pilot for service from St. Louis, Mo., to Fletcher's L'dg, Ark., at the rate of $150.00 per month. The services of these men were required to conduct the U. S. steamer "Success," with tow, from Quincy, Ill., to the works at Plum Point Reach, and it was impracticable to obtain authority previous to their employment. It is proposed to pay them from allotment for "Plum Point Reach," appropriation for "Improving Mississippi River."

Very respectfully, your obedient servant,

SMITH S. LEACH,
Captain of Engineers.

106

Following is a copy of the back or reverse side of the letter, showing office stamps, indorsements, etc. The perpendicular lines indicate the folds:

5402	ENGR. DEPT.	
B	Rec'd Dec. 17	1882

5591	WAR DEPARTMENT.	
A	Received Dec. 22	1888

MEMPHIS, TENN., *Dec.* 14, 1888.

LEACH, Capt. S. S.

In connection with transfer of Str. *Success* and tow from Quincy, Ill., to Plum Point Reach, reqs. approval of employment of a pilot from Quincy to St. Louis, $25, and of another pilot from St. Louis to Fletcher's Pt., Ark., at rate of $150 pr. mo.; to be paid from allotment for impg. Plum Point reach.

File.
J. C. P.
U. S. Engineer Office, Memphis, Tenn.
Received Dec. 31, 1888.
Recd. Engr. Dept. back Dec. 24, 1888. Approved.
Recd. Engr. Dept. back Jan. 3, 1889.

[1st indorsement.]

OFFICE CHIEF OF ENGINEERS U. S. ARMY,
J. C. P.   *Dec.* 21, 1888.
Respectfully submitted to the Secretary of War with recommendation of approval.
THOS. LINCOLN CASEY,
Brig. Gen. Chief of Engineers.

$\frac{5402}{B}$ 1888

Approved. By order of the Secretary of War:
SAML. HODGKINS,
Acting Chief Clerk.

WAR DEPT., *Dec.* 22, 1888.

Recd. Engr. Dept. Dec. 24, 1888.

[3d indorsement.]

OFFICE CHIEF OF ENGINEERS U. S. ARMY,
Dec. 27, 1888.
Respectfully returned to Capt. S. S. Leach, Corps of Engineers, inviting attention to the foregoing indorsement, by which he will be guided.
After such record as may be necessary has been made, this this paper will be returned to this office.
By command of Brig. Gen. Casey:
JAS. C. POST,
Major of Engineers.

$\frac{5402}{B}$ 1888

[4th indorsement.]

U. S. ENGINEER OFFICE,
Memphis, Tenn., Dec. 31, 1888.
Respectfully returned to the Chief of Engineers U. S. Army, as required in 3d indorsement, record having been made for the files of this office.
SMITH S. LEACH,
Captain of Engineers.

Recd. Engr. Dept. Jan. 3, 1889.

The history of this case shows, as nearly as can now be determined, that in its course from Captain Leach, through the War Department, including its return to that officer and its return again by him to the War Department, it was handled by officers and clerks seventy-six times, and including messenger service, ninety-four times.

The Chief of Engineers handled it six times: first, when it came into the office and he thus knew it was pending; second, when he approved of the action proposed; third, when he signed the indorsement containing his views; fourth, when the paper was returned to his office with the action of the Secretary of War thereon; fifth, when he approved the indorsement proposed to carry out the orders of the Secretary; and sixth, when he saw that the orders had been carried out and the case closed.

Maj. J. C. Post, Corps of Engineers, in immediate charge of the third division, which has charge of all matters relating to rivers and harbors, handled it twelve times: (1) when sent to him by the Chief of Engineers he read it; (2) after entry in the books he looked at it again and sent it to have indorsement drafted; (3) indorsement being drafted, he put his initials on it to show he approved it; (4) the draft being approved by the Chief of Engineers, he sent it to the clerk to put on the paper; (5) when indorsement was placed on the paper he initialed it to show it was correct; (6) when signed by the Chief of Engineers he saw it again, and thus knew the action of the office had been taken; (7) he next read the action of the Secretary and sent the paper to be "received back" on the books; (8) this being done, he sent to have indorsement drafted to carry out orders; (9) he put his initials on draft to show he approved it; (10) draft being approved by Chief of Engineers, he sent the draft to be placed on the paper; (11) it having been placed on paper, he signed indorsement; (12) paper having been returned by Captain Leach, he saw that action was complete and ordered paper filed.

Mr. Stevens (clerk of class $1,000) in charge of mail-wagon of War Department, handled the paper three times: (1) when he brought it from the post-office; (2) when he took it from the Department to the post-office, when it was returned to Captain Leach; (3) when he again brought it from the post-office upon its return by Captain Leach.

Mr. Warren, chief clerk, office Chief of Engineers (salary $2,000 per annum), handled it five times: (1) when he handed it to Mr. Hartman, messenger, to cut open the envelope in which it was contained—this saves time, as the envelopes are being cut while the mail, often large, is being assorted; (2) when he looked it over and sent it to General Casey with the time-slip attached; (3) at the time of its receipt back from the War Department; (4) when he at the time of its second receipt from Captain Leach handed it to Mr. Hartman to cut open the envelope; (5) when he again looked it over and sent it to General Casey.

Mr. Hartman, assistant messenger, office Chief of Engineers (salary $720), handled it four times: (1) when he brought it from the mail-wagon to Mr. Warren's desk; (2) when he cut open the envelope and replaced it upon Mr. Warren's desk; (3) when for the second time he brought it from the mail-wagon to Mr. Warren's desk; (4) when he cut open the envelope and replaced it upon Mr. Warren's desk.

Mr. Dempsey, clerk of class 4 and chief clerk of the third division, office Chief of Engineers, handled it eleven times: (1) when it was sent to him by Major Post, when he stamped it with the figures III in lower left-handed corner and sent it to Mr. Duryee, chief of record division, for record; (2) when it was returned to him after having been recorded and indexed, and was returned by him to Major Post; (3) when it was sent to him by Major Post to have indorsement placed upon it; (4) when it was returned to him by the clerk who had placed the indorsement upon it, when he again returned it to Major Post; (5) when Major Post returned it to him after the indorsement had been signed by General Casey; (6) when it was sent to him by Major Post after having been acted upon by the Secretary of War; (7) when it was returned to him from the record division, to which it was sent to have the action of the Secretary of War properly recorded; (8) when it was again sent to him by Major Post to have another indorsement placed upon it; (9) when it was returned to him by the clerk who had placed the indorsement upon it; (10) when it was returned to him by Major Post after the indorsement had been signed; (11) when it was sent to him by Major Post upon its return by Captain Leach after which it was filed.

Mr. Duryee, clerk of class 4 and chief of record division, office of the Chief of Engineers, handled it five times: (1) when it was sent to him by Mr. Dempsey for record; (2) when the press-copy of the indorsement was sent to him to be temporarily filed; (3) when it was sent to him by Mr. Dempsey to have the action of the Secretary of War recorded; (4) when it was returned to him after the indorsement of the Secretary of War had been properly noted and indexed; (5) when it was sent to him after its receipt back from Captain Leach to be permanently filed.

Mr. Nichols, clerk of class 1, office of Chief of Engineers, handled it six times: (1) when it was stamped, briefed, and recorded by him in book of letters received; (2) when he noted in the book of letters received the indorsement submitting the case to the Secretary of War; (3) when he stamped it upon its receipt back from the Secretary of War, and made notation of its approval; (4) when he made a notation charging the case to the third division; (5) when he made a notation of the indorsement returning the case to Captain Leach; (6) when he stamped it showing its receipt back from Captain Leach and made notation thereof, and of the case being filed.

Mr. Saxton, clerk of class 3, office Chief of Engineers, handled it twice: (1) when he indexed it at the time of its first receipt in the record division, office Chief of Engineers; (2) when he indexed the action of the Secretary of War.

Mr. Burgess, civil engineer, office Chief of Engineers (salary $3,600), handled the case twice: (1) when he prepared the draft of the indorsement submitting the case to the Secretary of War; (2) when he prepared the draft of the indorsement returning it to Captain Leach.

Mr. Kiner, clerk of class 1, office Chief of Engineers, handled the case once, having placed thereon the indorsement submitting it to the Secretary of War.

Mr. Jansen, clerk of class 3, office Chief of Engineers, handled the case three times: (1) when he press-copied the indorsement submitting it to the Secretary of War; (2) when he placed upon the case the indorsement returning it to Captain Leach; (3) when he press-copied said indorsement.

Mr. Johnson, skilled laborer, office Chief of Engineers (salary $720). handled it three times: (1) when he temporarily filed the press-copy of the indorsement submitting the case to the Secretary of War; (2) when he similarly filed the press-copy of the indorsement returning the case to Captain Leach; (3) when he placed the case in the permanent files.

Mr. Carrington, clerk of class 4, record division, War Department (at the time acting chief of the division), handled the case twice: (1) when he opened the envelope, looked the case over, and marked it for Major Adams; (2) when it was returned to the record division after the indorsement of approval had been signed.

Mr. Robinson, clerk of class 2, record division, War Department, handled the case once, for the purpose of indexing it in the index-book of letters received.

Mr. Smith, clerk of class 1, record division, War Department, handled the case twice: (1) when he entered it in book (A) of letters received; (2) when he noted in said book the indorsement of approval.

Major Adams, Corps of Engineers (on duty in office of Secretary of War), handled the case twice: (1) when he submitted it to the Secretary of War for his action; (2) when he prepared the draft of indorsement of approval.

The Secretary of War handled the case once, when he examined it and indicated his approval of the recommendation of the Chief of Engineers.

Mr. Randolph, clerk of class 4 (assistant to the chief clerk, War Department), handled the case twice: (1) when he placed the indorsement of approval upon the case; (2) when he received it back from the acting chief clerk, after the indorsement was signed, and sent it to the record division.

Mr. Hodgkins, chief of the record division, War Department (at the time acting chief clerk), handled the case once, when he signed the indorsement of approval.

This statement and this analysis show vividly every item of work that has been done in the case of the steamer *Success*, but it is not to be assumed that the effect of handling it by so many people has therefore been to delay it unnecessarily. The passing on from hand to hand has enabled those who have thus looked at it to keep fully abreast with the work of the office, to see that it is properly done, and thus to carefully supervise it. At the same time they are busily engaged with other matters. The Chief of Engineers, while he has apparently only looked at this paper, has satisfied himself that the action proposed is correct. It has taken only a moment, while at the same time he has been busy with visitors on official matters and with the important professional problems involved in the duties of the Corps of Engineers connected with the improvement of rivers and harbors and the fortifications of the country.

Major Post has handled it oftener than any other officer, but this is accounted for by the fact that it pertained to the duties of his division of the office. His experience has enabled him to pass upon it with a mere glance which has satisfied him that it is correct, and in the mean time he has been absorbed in perhaps some professional problem about the dredging of a river, the building of dikes or bridges, and other matters coming before him.

The chief clerk of the office guides the clerical force, distributes the mail to the proper divisions, keeps it going, sees that it is correct, and at the same time is busy with visitors on official matters and other duties for the performance of which he is responsible.

The several clerks in charge of divisions look at the work so that they may know to whom to distribute, and again see that it is correct, while, at the same time, by this distribution they keep all usefully employed. It is not, of course, necessary here to state all the duties performed by each official.

In the subdivisions of the office the duties are similar to those of chiefs of divisions, and finally the case comes to those who do the actual work of entering in books, noting, briefing, copying, indexing, etc. In this particular case, while at first glance it might appear that it was handled more frequently than was necessary, still it is to be remembered that each of these individuals have to perform but a fractional part of the work, which has occupied but a small part of the time, and that at other times they have been engaged upon other work which should fully occupy their time. For instance, the chief clerk may have been engaged upon some important matter to which he must give his own individual attention; writing up a report, or searching for something which is within his own knowledge. So the chiefs and subchiefs of division are also engaged. This will be apparent when it is considered that in the office of the Chief of Engineers there are five officers, forty-nine clerks, and thirteen messengers; that this force has accomplished the work devolved upon the Chief of Engineers in the river and harbor bill, the appropriations for which have averaged $10,500,000 annually, and in the fortification bill, the appropriations for which have averaged $215,000 for the fiscal years from 1883 to 1889, and in addition incidental questions coming up from the Army in regard to engineering matters, questions growing out of the late war in regard to positions of troops, maps of battle-fields, and of fortifications, etc.

It may be possible that the fact of passing through so many hands has delayed the work to some extent, and with a view of reducing this to the lowest possible limit the board took up the question of the messenger service, and upon its recommendation the Secretary of War issued an order providing for a half hourly collection and delivery of the mail, which, when put into operation in all the divisions of the several offices and bureaus of the Department, will effect the transfer of papers and of communications with an expedition not now possible, and at the same time enable it to be done with a smaller force of messengers than is now engaged upon the work, thus enabling the other messengers not thus engaged to be more constantly at the call of those who may need them to carry oral messages about the Department and to take care of the rooms and keep everything in proper order. The value of this system is evident after it is put into practical operation. In theory papers are moved as fast as they are ready, and this system seems useless as being an additional requirement. But when a messenger is wanted he may be away carrying a message and the paper is delayed. In some divisions the mail moves but two or three times a day.

By means of regular half-hourly messenger trips between the offices of the chief clerk of the several bureaus and of the Department each of the ten bureaus can transmit a paper to any one of the other nine bureaus and receive one from any of the other nine bureaus every half-hour. That is, papers can by this specific service be moved in (10 times 9=) 90 different directions by one round trip of the messenger, and experiment has demonstrated that he can easily accomplish such trips in twenty minutes. As fourteen such trips can readily be made a day by a messenger, he can accomplish or make possible (90×14=) 1,260 separate deliveries between the bureaus and the office of the Secretary of War; or in other words, 1,260 individual official papers can in one day be taken up in the different bureaus and delivered at their proper destination within half an hour after they are completed, no two papers being sent at the same time to the same destination by any one bureau.

Should two, three, or more papers be sent at the same time from one bureau to another this estimated number of exchanges of actual papers would be increased in a corresponding ratio. While on the one hand each bureau does not have occasion to send papers to every other bureau in every delivery, on the other hand some bureaus send many papers at a time. It may therefore not be improper to assume that the number of exchanges of actual papers between bureaus by this system will approximate the number of points of contact made by the messenger, which, as above stated, is 1,260.

The offices and bureaus of the Department comprise about ninety divisions. These divisions have the same occasion to transmit papers back and forth as the bureaus. The half-hourly messenger service should therefore be applied also to every division of each bureau, the division messenger including in his trips the office of the chief clerk of the bureau. By this means a paper requiring to go from a division of one bureau to a division of another bureau will reach its destination by transfer from and to the division messenger through the baskets of the chief clerks of the two bureaus.

By this method also every division of a bureau is automatically put in speedy communication with every division of all other bureaus. This messenger service, therefore, enables each of the ninety divisions to communicate with each of the other eighty-nine divisions, making (90×89=) 8,010 possible transfers of papers per trip. Fourteen trips a day will permit of (8,010×14=) 112,140 possible transfers throughout the Department, so that this number of individual papers could be transferred by this system without any two papers making the same journey at the same time, and without the necessity on the part of the sender of addressing and sealing an envelope, ringing for a messenger, waiting until he comes, handing him the paper, telling him where to go; nor on the part of the recipient of telling the messenger that there is or is not a reply.

It is estimated that this method of transfer can be accomplished by about twenty messengers, and that as the balance of the laboring and messenger force of the Department will thereby be relieved from the work of transmitting ordinary papers not requiring more speedy delivery than every half hour, they will be available for the carrying of oral messages, of papers requiring immediate transfer, and other necessary work of the Department.

To the criticism that the clerical work has been done by low-grade clerks, while those of a higher grade seem to have merely glanced at it and passed it on to others to do the work, it is to be remarked that there must be supervision, and in a large business many must be employed in doing fractional parts of work.

This is but one case of a ceaseless number. The high-grade clerk is experienced; a glance at many of the cases is sufficient to enable him to determine the next step necessary; other cases he must examine carefully; he is busy answering questions, directing, supervising: the clerks of the lower grades do the writing, searching, filing, and indexing. It is not asserted that all in the higher grades are better clerks than those in the lower grades, that they are more intelligent or more industrious, or that all of the clerks are usefully and necessarily employed, but it is believed this is true generally, for the work must be done satisfactorily and must not be allowed to accumulate. Chiefs of bureaus, being responsible for the character of the work in their respective bureaus, endeavor to secure the best men for responsible places, and to secure this they make their recommendations when there are vacancies, having also in view the result of the examination before the Civil Service Board of Promotion; and the appointment is made by the Secretary of War in accordance with such recommendation.

Whether there are any useless briefs, records, or notations made in this class of papers has already been partly considered and recommendation made that certain classes of paper be not recorded. This subject will be further considered in this report hereafter.

Whether there are any links in the chain that can be omitted has been reported upon in the paper upon "Administration."

It is evident that papers often pass through too many hands, and as this is a matter that can best be remedied by chiefs of bureaus, it is recommended that a circular be issued as follows:

[Circular.]

WAR DEPARTMENT,
Washington City, February, 1889.

In the matter of briefing and entering "letters received" and recording "letters sent" and indorsements in the respective bureaus and offices of the War Department, attention is invited to the case entitled "Salaries and Fees of United States Consuls," published on pages 25 to 37, inclusive, of volume 1 of the report of the Select Committee of the United States Senate, appointed under Senate resolution of March 3, 1887, to inquire into and examine the methods of business and work in the Executive Departments, etc.

With this case as a sample to be followed, chiefs of bureaus are requested to have an actual case selected, such as will show the average action or work upon cases in their respective bureaus or offices, then to have a history of the case prepared by the clerk in charge, showing in minute detail (including copies of briefs, office marks, indorsements, letters, entries in record, and index-books, etc.) the action from and including the receipt of the case in the office, through its various courses to and including its final disposition, in like manner as is shown in the case mentioned.

This history having been prepared as required, chiefs of bureaus will cause an investigation of the subject to be made, and having thereupon decided whether any unnecessary work has been done or any persons have been employed on the work more than were needed, and what possible improvements can be made in the methods adopted, they will apply the appropriate remedy and make report of their action to the Secretary of War, and transmit therewith a copy of the history of each case made up as above directed.

By order of the Secretary of War.

Chief Clerk.

It is believed this tracing of papers and writing down every step that has been taken, either by officers, clerks, or others will show the operation so clearly that it will be apparent that there is a possibility of improvement, and various steps that have been taken in the past will be cut off in future, and the work expedited. Thus the object desired by the Senate committee, and required by the order convening the board, will be accomplished and the remedy applied by the officers directly responsible for the work.

PENSION CLAIM OF THOMAS W. TAYLOR.

This case has been selected at random as showing delay, which will be remedied to a great extent by the foregoing circular and the order of January 18, 1889, requiring half-hourly mail collections and deliveries.

It has not been traced step by step like the case of the steamer *Success*. The circular just suggested requires cases to be selected in all of the divisions of the Department and traced step by step. A copy of this case will therefore be sufficient for the present purpose. The following is a copy of the papers in the case:

111

(1)

—— Mid., —— Division.

First call on Adjutant-General, U. S. A.

Claim No. 676347.
Thos. W. Taylor.
Co. I, 161st Ohio Vols.
Dec. 1st, 1888.

(2)

(3)

Mid. Div.
J. H. T., Ex'r.
No. 676347.
Thos. W. Taylor.
Co. I, 161st Ohio Vols.

(3-060)

Adjutant-General's Office,
Received Dec. 4, 1888.
Enlisted Volunteer Pension Branch.

DEPARTMENT OF THE INTERIOR,
BUREAU OF PENSIONS,
Dec. 1st, 1888.

SIR: I have the honor to request that you will furnish from the records of the War Department a full report as to the service, disability, and hospital treatment of Thomas W. Taylor, who, it is claimed, enlisted May 2d, 1864, and served as private in Co. I, 161st Reg't Ohio N. G. Vols.; also in Co.

and was discharged at Columbus, Ohio, Sept. 21st, 1864.
While serving in Co. I, 161st Vols. he was disabled by fever, deafness, lung and heart trouble, at Frederick, Md., Aug., 1864
Also

and was treated in hospitals, of which the names, location, and dates of treatment are as follows:
Regimental Hospital

Very respectfully,

JOHN C. BLACK,
Commissioner.

The ADJUTANT-GENERAL, U. S. ARMY.
13502—75 M.   O 6—002.

112

(4)

First division volunteer rolls and records.

Thomas Taylor, I Co., 161 Regt. Ohio Vols.

Regt'l Des. Book.	
Hospital records.	Not on file.
Con. M. Reports.	
Order Books.	
Letter Books.	
Co. Des. Book.	Ex.
Co. M. Reports	Ex.
Clothing Books.	
Co. Returns.	Not on file.
Casualties.	
Med. Certificates.	$\frac{377}{15}$
Furloughs.	
Files.	

(5)

Mr. Hesse:

No detachment or individual muster-out roll or certificate of disability on file. The records of this divison furnish no further evidence of disability.

Th. I. S.

1st Div., V. R. R.
Dec. 14, 1888.

(6)

$\frac{10894}{B}$	Adjt. Genl's Office Enlisted Br. Recd. Dec. 17.	1888

(7)

PENSION OFFICE,
Dec. 1, 1888.

Thomas W. Taylor, Co. I, 161 Reg't Ohio Vols.

Commissioner of Pensions requests full statement of service.

Wrapper.

123

$\dfrac{377}{15}$

3 — 378

(8)

Second Auditor's Office,
Dec. 22, 1888.
Mail Room.

WAR DEPARTMENT,
ADJUTANT GENERAL'S OFFICE,
Washington, Dec. 21, 1888.

Respectfully referred to the Second Auditor of the Treasury, with request that he will inform this office whether his files contain any record of payment to this soldier on final statements or muster-out roll, and, if so, the date, place, and cause of his discharge.
Please return these papers with the report.

C. McKEEVER,
Assistant Adjutant-General.
(199)

C.

Recd. back with report and 1 Enc. Jan. 31, '89.
J. K.

(9)

[Form 29.]

TREASURY DEPARTMENT,
SECOND AUDITOR'S OFFICE,
Washington, D. C., Jan'y 18, 1889.

4 W
5 "
6 "
7 "
8 "
9 "
10 "
11 "
13 "

SIR: Please give the last payment, and any ordinary or add. bounty payments, when and by whom made to Thomas W. Taylor, —— late Pvt. —— Company "I" 161 Ohio —— Volunteers, who was discharged after the 2d day of Sept., 1864 (Notation on M–O roll; "certif. to Maj. Sabin, Aug. 14, 1865.")
Very respectfully,

J. F. K. 80.

WM. A. DAY,
Auditor.
By F. E. G.

Paymaster General's Office,
U. S. A.
Rec'd Jan. 21, 1889.
Vol. Record Division.

To the PAYMASTER-GENERAL.

(10)

Second Auditor's Office,
Jan. 22, 1889.
Mail Room.

WAR DEPARTMENT,
PAYMASTER-GENERAL'S OFFICE,
Washington, D. C., Jan. 21, 1889.

SIR: It appears on record that Thos. W. Taylor, —— late —— pt. —— Company —— I —— 161st —— Regiment —— Ohio —— Volunteers, was last paid by Major J. A. Sabin, 6678, on the 21st day of Aug., 1865. ——.
No record of A. B.
Very respectfully,

WM. B. ROCHESTER,
Paymaster-General.
By B.

To the SECOND AUDITOR OF THE TREASURY.
[Ed. 7-29-87-20,000.]

(11)

[Form 113.]

TREASURY DEPARTMENT,
SECOND AUDITOR'S OFFICE,
January 26, 1889.

Respectfully returned to the Assistant Adjutant-General.
Thomas W. Taylor, late pvt., Co. "I," 161 Ohio U. S. Vols., was last paid on Form 5 to include Sept. 1st, 1864.
No final statement with voucher; data obtained from M | O roll of company.
1343-1914.

WM. A. DAY, *Auditor.*
By J. H. B. JENKINS.

J. F. K. 80.
[Ed. 1-27, '87—5,000.]

(12)

O

WAR DEPARTMENT,
ADJUTANT-GENERAL'S OFFICE,
Washington, Feby. 2, 1889.

Respectfully referred to the Surgeon-General U. S. Army for information, with request that these papers be returned with report.
By order of the Secretary of War.

C. McKEEVER,
Asst. Adjutant-General.
(123)

O. E. C.   O

(13)

```
        R. & P. DIV.
1889.      530460      Feb. 5,
          S. G. O.
```

(14)

Name.	Rank.	Co.	Regiment.	Date of admission.	Record of—	Diagnosis.	Disposition and remarks.
Thos. W. Taylor.	P........	I...	161 Ohio	1864. Aug. 14...	Gen. Hosp., Frederick, Md.	Typhoid fever.	Returned to duty Sept. 19, '64.

Note._____

115

(15)

Case of Thomas W. Taylor, P, Co. I, 161 Reg't Ohio V.

Claim No. 676347.

WAR DEPARTMENT,
SURGEON-GENERAL'S OFFICE,
RECORD AND PENSION DIVISION,
Washington, D. C., Feb. 7, 1889.

This transcript from the records on file in this office is respectfully furnished for the information of the Adjutant-General, U. S. A., and embodies all the information which has been found on a search of those records made in full compliance with the inclosed request.

All papers pertaining to the case are herewith returned.
By order of the Surgeon-General.

F. C. AINSWORTH,
Capt. and Assistant Surgeon, U. S. A.
Per

R. & P. Div., No. 530160.
J. C. F.

(16)

676347

WAR DEPARTMENT,
ADJUTANT-GENERAL'S OFFICE,
Washington, ———, 188 .

Respectfully returned to the Commissioner of Pensions.
Thomas —— Taylor, a private of Company I, 161st Regiment Ohio Volunteers, was enrolled on the 2d day of May, 1864, at Findlay, Ohio (100 days), and is reported on muster-out roll, dated Camp Chase, Ohio, Sept. 2, 1864, "sick at U. S. Gen. Hospital, Frederick, Md." Muster and muster-out roll only on file. Reg'l returns for May and July, 1864 (only on file), do not report him absent. Co. returns not on file. Reg'l hospital records not on file.
Name also borne as Thomas W. Taylor.

R. C. DRUM,
Adjutant-General.
By

Th. I. S.

C. 3–019.

(2.)

From the foregoing it appears that the Commissioner of Pensions wrote to the Adjutant-General for a report in the case on December 1, 1888, but the letter was not received in the Adjutant-General's Office until December 4, 1888, a delay of three days. The case was undergoing search in the Adjutant-General's Office until December 21, 1888—seventeen days—when it was sent to the Second Auditor of the Treasury for information. Twenty-eight days thereafter—January 18, 1889—the Second Auditor wrote to the Paymaster-General for information, but the letter was not received in his office until January 21, 1889—a delay of three days—and was answered on the day of its receipt, the answer having been received in the Second Auditor's Office on the following day—January 22, 1889. The case was returned by the Second Auditor to the Adjutant-General by indorsement dated January 26, 1889, the latter date being thirty-six days subsequent to that on which the case was sent to the Auditor. A notation on the case shows it to have been received back in the office of the Adjutant-General January 31, 1889. It is hardly supposable that an interval of four days—or five days including either the date of the indorsement or that of the notation mentioned—could have been consumed in the transmission of the case between the two offices, and as the mail coming into the Adjutant-General's Office is opened by the clerk in charge of the mail-room, from which it is taken by messengers at irregular intervals to the divisions to which it respectively pertains, and is not stamped to show the date of its receipt until after it reaches the division to which it belongs, it is thought probable that the case may in fact have been received into the office prior to the date given in the notation, and this may be true of the other delays in transmission mentioned. On February 2, 1889, seven days subsequent to its return as per the indorsement of the Second Auditor, the case was returned by the Adjutant-General to the Surgeon-General, but did not reach the office of the latter until

February 5, 1889—a delay of three days. Two days thereafter—February 7, 1889—the Surgeon-General returned the case to the Adjutant-General, where its record was completed and made ready to send to the Commissioner of Pensions February 14, 1889.

The advantages of the half-hourly messenger service, which was put in operation the 1st instant, has already been clearly demonstrated in the division of requisitions and accounts, office of the Secretary of War. Under the former system, while a paper received one day may have been sent out the same day, it would not have come back, unless made "special," the same day. Now a settlement certificate is received, charged out, returned, the requisition is prepared, signed, entered, and sent to the Treasury on the same day, and this rapidity of movement is had without the least inconvenience.

METHODS OF GOVERNMENT DEPARTMENTS AND COMMERCIAL ESTABLISHMENTS.

It now becomes proper to state the method adopted by the board in its investigation of this subject. Having a practical knowledge of the business of the Department and the manner of keeping the records, it was deemed essential in the first place to ascertain the methods of business relating to correspondence adopted by large corporations and commercial establishments. Accordingly, with the sanction of the Secretary of War, the board, on December 14 last, proceeded to Philadelphia, New York, and Boston, and visited the offices of the Pennsylvania Railroad Company, Philadelphia; the agent in Philadelphia of the New York Mutual Life Insurance Company; the Southern Pacific Railroad Company, New York City; the Equitable Life Assurance Society, New York City; the Mutual Reserve Fund Life Association, New York City; the Metropolitan Life Insurance Company, New York City; the New England Mutual Life Insurance Company, Boston, and the establishments of Messrs. W. & J. Sloane and Edwin S. Greely, of New York City, and John Wanamaker, of Philadelphia. On December 24 the board returned, having been afforded every facility to accomplish the object in view. As the work of the Department would not admit of a prolonged absence the investigation was confined to the system adopted by the companies named, of receiving, listing, answering, and filing correspondence. It was found to differ greatly from that adopted by this Department.

In corporations and commercial establishments correspondence is acted upon and answered before any record is made of it. In Government offices the reverse is the rule. In the one case delay is of rare occurrence, in the other there is more or less delay in many cases. The cause is due to the essential difference in the business.

The principal business of corporations and commercial establishments is that for which they are organized, viz., the transportation of freight and passengers, the insurance of lives, the buying and selling of goods, etc.; the incidental business is correspondence which relates almost entirely to current business and is at once disposed of; such correspondence rarely requires an examination of old records before it can be answered. While the correspondence is perhaps of equal or greater volume, the commercial house has little or no occasion to refer to any of its files of letters received or sent after the business matters involved have been brought to a conclusion. The business of the War Department is transacted to a great extent by correspondence, and except where the matter is purely routine an examination of records or a report from some official is required before a satisfactory answer can be made. This correspondence constitutes the actual stock or matter of business of the Department in its dealings with creditors and claimants for all time. There is no general statute of limitations affecting Government claims, so such claims, with a few exceptions, must be considered without regard to their antiquity; and even the cases which have been specially barred by law are liable to be called up by means of a petition to Congress, praying for relief.

The following table shows the contrast, in some particulars, between the two methods of business:

In private establishments.	*In Government offices.*
Correspondence is opened as soon as received.	Same.
Envelopes retained for a stated period, averaging forty-eight hours.	Envelopes not retained.
In some offices a running list, by name only, is made each day, and letters at once distributed to the proper departments for action. The action is noted on the letter, which is sent back to the clerk to answer and file. Prior to filing a list is made, by date only, of each letter, showing name, subject, and answer. This never exceeds one line. Each line is numbered, and the corresponding number only is placed on back of letter. The letters are filed away in even hundreds for ready reference. The answers, or "letters sent," are press-copied only and indexed by	Each "letter received" is briefed on the back, which brief is entered in a book known as the "Letters-received book," numbered, and the name of the writer, and all proper names in the letter, as also the subject, are carefully indexed. When this is done the letters are distributed to the proper officials for action. Important letters are given the preference in entry, etc. The action on papers is either by indorsement or letter. An indorsement is noted in the book of "letters received," in the appropriate column, opposite the entry of the letter, or if long recorded

name. Many houses use the indexed letter file-cabinets, Cameron, Amberg & Co. (or similar books), for filing away letters.

When a letter can not be answered at once its receipt is acknowledged.
Correspondence, as far as it can be controlled, is confined to one subject.

in the book of "letters sent." Letters sent are press-copied, these are copied into a permanent book of "letters sent," and the press-copies filed with the papers. A list of letters received and sent which are not recorded has already been given on pages 6 to 23.
This is rarely done.

No rule on the subject, but one recommended in paper on "Administration." See Appendix No. 8.

In addition it may be said that competition in trade, the personal interest of proprietors, the present or prospective interest of superintendents and heads of Departments, and the direct control and discharge of employés, which gives greater moral force to a caution or a reprimand, explain in part the cause of the difference between the business methods of commercial establishments and the Government Departments.

NECESSITY OF RECORDING IMPORTANT PAPERS—DUPLICATION OF ENTRIES TO BE AVOIDED.

If all letters were filed in the office where received, a mere index of names and a bare statement of the subject would be sufficient to enable the searcher to find the letter itself. But all the letters are not filed; many are returned or referred with orders, reports, information, or expressions of opinion indorsed thereon, and do not come back. The practice of indorsing orders, etc., on letters is old and expedites business; it saves letter writing, and at times the copying of the letter on which the indorsement is placed. Letters so indorsed are often of great importance. It eventually becomes necessary to refer to one or more of them in a case involving a similar principle or which pertains to or is a continuation of the same subject. In the absence of the papers the entry on the book of letters received is the next best evidence; it contains a statement in the nature of a syllabus of the contents of the paper desired, and also of the date of receipt, the action thereon if by indorsement, or the page of the letter-book if a letter was written.
It is evident that it takes considerable time to do this properly, and when there is a large correspondence, many clerks—clerks to receive the mail, to brief, enter, and index it, to make notations and searches, and to file away papers. In many of the offices the correspondence is large, and to keep trace of it it is entered before it is acted upon. This is a delay at the inception which is most marked, especially in cases which it is known are pending and require immediate action. So it is the rule to make such cases "special," and hurry them through the record books ahead of the other mail. Again, when an important paper is acted upon by indorsement, of course it should go out at once, but the inevitable delay of recording again occurs. To reduce this to the lowest limit it is again made special and sometimes the indorsement is dictated to a stenographer so the record may be made on the books while the paper goes on its way.
Short methods are adopted consistent with a record that shall be of value for future reference. But is such a record necessary in all cases? Not by any means. Only important papers should be recorded. But the practical difficulty of deciding this question has led to the entering of many letters received, the recording of many letters sent, and indorsements which are not important. To meet the difficulty in part, lists have been prepared in the several offices of classes of correspondence which should not be recorded. These lists are given on pages 92 to 98 of this report.
Important "letters sent" are recorded in permanent books, because there is no copying ink in use which is permanent for the purposes of the Government. Press-copies are good for many years—ten, twenty, thirty perhaps—but they begin to change color after a few years, and some soon fade so as to be illegible, while it may be necessary to consult a record after the lapse of one hundred years. An ink that will last for an indefinite period is therefore required for governmental use. Another reason is that, if press-copy books alone were used, they would soon become dilapidated by constant use.
Further, the press-copy of the reply to a letter is filed with the letter, thus making the case as filed complete in itself. This practice is a great convenience when a case is being made up from the papers themselves, especially when they are numerous, and saves the time which would otherwise be required to consult the records. If press-copies were not recorded, they must be kept in books and indexed, then in making up a case it would be necessary to search the records for replies to letters, to make notes of the replies, and it would often be necessary to extend the search to other offices of the Department, where action had been communicated by letter. This is saved by the present system of recording letters and filing the press-copies with the proper papers.
This elaborate system of recording has been in use for many years. It works smoothly but slowly; slow at first, but it undoubtedly saves much time when it becomes necessary to refer to previous papers. It takes but a comparatively short time to say defi-

nitely whether a paper has been filed in any of the offices of the War Department, say within the past twenty years. In the office of the Secretary it can generally be told in from one-half to three-quarters of an hour.

The following is the result of an actual test made on the 17th of January: Search was made from January 1, 1868, to January 1, 1889, for the name J. T. Smith or Joshua T. Smith. The name was found once in 1870, once in 1882, once in 1883, twice in 1884, once in 1885, once in 1886, and once in 1887. The time occupied was fifty minutes.

The name Harry Barton was searched for from 1868 to 1889, inclusive. It was found once in 1883 and twice in 1888. Time consumed in making the search, twenty-three minutes.

The name Horace Williams was searched for from 1868 to 1888, inclusive, and not found. Time consumed in search, forty minutes.

But with this system there is undoubtedly a duplication of entries. A paper addressed to the Secretary of War is entered in his office; if referred to the Adjutant-General it is entered in his office; and so it is entered in any office to which it is referred. This duplication of entries will be remedied to a great extent by the order issued on the 13th instant on the subject of "Administration." As all the offices and bureaus are now in one building (except the Signal Office) the records are easily accessible, consequently the original entry of a paper should be sufficient for all purposes. When a paper is referred to another office the action there taken can, if necessary, be noted, and the notation should show the action taken, followed by the office-mark of the paper where it was first recorded; then when the paper is needed it can be obtained from the office where it is filed.

If this rule is adopted can a particular paper be found on which action was indorsed? Yes, (1) if the indorsement sets forth the names of persons and things, or the subjects concerned, sufficiently for indexing purposes; (2) if it does not and important action on many papers is simply indicated by the word "approved" or "recommended," etc., the paper in such a case can be found by indexing from the paper itself, as is now done in most cases, and by inserting in the index the number of the paper as shown by the office-mark where the paper was first entered, it being assumed that that office has jurisdiction of the subject-matter. This will also apply to cases where the action is communicated by letter instead of by indorsement.

Of course the index will only point to the paper, and to ascertain the action taken in the second class of cases mentioned above it will be necessary to send for the papers, but this is only a few steps farther for the messenger than he takes at present. It is a pertinent question whether it is necessary to even index the second class of cases, or to record and index many of the first class in any office other than where the paper is first recorded. It is true the action may be important in itself, but unless it forms a precedent for action in other cases, one record is sufficient for reference. The subject of precedents and their notation will be considered under the heading "card index of decisions or precedents." The present system would be too slow for a time of war, when things must be done in a hurry, and therefore a system applicable to all times should be adopted.

RECEIPT OF MAIL—FIRST ACTION ON.

If the clerk in charge of any record division is not present at 9 o'clock or any other time when mail is received the mail should not be delayed on that account; nor should it be delayed when he is present to enable him to read it. At 9 o'clock, and whenever received, a sufficient number of clerks in the several record divisions should be required to suspend all other business and open the mail. As each clerk reads a letter he should underscore in blue pencil all names of persons and of things written about, unless it should include a list of persons or things, when the underscoring may be omitted. He should also draw a line in blue pencil along the margin of the letter where the subject is stated or a question is asked. This will take but little more time than it does to read the letter and will be facilitated if the subject of correspondence is indicated by the writer at the upper left-hand corner of the first page of the letter or report, as recommended by the board in the report upon "Administration." The letters pertaining to the business of the office should then be separated from those that pertain to the business of other offices. Those pertaining to the business of other offices should be noted on the brief cards hereafter recommended if chiefs of bureaus deem it necessary to keep trace of such papers. This mail should then be marked with the initials of the office to which it pertains, the clerks being guided in this respect by the lists to be published showing the jurisdiction of each office, and the mail being then handed to the chief of the division, section, or room, he or the person acting for him should at once send it to the proper offices. This should all be completed within half an hour after receipt of the mail, and then the papers which pertain to the business of the office should be taken up, briefed, and entered, except the classes of letters heretofore noted, which it is recommended be not entered.

The briefers should note on each paper in lead pencil the name of the official in the office to whom it is to be sent for action, being guided by a list which should be prepared in each office or bureau showing the class of work each official acts on. As fast as entered, and not exceeding intervals of one-half an hour, the mail should be handed to the chief of the division, section, or room, in order that he may read the briefs and inform himself of the nature of the communications passing through his office; having done this he should at once send them to their destination.

None of these suggestions, of course, to interfere with special cases, but if this course is thoroughly carried out all will go through with the rapidity of special cases.

BRIEFING AND INDEXING.

The rules for briefing contained in the instructions should be carefully followed. The tendency is to make them too long by the use of superfluous words and reference to immaterial matters. The subject should be stated in the fewest possible words, so as to show in the absence of the paper what in particular was written about, bearing in mind that it is generally necessary to read the paper before it can be finally acted upon. The brief enables the paper to be passed rapidly from one to another until it reaches the authority competent to decide. The attention of the board has been called to some briefs which are in fact longer than the letter.

The principal subject should be indexed so as to clearly indicate the paper sought. With the adoption of the card-index in lieu of letters-received books, the brief, reply, notations, and all about the paper will be written on a card, having the principal subject written at the top, and under that title it will be filed. The principal subject is the word or words finally remembered, as "Bridge" when a particular bridge is forgotten, "Absence" instead of "leave of absence," "Subsistence supplies" or "Transportation" instead of particular articles, the articles following the title of principal subject, thus: "Subsistence supplies—pork," "Transportation—wagons;" such cards will fall into the appropriate subdivisions of the principal subjects, and all papers about subsistence supplies or transportation will come together, the subdivisions following in alphabetical order, as also the cards of each subdivision. Thus, if Jones writes about wagons the card will be found in its proper alphabetical place of the sub-division "wagons" of the subject or division "Transportation." To know that one should look for Jones' letter about wagons under "Transportation." Let rules be prepared and printed for the guidance of those who make the cards and those who file them, showing in two columns lists of principal subjects and their subdivisions (see Exhibit C); thus, if a letter about the "Eastern Branch Bridge, Potomac River," is looked for, instead of turning to the letter "E" in the file-boxes he will know by the rules that all bridges are filed under the word "Bridge," and turning to "E" of bridge he will find the card. This system will save indexing subjects under many heads. Under the present system the bridge supposed would be indexed under "Bridge," "Eastern Branch," and "Potomac River," and probably "Chief of Engineers," as the business pertains to his office. One subject will generally be enough, proper names being indexed on separate cards with reference to the "principal subject" and filed by themselves alphabetically as cross-reference cards.

CONSOLIDATION OF RECORD DIVISIONS.

It has been suggested that the records of "letters received" and "letters sent" in each bureau be consolidated into one general record and file division, thus saving labor and simplifying the work, while classification and distribution lead to complication and duplication.

It is true that less clerks can do this work in one division than if it is in several, and when practicable there should be but one record division in a bureau. To facilitate the work of those who act on cases, or prepare them for action, it is considered important that they should be near the record, and if classified the record is thought to be more accessible.

It was the object of the board which compiled the 1870 instructions to have but one record and file-room in each bureau, but in practice several have been authorized in some of the bureaus. *In any event duplication of entries should be avoided and record divisions should not be multiplied in any bureau except after careful investigation, and for imperative reasons, and only when approved by the Secretary of War.*

It should be borne in mind that several record divisions in one bureau tend to confusion, unless the subdivisions are natural and the boundaries plainly and definitely marked. Vagueness in any respect causes uncertainty where to search for papers, and much loss of time.

In view of the great number of record books in the Department, it is evident that a preface or introduction is necessary in many of them to show the purpose they were intended to serve, for public records ought not to need the skill of experts or the memory of officials to understand them. A copy of one such introduction, kindly furnished by the chief clerk of the Surgeon General's Office, is here given more as a suggestion of the need of such an introduction than as a particular form to be followed:

"This book was made up in 1885, and was intended to contain, as far as could be ascertained, the names of all persons and quasi-persons paid by medical disbursing officers, beginning with July 1, 1862, and ending with Abstract Books 18, 19 and 20. The several accounts in these are brought down to very different dates; some no farther than April 30, 1867, and others as far as July, 1874.

"The books referred to are an old ledger, lettered G, commencing July, 1862, and Abstract Books 2 and 4 to 20, inclusive. There never was any Abstract Book 1 or 3. Formerly these abstracts were made on loose sheets and then copied in the ledger. The books were made to save this double writing. When they were ordered it was thought there would be loose sheets enough to make three thin volumes, and so they were numbered from 4 upwards. When the books came from the binder those loose sheets that were of nearly uniform size were bound into one thick volume numbered 2. The remainder of the papers, which were of various sizes and patterns, were copied into Ledger G.

"As several persons may have the same name, and on the other hand the same person may recur in several places, fulfilling different functions, no attempt has been made to separate them. On the general roll of artificial limbs eleven men bear the simple name of John Smith, while in the books here indexed the name occurs thirty-six times. How many persons it represents is unknown. The reason for not attempting to discriminate is that but a small percentage will ever be inquired for, and when they are wanted it will be as easy to separate them as now. The labor will thus be saved of analyzing names that will never be called for.

"Although considerable pains have been taken, many names are no doubt incorrect. They were at first taken down hurriedly on pay-rolls by clerks who caught them by ear as best they could, and did not always write them in a very legible manner."

SUGGESTIONS OF THE CHIEF SIGNAL OFFICER.

The Chief Signal Officer recommends the following as improved business methods for the War Department:

"*Letters received* should be marked with a dated receiving-stamp, and numbered consecutively. The letters-received book should be dispensed with as an unnecessary elaboration, which is kept up by no business man in the world. The consecutive numbering of letters received and very full index books of names, places, and subjects (which are now kept) are sufficient for practical purposes. Not more than one letter out of a hundred in this office is ever consulted after once going to the files, and not more than one in five hundred quits the office files. When letters leave the office a concise summary of the contents should be retained for file in place of the letter sent out. The adoption of this plan would be worth three clerks to this office, and allow that reduction in force another year. If, however, letters must be briefed, press-copies instead of written copies of the brief should be adopted, and for the letters-received book a complete index of briefs be substituted. Whenever the number of communications on any subject is sufficiently large to justify it there should be a separate series of numbers, and a letters-received book or index for each class alone, thus obviating the necessity of recording or indexing the subject.

"*Letters sent.*—Press-copies only should be made, and in case of indorsements press-copies on loose sheets should be placed in the files of the letters received. Separate books should be kept for separate classes of subjects whenever the number of communications on any subject is large enough to justify it. As far as practicable, skeleton letter-forms, in copying-ink, should be used, thus reducing to a minimum the amount of pen-work. Letters sent, based on letters received, should be filed with letters received, so that the copy of the action and the communication would be together."

From the foregoing it appears that not one letter in a hundred in the Signal Office is consulted after it is filed, and not one in five hundred quits the office files. Under these circumstances it is evident that the business is entirely current, and when disposed of is rarely, if ever, referred to. This statement of facts is like the hypothetical case stated on page 117, as follows: "If all letters were filed in the office where received, a mere index of names and a bare statement of the subject would be sufficient to enable the searcher to find the letter itself." As, therefore, all letters are filed in the Signal Office, except one in five hundred, no objection is seen to the adoption in that office of the system proposed by the Chief Signal Officer.

But a very different state of facts exists in other bureaus, and the system should not be adopted elsewhere, at least for the present. It is a radical change from the system in use and will lead to confusion, if adopted, while the changes here recommended are being put into operation.

CARD-INDEX BRIEFS.

With reference to that portion of the mail which is addressed to the Secretary of War, but to answer which it is necessary to obtain information or an expression of opinion from another office of the Department, it is recommended that the following course be pursued: Let such mail be immediately separated from the rest and handed to a sufficient number of clerks to make card-index briefs of it, the entire time occupied not to exceed half an hour; the cards to be in size, 8 inches long by $3\frac{1}{2}$ inches wide, as follows:

[Face of card.]

```
*                                          1889.

            Letters Received
         Office Secretary of War
                   on
        Business pertaining to bureaus.

Date_____[Place]_____
              [Date]_____
From_____[Writer]_____

Subject_____
_____
_____


        No. of Inclosures ____.

Received_____M_____1889.
Sent same date_____M to_____
Acknowledged same date_____M_____
Recd. back____M_____1889.
Bureau office mark_____
Action_____
_____
_____
_____
_____
_____

Prepared by____[Signature of clerk.]___
```

[Reverse of card.]

Letters received at the office of the Secretary of War pertaining to bureaus will be entered on brief cards and the letters sent to the proper bureaus. Such letters to remain in the office of the Secretary not to exceed one-half hour.

Letters of acknowledgement on blank forms to be filled out from these cards after the letters are sent to the bureaus, and mailed on day of receipt of letters.

Brief cards to be filed alphabetically by surname.

No other entry to be made, and no marks to be placed on such letters or inclosures, except office date of receipt and name of office to which it pertains and number of inclosures, these to be placed on first page of each letter.

* First three letters of surname.

The letters to which this would apply in the Secretary's office are those from Senators, members of Congress, and others, to which he is expected to reply; but to do so he must first obtain a report from some source outside of his own office.

A subject index of these cards will not be needed. Subjects are usually called for by those who do not remember the name of the writer, but in the office where the cards are made the papers will generally be seen only by the clerks who make the cards, hence in that office subjects will not be called for of such papers, and they can only be called up by the writers.

The object of the brief card, as will be seen, is to get the paper under action at once, so that the reply will be delayed as little as possible, and also to enable the letter to be traced, if necessary. When a paper of this class is returned to the office of the Secretary, if of sufficient importance, it may be entered on the book of letters received, or on the permanent record card, if the recommendation under the head of "Card Index" is approved, and the brief card destroyed, having served its purpose; all papers finally to be sent or returned for file to the chief of the bureau having jurisdiction of the subject treated of, as proposed in the report upon "Administration." Many cases must be returned to the Secretary of War, because courtesy demands that he should reply to the writer, but which are not of sufficient importance to warrant a permanent record. In such cases the fact of final reply should be noted on the proper brief card and the letter and press-copy of reply filed in the office furnishing the information. In case a letter received is not entered on the permanent record, and it is decided to record the reply, the record of the letter on a record card will, in most cases, be sufficient, especially if the bureau office-mark of the paper is noted thereon, and then the paper can be sent for when needed. This applies with equal force to indorsements. See remarks on this subject under the heading "Duplication of entries."

In the bureaus of the Department a record of papers of merely transient importance can also be kept on brief cards, which need not be entered on the permanent records of the office.

ACKNOWLEDGMENTS.

(1) When the reply to a letter will be delayed for a short time; (2) when a letter is sent elsewhere for report before it can be answered; (3) when the letter is upon a subject over which the official addressed has no jurisdiction, and (4) in other cases which will suggest themselves in actual practice, it is recommended that an acknowledgment of the receipt be sent in any case where the writer may be in doubt whether his letter has been received or not.

For the acknowledgment of letters from persons who rarely write to the Department a postal card may be used, with a suitable form printed thereon, having the fewest possible blanks to be filled, as follows:

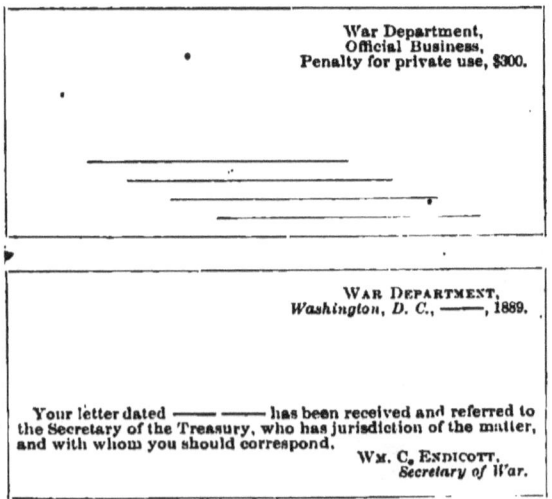

A number of different forms might be printed for use in the Department and its bureaus, only requiring the name and address of the writer to be inserted on one side and two dates on the other.

When, however, many letters are received from one individual or a member of either House of Congress, or any other official refers letters from his correspondents, it will be necessary to use a blank letter form in which can be inserted the name and address of the correspondent and the subject. This will remove doubt as to what particular letter on a given date is acknowledged, and the law (22 Statutes, 563) can then be complied with, which requires letters to Senators, Representatives, and Delegates to be accompanied with envelopes addressed to their correspondents.

The following forms are suggested as embodying the idea intended to be conveyed:

WAR DEPARTMENT,
Washington, D. C., ———, 1889.

_____

_____

SIR: Your letter of _____ [date] _____
_____ [subject] _____
_____ is received.

As soon as the information desired by you is obtained you will be duly advised.
Respectfully,

WM. C. ENDICOTT,
Secretary of War.

WAR DEPARTMENT,
Washington, D. C., ———, 1889.

_____

_____

SIR: I have the honor to acknowledge the receipt of your reference of a letter dated _____
[place] _____ [date] _____
from _____ asking
_____ [subject] _____

The information desired by your correspondent has been called for, and will be communicated to you when received.
Respectfully,

WM. C. ENDICOTT,
Secretary of War.

When acknowledged such letters should be stamped on the first page as follows:

> Office Secretary of War,
> January ———, 1889.
> Acknowledged.

CARD INDEX.

A card index is not of necessity a card. It may be of any size and on paper of any kind. It should be of suitable size and on good, stiff white linen paper. The form and size suggested by the board on which to list papers pertaining to the business of other bureaus is good for many purposes. The size and form of the card depend on the use to be made of it. If at the end of each year it is desired to preserve the information contained on the cards in book form the cards should be as large as the proposed book to avoid re-copying, with a sufficient margin on the left to enable the cards to be bound without obscuring the writing, and a margin at the top and bottom and on the right, so that the edges may be trimmed and the pages numbered when bound. Such cards become at once a card record and a card index—a card record of the things recorded arranged alphabetically by principal subjects, with cross-reference cards for names and subordinate subjects. These cross-reference cards should be no larger than the index-brief cards already recommended, and should be consolidated at the end of the year and inserted at the end of the volume; or, if numerous, they should be bound separately.

On the record card can be recorded all that is now contained in the books of letters received, the arrangement to be similar to the form suggested under the title "Card-index brief." The blank spaces on the front and back afford room to record, in full if necessary, the action taken, whether by indorsement or letter. This record card therefore combines in itself four books, viz, the book of letters received and its index and the book of letters sent and its index. A letter originating in the office not based on any paper, if necessary to record, can be also recorded on a card and filed under its appropriate subject.

This system has many advantages not possessed by that now in use.

(1) It is easier to write on a single sheet of paper than in a book.

(2) The clerk is not interrupted in his work by frequent reference to the book in which he is writing, as is now the case.

(3) A card can be sent within the Department where needed. This saves the labor of making notes, and the delay caused thereby to the official and to the person who has called for the information. It is an easy matter to make an accurate charge of such card, so it may be recalled to the files when no longer needed elsewhere.

(4) Subjects are arranged topically and compactly. This in itself saves much labor. By the present system there is no arrangement of subjects; papers are entered as they arrive, the subjects are indexed, and the time is consumed in making extracts from the records when it is necessary to bring one subject together, or in making notes of numbers, and hunting through the books to see where the papers are, prior to collecting the papers.

This card-record book is more elaborate than the "card-index of decisions" suggested in another part of this report. These would be bound by years. The decision cards run through many years, and are really the working data for intricate cases; that subject and its advantages are treated of more fully under the appropriate heading.

By the card-index system papers are entered as received, but the cards must be filed alphabetically. This system does not therefore give a list of papers in order of date; if it did it would be but little better than the book of letters received. This objection is, however, met by the use of the numbered charge book hereafter recommended. The clerk in giving a number to papers should place in the margin of the book the date opposite the first number used each day; then, the subject being stated opposite each number, it is easy to look up the papers of any date when necessary.

There is only one reason in favor of entering papers as they are received in the order of date, viz: It can be ascertained what papers were received on a given date. But what advantage is that? Simply this, by running over all the entries of one or more days a paper may be found that is forgotten. This is very rarely necessary, and does not often accomplish the purpose. It must be assumed as true that unless something is remembered about a paper it can not be found. An elaboration of records will effect nothing in such a contingency. For instance, one must either know the name of the writer, some proper name mentioned in the letter, or the subject of the correspondence, else a search will be without avail. The decision may be remembered in a general way, but the possibility of finding it is more remote than if one of the other three elements is known. Hence the need of an index of decisions or precedents which is elsewhere suggested.

It is as easy to give papers a number for filing purposes under the card-index system as under any other method. Give the papers pertaining to the office, and which should be entered a running number, keeping tally of the numbers used on a card as is now done in some offices, or in a book, as suggested under the title "To keep trace of cards and numbers on paper," which is believed to be preferable as it will show the particular numbers which belong to a given date, which may be important if it should ever be essential to show that a number on a paper was not correct because it was a different number from the numbers used on the date in question. Such a contingency might never arise, but it is as little trouble to keep the numbers in a book as on a card.

The arrangement by subjects is the best method, as subjects are remembered when names are forgotten. To illustrate: A writes about the bridge across the Eastern Branch of the Potomac River. The principal subject is "Bridge." All papers received on that subject during the year fall together, each bridge by itself. The card is therefore filed under the principal subject, "Bridge," with cross references on other cards as suggested under title "Briefing and indexing." Again, suppose B writes about the claim of Richard S. Williams and files evidence. The principal subject is "Williams, Richard S.," with cross-reference: "B. About claim of Williams. See Williams, R. S." It involves no difficulty. Having found the card of the principal subject, it gives the number of the paper so it can be found, or the action if it is not in the office.

It is objected that cards may be lost or mislaid. This may happen; so papers may be lost or mislaid, and other mistakes may be made, but such things are liable to happen with any system. Care is therefore as necessary here as in other matters. An absolutely perfect record is an ideal rarely attained, and certainly not worth the time, trouble, and cost when something less perfect will serve the purpose as well. When required it is made, and can be made again, but it is only necessary in a few cases.

That the danger of losing index record-cards is infinitesimal, if ordinary care is exercised in handling them, is fully established by the experience of the record and pension division of the Surgeon-General's Office. In that division over three and one-half million cards, representing the medical histories of sick and wounded soldiers, are on file. These cards are used in furnishing information to the Adjutant-General, the Commissioner of Pensions, the Second Auditor, and others in pension and other claims against the Government. Since the 12th of March, 1888, when the cards were first used for this purpose, over 57,000 cards have been removed from the files to accompany cases, all of which have been passed through the hands of the various searchers, examiners, and indorsers in two separate buildings located in different portions of the city, and yet only two of the cards so removed from the files have failed to be returned. The numbers of these two cards having been recorded at the time they were taken from the files it was a matter of no difficulty whatever not only to reproduce them from the original records, but to determine as well the individual clerks who were responsible for their loss.

So with the card index here suggested; if a card is lost the book shows the number and subject, and from the paper, generally on file somewhere in the Department, the card can be reproduced.

The following table shows the number of pages of record of letters received and letters sent in the several offices and bureaus of the War Department during the calendar year 1888, the average number of lines of record required for each letter received, etc.:

126

Letters received, and letters sent, indexed, and recorded in War Department during year 1868.

Office.	Book.	No. of vols. recorded.	No. of pages recorded.	Lines per page.	Lines recorded.	Total lines recorded.	Lines recorded each day of 300 days to year.	No. of clerks employed.	Lines recorded each day by 1 clerk.	Average No. of sheets to a page.	Pages recorded each day by 1 clerk.	Size of pages.	Total No. of letters received.	Av. No. of lines to the record of each letter rec'd, sent, and indexed.	Remarks.
Sec'y of War	L. R	3	2,550	52	132,600	326,677	1,089	9	121	42	2.9	11 x15½	17,133	19	Of the force employed 1 is in charge, 1 ass't, 1 searcher. The pages recorded 326,677÷17,133, the No. of letters received = 19 lines, the entire record of each letter received, sent, and indexed. One clerk in charge and five others.
	Index L. R	1	978	35	34,230							12 x15			
	L. S	4	2,925	47	137,475							11 x16			
	Index L. S	1	658	34	22,372							12 x15			
Adjt. Gen.: Misc. rec. div. (permanent records).	{ L. R	{2 2	1,214 629	34 30	42,296 18,870	166,130	553	6	92	39.20	2.35	16½x11 13 x 8	10,967	15.15	One clerk in charge and three others.
	Index L. R	1	428	48	20,544							17 x11½			
	L. S	4	1,910	42	80,220							16 x11½			
	Index L. S	1	102	42	4,200							16 x11			
A. C. P. div	L. R	2	1,394	34	47,396	122,160	407	4	102	37.	2.76	16 x11	6,639	18.40	One clerk, one ass't, and six others.
	Index L. R	1	314	38	11,932							17 x11½			
	L. S	2	1,290	40	51,600							15 x10			
	Index L. S	1	312	36	11,232							16½x11			
Vol. ser. div	L. R	4	2,570	33	84,810	306,625	1,022	8	127½	35.	3.65	13 x 8	20,250	15.14	One clerk in charge and sixteen others.
	Index L. R	2	500	33	16,500							16½x11½			
	L. S	5—7	4,400	41	180,400							13½ x 8			
	Index L. S	12	10,320	35	361,200							14 x10			
Enl. br	L. R	2	1,800	35	63,000	824,775	2,749¼	17	161.75	35	4.62	14 x10	55,699	14.91	One clerk in charge and one other.
	Index L. R	13	10,585	35	370,475							15 x10½			
	L. S	1	860	35	30,100							14 x10			
	Index L. S	†1	164	34	5,576							15 x10½			
Mil. acad. br	L. R	†1	11	53	583	8,601	28¾	2	14	40	3	15 x10½	*678	9.80	*Number recorded. Large number not recorded. †Part. One clerk in charge and two others.
	Index L. R	†1	60	37	2,220							15 x10½			
	L. S	†1	6	37	222							15 x10¾			
	Index L. S														
Mil. Pris. div	L. R	1	126	37	4,662	15,735	52½	3	17.50	41	2.34	16½x11	1,116	14.12	One clerk in charge and one other.
	Index L. R	1	25	44	1,100							15 x10			
	L. S	1	231	40	9,240							16½x11			
	Index L. S	1	17½	43	753							15 x10			
Inspector-General	L. R	1	249	37	9,213							15 x11			
	Index L. R	(‡)	35									15 x11			

	L. S.	1	171	40	6,840							15 x10			
	Index L. S.		(‡)	35				2				15 x11	1,352		‡Reported "unknown."
Judge Advocate-General	L. R.	1	235	38	8,930							16½x12½			
	Index L. R.	1	144	27	3,888							10½x8½			
	L. S. ‖														‖Reported as impossible to state.
	Index L. S.					12,318	42¾	1	42¾	37.50	1.13		1,706	7.51	
Q. M. G.:															
Inspection branch	L. R.	2	834	45	37,530							17 x11			One clerk in charge and two assistants.
	Index L. R.	1	200	45	9,000							17 x11			
	L. S.	1	431	34	14,654							15 x10½			
	Index L. S.	1	161	45	7,245	68,429	228	3	76	42.25	1.8	17 x11	6,923	9.88	
Clothing supply br.	L. R.	1	804	45	36,180							17 x11			One clerk in charge and three assistants.
	Index L. R.	1	430	45	19,350							17 x11			
	L. S.	4	1,205	34	40,970							15 x10½			
	Index L. S.	1	279	45	12,555	109,055	363¼	4	91	42.25	2.15	17 x11	3,840	23.40	
Transportation br.	L. R.	2	846	46	38,916							17 x11			One clerk in charge and two assistants.
	Index L. R.	1	145	46	6,670							17 x11			
	L. S.	6	1,450	30	43,500							15 x11			
	Index L. S.		150	40	6,000	95,086	317	3	106	40.50	2.62	15 x11	4,479	21.23	
Claims branch	L. R.	1	370	47	17,390							17 x11			One clerk in charge and three assistants.
	Index L. R.	1	400	39	15,600							17 x11			
	L. S.	1½	988	46	45,448							17 x11			
	Index L. S.	1	600	42	25,200	103,638	345¼	4	86¼	43.50	1.92	17 x11	4,218	24.57	
Accounts branch	L. R.	2	1,028	45	46,260							17 x11			One clerk in charge and two assistants.
	Index L. R.	1	360	45	16,200							17 x11			
	L. S.	8	2,697	34	91,698							15 x11			
	Index L. S.	1	360	45	16,200	170,358	568	3	189¼	42.25	4.48	17 x11	9,511	17.91	
Cemeterial br.	L. R.	1	267	45	12,015							17 x11¼			One clerk in charge and two assistants.
	Index L. R.	1	154	45	6,930							17 x11¼			
	L. S.	1	301	45	13,545							17 x11¼			
	Index L. S.	1	175	45	7,875	40,365	134½	3	44.83	45.00	1.00	17 x11¼	1,887	21.31	
Branch "A," (Finance).	L. R.	1	457	48	21,936							17 x11			One clerk in charge and two assistants.
	Index L. R.	1	55	45	2,475							17 x11			
	L. S.	2	634	36	22,824							15 x11			
	Index L. S.	1	59	45	2,655	49,890	166	3	55.33	43.50	1.27	17 x11	3,768	13.24	
Division "C"	L. R.	1	373	45	16,785							17 x11¼			One clerk in charge and two assistants.
	Index L. R.	1	247	45	11,115							17 x11¼			
	L. S.	3	345	46	15,870							17 x11¼			
			685	34	23,290							15 x11			
	Index L. S.		186	45	8,370							17 x11¼			
			180	46	8,280	83,710	279	3	93.00	43.50	2.14	17 x11¼	2,584	32.40	
Division "G," barracks and quarters.	L. R.	1	598	45	26,910							17 x11¼			One clerk in charge and two assistants.
	Index L. R.	1	300	45	13,500							17 x11¼			
	L. S.	4	1,200	33	39,600							15 x10½			
	Index L. S.	1	300	40	12,000	92,010	307	3	102.00	41.00	2.50	15 x11	2,656	34.64	
Branch "E," regular supplies.	L. R.	4	2,296	45	103,320							17 x11½			One clerk in charge and four assistants.
	Index L. R.	1	521	45	23,445							17 x11½			
	L. S.	3	1,639	35	57,365							15 x11			
	Index L. S.	1	560	45	25,200	209,330	698	5	139.50	42.50	3.28	17 x11½	8,279	25.28	
Branch "I"	L. R.	1	486	46	22,356							17 x11			One clerk in charge and two assistants.
	Index L. R.	1	168	46	7,728							17 x11			
	L. S.	4	1,031	36	37,116							15 x11			
	Index L. S.	1	168	40	6,720	73,920	246	3	82	42	1.95	15 x11	2,132	34.67	

Letters received, and letters sent, indexed, and recorded in War Department during year 1888—Continued.

Office.	Book.	No. of vols. recorded.	No. of pages.	Lines per page.	Lines recorded.	Total lines recorded.	Lines recorded each day of 300 days to year.	No. of clerks employed.	Lines recorded each day by 1 clerk.	Average No. of ~~clerks~~ lines to a page.	Pages recorded each day by 1 clerk.	Size of pages.	Total No. of letters received.	Av. No. of lines to the record of each letter rec'd, sent, and indexed.	Remarks.
Com. Gen. of Sub.: Misc. div	L. R	1	624	40	24,960							17⅛x11			
	Index L. R	1	60	42	2,520							17 x11½			
	L. S	2	1,461	42	61,362							17½x11⅛			
	Index L. S	1	56	42	2,352	91,194	304	3	101¼	41.50	2.44	17¼x11⅛	2,530	36	
Accts. and ret. div	L. R	1	603	40	24,120							17⅛x11			
	Index L. R	1	43	42	1,806							17 x11½			
	L. S	2	1,446	42	60,732							17½x11⅛			
	Index L. S	3	157	42	6,594	98,252	310¾	2	155¼	41.50	3.74	17¼x11⅛	4,310	21.64	
Contract div	L. R	1	482	40	19,280							17⅛x11			
	Index L. R	1	37½	42	1,575							17 x11½			
	L. S	1	804	42	33,768							17½x11⅛			
	Index L. S	1	40⅝	42	1,708	56,331	187¾	2	94	41.50	2.27	17¼x11⅛	2,522	22.34	
Claims div	L. R														None reported.
	Index L. R														Do.
	L. S	2	1,744	42								17⅛x11⅛			
	Index L. S	4	308	42				1				17¼x11⅛			
Surgeon-General: A. and M. div	L. R	5	3,270	50	163,500							16⅛x13⅛			One clerk in charge and eight others.
	Index L. R	1	692	32	22,144							16¾x13¾			
	L. S	5	3,193	39	124,527							16 x11			
			807	40	32,280							16¾x11¼			
	Index L. S	2	518	43	22,059							16¾x11⅛			
			155	58	8,990	373,500	1,245	9	138⅓	43.66	3.17	15¾x10⅜	22,216	16.81	
Property div	L. R	2	1,154	49	56,546							16 x13⅛			One clerk in charge and two others.
	Index L. R	1	175	58	10,150							15⅛x10⅛			
	L. S	1	1,075	37	39,775							15⅛x10¼			
	Index L. S	1	109	39	4,251	110,722	369	3	123	45.75	2.69	15⅛x10	5,800	19	
Mus. and lib. div: Mus. section	L. R	1	109	36	3,924							16¾x11¼			One clerk in charge and two others. The volume is alphabetically arranged, and is therefore an index in itself.
	Index L. R														
	L. S	1	437	39	17,043							15 x10¼			
	Index L. S		20	39	780	21,747	72½	3	24¼	38	½		549	39.61	

Library section	L. R	1	53	50	2,650							16½x13			One clerk in charge and one other.
	Index L. R	1	26	50	1,300							16¼x13			
	L. S	2	540	38	20,520							15¾x11			
	Index L. S	2	102	38	3,876	28,346	94½	2	47½	44	1	15¾x11	993	28.55	
Rec. and pen. div	L. R	2	145	39	5,655							13½x 8½			
	Index L. R	1	13	39	507							15½x10¼			
	L. S	2	315	39	12,285							13½x 8¼			
	Index L. S	1	20	39	780	19,227	64	2	32	39	¼		910	21.13	
Finance div	L. R	1	11	39	429							16 x14			One clerk in charge and one other.
	Index L. R	1	⅔	40	26							16 x11			
	L. S	1	134	38	5,092							16 x10			
	Index L. S	1	7½	43	323	5,870	19½	2	9.75	40.00	¼	15½x10½	66	89.00	
Paymaster-General	L. R	2	928	47	43,616							19¼x15			One clerk in charge and three others.
	Index L. R	1	271	48	13,008							19½x12			
	L. S	3	1,085	42	45,570							16 x12			
	Index L. S	1	202	42	8,484	110,678	368	4	92.00	44.75	2.66	16½x12	10,132	10.93	
Chief of Engineers	L. R	3	3,028	37	112,036							14½x10			One clerk in charge and nine others.
	Index L. R	1	750	18	13,500							15 x11			
	L. S	4	2,927	40	117,080							14¾x10			
	Index L. S	1	750	18	13,500	256,116	853	10	85.30	28.25	3.00	25 x11	14,840	17.25	
Chief of Ordnance	L. R	2	1,428	48	68,544							17¾x13½			One clerk in charge and five others.
			450	45								18 x13¾			
	Index L. R	2	230	35	20,250							15 x11½			
					8,050										
	L. S	8	2,885	43	124,055							19 x11			
			460	45	20,700							18 x13¾			
	Index L. S		240	35	8,400	249,999	833½	6	139.00	42.00	3.30	15 x11½	8,547	29.25	
Signal Office:															
Cor. div	L. R	4	1,711	35								15½x10½			One clerk in charge and five others.
	Index L. R	3	337	38								15½x10½			
	L. S											12 x 9			Only press copies preserved.
	Index L. S	16	7,092	33				6				12 x 9	16,687		
Exam. div	L. R	2	391	35								15¼ x 10¼			
	Index L. R	2	137	35								15¼ x 10¼			
	L. S											10½ x 9¼			Only press copies preserved.
	Index L. S	3	80	64				1				10½ x 9½	2,287		
Prop. and disb. div	L. R	3	2,400	35								15¼ x 10¼			One clerk in charge and eight others.
	Index L. R	4	320	47											
	L. S											10½ x 9½			Only press copies preserved.
	Index L. S	39	1,932	64				9				10½ x 9½	23,603		
Publication div	L. R														One clerk in charge. No record book; only index for this series.
	Index L. R	1	435									10½ x 9½			
	L. S														
	Index L. S							1							
Records div	L. R	2	308	35								15½ x 10½			
	Index L. R														Not indexed.
	L. S	4	92									10½ x 9½			
	Index L. S							3					3,649		

From this table it appears that in the year 1888 there were 4,296,314 lines recorded in the books of letters received and letters sent and indexes thereto; that 238,070 letters were received (exclusive of the Signal Office, in which the lines recorded are not given) which is equal to 18 lines for the complete record of each letter received.

A card, therefore, of 8 inches by 10½ inches, with an interior space within lines of 6½ inches by 8½ inches will contain for record purposes on both sides of the sheet more than 50 lines, amply sufficient for the purpose. A record card of the size suggested will be large enough to record all that is done with most letters received; *i. e.*, on it the brief can be entered, the action noted or recorded, and the reply recorded in full, and when a long letter is written in reply other sheets can be added with the proper index words at the top of each sheet, then to be tied or fastened together at the upper left-hand corner until the volume is bound. The following is submitted as a sample of a record card that will answer the purpose:

[Face of record card.]

Transportation.	Wagons.	Jones, J. R.
Office Secretary of War.	No.	1889.

Return to Record Division, Room 235, as soon as read. If a copy is desired it must be made at once, so this card can be returned to the files.

Date_____ [Place]_____ [Date]_____
From_____
Subject_____
_____
_____
_____
_____

No. of inclosures_____
Received _____ 1889. Sent to _____ 1889.
Acknowledged_____ 1889. Received back _____ 1889.
                                        Bureau office mark _____
Action_____
_____
_____
_____
_____
_____
_____
_____
_____
_____
_____
_____
_____

[To be ruled on back within exterior lines, for recording letters sent that cover more than first page. The blank space outside of lines must not be written on; it is for binding purposes.]

[Reverse of record card.]

FILE-CASES FOR RECORD CARDS.

If index-record cards are adopted they should be filed away flat until bound. If stood on edge the size of the card will cause them to bend, and thus they will get out of order. It is believed that cabinet letter-files, suggested under the head of "General remarks," will be found most convenient to use for this purpose. Such a letter-file of thirty-six boxes will contain eleven thousand cards. Before an order is given for cabinet files the index-book of letters received for 1888 should be studied to determine the arrangement of the indexes for the boxes. As each box has provision for twenty-five subdivisions, the thirty-six boxes will embrace nine hundred subdivisions. The indexes should therefore be so arranged as to make, as nearly as practicable, one nine-hundredths of the total number of record cards fall into each subdivision. A careful count of the names of persons and of subjects on the index books of last year should be made, keeping in mind that the cards to be filed under subjects are to be arranged alphabetically under the heading of the principal subject to which they belong. By this means approximately uniform divisions can be made so that each of the twenty-five subdivisions in a box will receive a due share of cards, and none be unnecessarily crowded. Where a principal subject is likely to embrace about one thirty-sixth of the whole number of cards a whole file-box should be devoted to it for convenience of reference; for instance: "Army," "Subsistence stores," "Transportation," "Papers awaiting final action," etc. A specimen of arrangement of principal subjects and subdivisions is herewith submitted as a guide. (See Exhibit C.) The cross-reference cards are recommended to be made the size of "brief cards." These should be stood on end, and a stiffer paper should be used. A linen record paper, twenty pounds per ream, is suggested, the cards to be filed for easy reference in Woodruff or similar file-boxes.

INDEX OF NAMES ON RECORD CARDS.

Proper names should be indexed on "cross-reference cards" (see Exhibit D), and refer to the subject under which the record card is filed; the date of letter should also be given. This will often save looking at many subjects, or many cards on the same subject, when there are many letters from the same person, thus:

"Jones, J. R............see Transportation wagons ....January 12, 1889."

The same rule as to the use of black and red inks should prevail as at present, viz: Black ink for the person who writes, and red ink for the person, etc., written about.

TO KEEP TRACE OF CARDS AND NUMBERS ON PAPERS.

The record cards should be numbered consecutively, commencing with number one on the first of each calendar year.

Each paper should have the same number as its record card, and be filed numerically. One clerk should be in charge of the cards. He should have a charge-book with each line numbered consecutively through the book and containing a few more numbers than the number of letters received during the last preceding year.

This book should have four columns, the first for the numbers, the second for the index word at the head of the record card, as for example—No. 301—Transportation—Wagons—Jones, J. R.—the third column for charges for record cards, showing the names of persons to whom cards are sent, including time and date. The fourth column for charges for papers, showing the names of persons to whom papers are sent, including date. When a record card is withdrawn it should be immediately charged in lead pencil to the person to whom sent. It should be the duty of the clerk in charge of cards to see that a record card is returned within one-half hour after it is charged out, if possible, and he should report to the chief of the division any cards not returned, at the close of the day. The cards should have printed on them "Return to Record division, —— Room ——, as soon as read. If a copy is desired, it must be made at once, so this card can be returned to the files." When returned the lead-pencil charge must be at once erased. When a charge has remained on the charge-book more than one day the clerk in charge must immediately search the card-file to see if it has been returned, and if not, every exertion must be made to find the missing card. By searching for cards, within a short time after they have been charged out, the danger of loss will be almost entirely removed. Practical experience in the Surgeon-General's Office shows that the danger is slight.

The average number of letters received in one day in the office of the Secretary of War is fifty, so the charge clerk will have but fifty lines to write in his charge-book, and this he can do at intervals as he receives cards for file.

If it appears from this book that a paper has been charged to some person for six days the charge may be posted to the record card; but it is believed this will not be necessary as this book will serve every purpose as a charge-book, and thus the cards need not be so often referred to and a more careful watch can be kept of papers. Papers charged out over one day should be looked up. Under the present system many papers are charged to persons who have returned the papers to the files, perhaps with other papers, and the charge has through oversight not been removed. Subsequently the papers are found on the files or returned from some other office and the charge removed. Such charges are misleading and cause trouble. The danger of oversight will be largely reduced by the use of this book, and by making it the duty of the proper clerk to see that papers charged out are looked up at intervals and returned to the files as soon as possible. The incidental effect of thus looking up papers will be to hasten the action thereon.

For ease and rapidity of reference the card-record charge-book should have fifty lines to the page, and each line being consecutively numbered will give a list of one hundred papers wherever the book is opened. For 15,000 letters received a book of 300 pages will therefore be required. The book should be tagged at each 1,000 numbers with pages cut on the margin for each 100 numbers. Thus it will be possible by two movements to turn to the number wanted. The numbers on all the pages should be as follows: The left-hand pages from 0 to 49; those on the right-hand from 50 to 99; then but one, two, or three figures will need to be added at the top of each page.

The following is a sample of the book suggested:

N	Subject.	When and to whom record card sent.	When and to whom papers sent.
5500			
01			
02			
03			
04			
05			
06			
07			
08			
09			
5510			
11			
12			
etc. to 49			

NOTE.—The page should be 10 inches wide, the numbered column 1 inch wide, the subject column 4½ inches, and each of the charge columns 2 inches wide.

PAPERS AWAITING FINAL ACTION.

There should be a temporary file, of course, arranged alphabetically, of record cards, in which should be placed the cards of cases awaiting final action. Such cards would be most frequently referred to in answer to inquiries and to place notations upon them. By this means it will be possible to call up the unanswered mail of the office. Such cards when finally acted upon, that is, when the decision had been noted or the office reply recorded, should be put in their proper places in the permanent card boxes.

CARD INDEX OF DECISIONS OR PRECEDENTS.

An index of decisions or precedents differs from an index of subjects in that the latter is a brief index pointing to the papers on a subject which must be referred to in order to ascertain the decision thereon, while the former is a concise statement of the decision itself in leading or novel cases, thus in the course of time grouping together precedents to form a rule or serve as a guide for future action.

The instructions now in force for keeping the records and transacting the clerical work of the Department require:

"A copious index of subjects of general interest, or involving principles applicable to similar cases likely to arise hereafter, should be compiled from individual cases after they have been recorded in the entry books, and have received the action of the proper authorities. This index should extend to the business of the entire bureau, and should embrace the records of as many unbroken years as is consistent with convenience of size and handling. The design of this book of reference is to aid in securing uniform, just, and speedy decisions upon certain classes of cases of frequent occurrence, which might otherwise require each of them a lengthened search and study of principles, authorities, and precedents. Great care should be given to the preparation and keeping of this index."

In lieu of this book of reference it is recommended, however, that the card-index system be adopted. The benefits of the card index wherever it can be used are so great that it has generally been adopted in large libraries for names and subjects. If applicable to libraries of hundreds of thousands of volumes of course it is applicable to this subject. It is capable of indefinite expansion, and each subject is compact and complete in itself, while with record books the subject is scattered and reference to several volumes may be necessary. It saves time, as the information is always available; it also saves the labor of copying or the making of notes or memorandums from the books, and as all the cards on the subject under consideration can be sent for when needed in the office and without interrupting the work of indexing. Further, a book of reference must be indexed, which is not necessary with cards. They are arranged alphabetically like a dictionary or encyclopedia, cross reference being made where necessary to insure the finding of the subject. Cross references are made now, so that is not additional work.

A good card index of decisions is a great desideratum. If when a subject is under consideration the cards are available to show the current of decisions upon the subject, the line of action pursued at different periods, the reasons for changes being shown by reference to laws and orders, the subject at once becomes clear and easily understood without dependence upon memory or experience.

The card index takes the place of memory and experience, and thus the affairs of an office are administered with ease and certainty, and decisions become stable and progressive. The decisions noted in the books now required to be kept are difficult of access because scattered through many volumes in the various bureaus. With this system inaugurated it becomes possible to collect the cards in the various offices and bureaus on a given subject, and with the information thus obtained, to prepare a paper which shall show its history, development, customs of the service, laws, and orders, and thus a book can be formed by topics somewhat like Clode's "Military Forces of the Crown," which would be of the greatest value for the practical use of the Department in the transaction of every-day business.

Such a book, showing why certain lines of action have been modified, changed, or abandoned, gives the new official the experience of his predecessors and enables him to continue improved methods instead of adhering to old systems which experience has proved imperfect.

As a suggestion of a plan for such an index, see Exhibit B, in which could also be included drafts of important letters; for instance, in a certain case, care has been given to the drafting of a reply to a letter so that it will fit the case and other like cases. Suppose the subject is "eight-hour law;" with this subject at the head of the card a draft of the letter is copied thereon, and it is then always available for like cases without further search.

The cards for the card index of decisions or precedents in the several bureaus should be alike in size, with the name of the office plainly printed thereon, and when a copy of a card is made it should be marked "copy." A copy furnished to another office may be filed with other cards in that office, as the word "copy" written or printed thereon in large letters shows it need not be returned.

ABBREVIATIONS.

It is suggested that this list of abbreviations be pasted on first fly-leaf of all record books or of bound volumes of record cards.

The following abbreviations should be used in records in lieu of such words written in full in letters, orders, etc. When a copy is made therefrom all abbreviations should be written in full, as shown by this list:

W. D.	War Department.	J. A. G. O.	Judge-Advocate-General's Office
W. D., W. C.	War Department, Washington City.	Q. M. G.	Quartermaster-General.
Jan	January.	Q. M. G. O.	Quartermaster-General's Office.
Feb	February.	C. G. S	Commissary-General of Subsistence.
Mch	March.	O. C. G. S.	Office of Commissary-General of Subsistence.
Apl	April.	S. G	Surgeon-General.
May	May.	S. G. O.	Surgeon-General's Office.
June	June.	P. M. G.	Paymaster-General.
July	July.	P. M. G. O.	Paymaster-General's Office.
Aug	August.	C. of E	Chief of Engineers.
Sept	September.	O. C. of E	Office of Chief of Engineers.
Oct	October.	C. of O	Chief of Ordnance.
Nov	November.	O. C. of O	Office of Chief of Ordnance.
Dec	December.	C. S. O	Chief Signal Officer.
A. G.	Adjutant-General.	O. C. S. O.	Office of Chief Signal Officer.
A. G. O.	Adjutant-General's Office.	Resp'y	Respectfully.
I. G.	Inspector-General.	S. of W	Secretary of War.
I. G. O.	Inspector-General's Office.	C. C.	Chief Clerk.
J. A. G.	Judge-Advocate-General.		

Space is saved in the records by the use of these abbreviations, and hereafter the place and date should be placed on one line, and the conclusion of the letter also on one line, thus:

W. D., W. C., Jan. 16, 1889.

Resp'y., Wm. C. Endicott, S of W.

REPLIES TO LETTERS.

An answer to a letter should be short, clear, and concise, and where it must be studied to understand the meaning the answer should be recast. The opening paragraph should give the date of the letter to which it is a reply, and state the subject in a general way in a few words when practicable. Questions asked should be answered in order in the body of the letter. If possible, letters should be on one subject only. Adherence to the foregoing will save the time of the clerk who writes the letter, of the officer who signs it, and of the clerk who records it. These remarks, of course, do not apply to forms of letters that have been printed, but they should be considered in the preparation of forms.

In one of the letters received by the board in answer to the invitation of the Secretary it is suggested that the words, "your obedient servant," be omitted from letters, and the following calculation is made: "In this office we record about 2,800 pages of letters sent each year, with an average of two letters to each page containing 'your obedient servant.' This will make 5,600 lines of the books used each year, and, there being 47 lines to the page, 122 pages are wasted, not counting the labor expended by the clerks who write and copy the letters." He also suggests that in the place of "very respectfully," the letters close with the word "respectfully," thus effecting another saving. For the reasons so graphically shown the board concurs in the suggestion made, believing that a due regard to courtesy will be shown by the use of the word "respectfully" at the close of the letter, or at most by the use of the words "very respectfully," with but a few exceptions which may occur in correspondence of a diplomatic character.

In connection with the suggestions made upon this subject the following example, taken from the records, is given of a letter that is not concise:

WAR DEPARTMENT,
Washington City, April 3, 1888.

SIR: In reply to your letters of the 12th and 26th ultimo, requesting that the official records of the War of the Rebellion, which have heretofore been mailed to you at Turner Centre, Me., be mailed to you in the future at Canton, Me., I have the honor to advise you that the change of address has been made as requested, and that the future volumes of the work in question will be sent to you at Canton, Me.

Very respectfully, etc.,
Mr. ———— ————

The following would have been sufficient:

WAR DEPARTMENT,
Washington City, April 3, 1888.

SIR: In compliance with your request the address for your copy of the Rebellion Records has been changed to Canton, Me.

Respectfully, etc.,
Mr. ———— ————

These examples will show how replies to letters may be reduced to a few words and serve the purpose as well.

GENERAL REMARKS.

Cabinet letter files.—Letters of slight importance which need not be entered or even listed, but which it is desired to retain for a short time, should be filed in index files for ready reference, thus saving the labor of listing many papers. The letter-file cabinets manufactured by Cameron, Amberg & Co., of Chicago, and by Brower Brothers, of New York City, will serve as an illustration of the kind of files referred to.

Files.—To save space in the files, communication which do not contain information necessary to be retained, should be returned by indorsement containing the information desired.

Indorsements.—Papers which are referred within the Department for "report" or "remark" or "to note" should not be formally indorsed and signed when it can be avoided, and a red-ink notation following the brief or last indorsement is generally sufficient, as "A. G. report." "J. A. G. to note." "Noted in J. A. G. O., and returned." It will not often be necessary to do this under the rules contained in the circular on "Administration."

Letters for immediate attention.—There are some letters which should at once be brought to the attention of the official addressed—these will readily suggest themselves—they are of more than ordinary importance and in no sense routine—he should know they have been received, so he can indicate the action thereon before they have been sent elsewhere.

These are the exceptional cases, outside the rules, even though the subject treated of is one pertaining to the business of another bureau, which will probably be consulted before reply is made. In this class are letters, not routine, from the President, heads of Departments, resolutions of Congress, letters from members of either House of Congress, from governors of States, etc., not necessary to indicate further, as they will be readily recognized when received.

Lists.—When a list of names is to be prepared, either of persons or things, if an alphabetical arrangement will serve the purpose as well as any other it should be preferred, being more convenient for reference.

Notations.—A short indorsement placed upon a letter as follows: "War Department, Jan'y 21, 1889. Respectfully referred to the major-general commanding the Army, for remark. Wm. C. Endicott, Sec'y of War," should not be recorded in full, a notation as follows is sufficient: "Comdg. gen'l for remark, Jan. 21, '89," and this course should be followed in other simple indorsements not in themselves important.

Papers pertaining to several bureaus.—When a communication is received which calls for information or action in several bureaus, it should be passed from one to the other until the information is complete, then to be returned for final action to the bureau which has jurisdiction over the principal subject involved in the communication—where it will be filed. In such cases the initials of the several bureaus will be indicated on the paper in red ink in the order in which the information is required.

Red ink.—The red-ink ruling on papers is, in most cases, more ornamental than useful, and should be discontinued. Where necessary, words can be underscored more quickly with a colored pencil, as has been recommended in another part of this paper. This does not refer to the use of red ink in the ruling of tables, forms, etc.

Result of search to be preserved.—Whenever necessary to search for decisions, laws, orders, customs, and precedents, bearing upon any particular subject the result of such search should be filed under its proper subject for future reference. To enable this to be done with little or no extra labor the searcher should be provided with card-index blanks of proper size upon which to make a record of the search.

Secretary's office.—As the office of the Secretary is, to a great extent, the bureau of information for the entire Department, it will be necessary to make a note of many cases which strictly belong to the business of particular bureaus, but as the law places them all under his direction the record of his action should be noted in his own office, in order that he may have easily accessible the record of his own acts, and thus be enabled to at once answer inquiries.

Unanswered mail.—It is customary in some corporations for the president to call at intervals for the unanswered mail and ascertain the cause of delay. This custom can be adopted in the Department by the use of the temporary file of record cards of cases awaiting final action, heretofore recommended.

MISCELLANEOUS.

At several of the establishments visited by the board there were in use appliances called "mail chutes," for the conveyance of mail matter from the upper stories to the ground floor. These were perpendicular conductors extending through the intervening rooms or corridors, to the basement, with openings on each floor large enough for the insertion of letters. Where visible they had glass fronts, so that any mail matter that was lodged could be seen. The chutes ran into locked boxes on the ground floor, to which the post-office letter-carriers hold the keys. A modification of this arrangement could be applied with advantage to this building. The following diagram will serve as an illustration:

Mail chutes.

Fifth floor, library...	...	...	...	...
Fourth floor, mail for C. G. S. and P. M. G..	...	...	...	...
Third floor, mail for Q. M. G. and S. G..		...	...	...
Second floor, mail for S. of W., A. G., and J. A. G...................................			...	...
First floor, mail for C. of O. and C. of E..				...
Basement, mail for post-office, supply div., Supt. P. B. & G. and depot Q. M........				...

By this arrangement mail could be dropped to any floor of the building and taken to its destination by the half-hourly mail messengers on their rounds, or sooner, if a messenger with a key happened to be passing. The elevator service could likewise be utilized to convey mail to the upper floor.

In the office of the Metropolitan Insurance Company of New York pneumatic tubes are in use for the conveyance of mail between rooms and floors with the utmost rapidity, and that company also uses a cheap and convenient telephone service, known as the village telephone. It is entirely independent of the commercial line, and is confined exclusively to the building. Each telephone has a switch-board, by which it is possible to call up and converse with any one of the forty or fifty stations in the building. It is much cheaper than the regular service and is more convenient and rapid for the transmission of messages where there are a number of offices under one management in the same building.

CONCLUSION.

In conclusion the board desires to state that to have investigated each particular class of work in the Department would have required a long time and delayed the report longer than appeared to be necessary, hence types were selected, and as the recommendations made are of general application, it is believed they will accomplish, if carried into execution, the result desired. But in order that the work thus commenced shall continue it should be generally understood that it is the duty of all persons in charge of any class of work to study it with a view to the adoption by proper authority of such short methods as will secure simplicity of routine as well as safety of record, and the elimination of whatever is unnecessary either in the entry or handling of papers, and to endeavor to make not an absolutely complete and perfect record, but one that will be sufficient for the purpose.

It is not to be presumed that this is not done now by some, but it is the duty of all. Routine clogs the actual work of which it is but an incident; more thought must therefore be given to the routine or mechanical part of the work, if the expression is allowable, in order that the actual work of the Department may be more nearly assimilated to that of the business of the country, and enable it to do in time of peace what must be done in time of war.

Routine and custom run in grooves which deepen with age, and anything involving change in fixed habits is looked upon with little favor. So while it is possible to state the advantages of quicker methods, and to make rules providing for their adoption, the enforcement of the rules and the prevention of retrogression can only be accomplished by constant supervision, which must also be directed to the prevention in future of the growth of unnecessary routine. This is a difficult task and will be met with many obstacles which can only be overcome by giving the necessary power to those who must supervise, subject, of course, at all times to confirmation or rejection by the head of the Department or other proper authority.

A willing and cheerful execution of orders will carry out the rules so as to accomplish the result desired, and the business of the Department will be transacted with the greatest possible dispatch; while, on the contrary, the best rules can be so carried out as to prove to a great extent worthless.

The recommendations and suggestions made herein, if approved, will reduce the work in many of the offices. A number of clerks can therefore be spared for duty in preparing the card-index record of the rolls of the volunteer army during the late war.

It will be observed that the recommendations contained in this report relate to the clerical part of the work of the several offices and do not affect the duties or prerogatives of the Secretary of War or chiefs of bureaus. The object is to facilitate the work and hasten the execution of what has been decided.

Respectfully submitted.

JOHN TWEEDALE,
L. W. TOLMAN,
JACOB FRECH,
Members of Board.

Hon. WILLIAM C. ENDICOTT,
   Secretary of War.

WAR DEPARTMENT, *February* 15, 1889.

The result of experience in the War Department convinces me that delay in the transaction of business can be remedied with no loss of security by the adoption of more rapid methods.

I am more confident that this is true from my experience in the pension work of the Surgeon-General's Office. It was the opinion of the officer in charge that a large accumulation of unanswered calls was necessary in order that the work might be economically performed, and as his opinion could not be changed he was relieved and another officer was detailed in his place. This has been followed with the most satisfactory results. There are no delayed cases now, and the records of the office have been put upon cards as easily referred to as a dictionary. When the regimental hospital records, now in the Adjutant-General's Office, are transferred to the Surgeon-General's Office, the entire medical history of each soldier in service during the late war will be placed on a series of cards filed together in one place. These cards can all be completed within a year, and thereafter it will be possible to give the entire medical history of a soldier in one or two days after the receipt of a call for such history. The system is easy and practicable, but to make it successful it required the constant individual attention of the officer in charge.

After carefully reading the report upon the subject of "correspondence," during its preparation and since its completion, I fully concur in the recommendations and suggestions made by the board. The report is the result of long practical experience combined with an extended investigation of the whole subject.

The success of the system, so fully and carefully explained, depends, as stated by the board, upon a willing and cheerful compliance with orders; and the clerks will be required to study the system and to become perfectly familiar with its requirements. The recording and index of letters received is similar work, only more elaborate, to the cataloguing of a library. The "letter received" in the Department is like a volume in a library; the entering and indexing is like the work of cataloguing. The card-index system has met with complete success in great libraries; if it fails in its application to Department work it will be the fault of those intrusted with its execution rather than of the system which has stood the test of actual trial.

The necessary orders will be issued to carry into effect the recommendations and suggestions of the board

WILLIAM C. ENDICOTT,
Secretary of War.

[Circular.]

WAR DEPARTMENT,
Washington, D. C., February 15, 1889.

The report of the Board on Business Methods upon the subject of "Correspondence" has been approved and a copy transmitted to the chairman of the select committee appointed under the resolution of the Senate of March 3, 1887, to inquire into and examine the methods of business and work in the Executive Departments, etc.

When copies of the report shall have been received from the Public Printer, chiefs of bureaus will require the report to be studied by those employed upon work of the kind treated of in the report, and will put into execution the various recommendations and suggestions in such order as will prevent confusion. As the success of the system in the matter of speed depends to a great extent upon the rapidity with which papers are moved, when ready, in rooms, sections, and divisions, the half-hourly mail messenger service, required by orders of the 18th ultimo, will be put into operation in all of the divisions and subdivisions of the Department.

Requisitions will be made upon the Public Printer for the necessary blanks and books to carry out the recommendations and suggestions, and estimates will be submitted of the number of Cabinet letter files required in each office. Before orders are given for such letter files, the indexes to letters received for the year 1888 will be carefully studied to determine the proper alphabetical and subject arrangement, as suggested by the board.

These orders will be carried into effect as soon as printed copies of the report are received.

WILLIAM C. ENDICOTT,
Secretary of War.

[NOTE.—The regimental medical records on file in the Adjutant General's office were transferred to the Surgeon General's office to be card indexed, under orders from the Secretary of War, dated February 19, 1889.]

EXHIBIT A.

INSTRUCTIONS FOR KEEPING THE RECORDS AND TRANSACTING THE CLERICAL BUSINESS OF THE WAR DEPARTMENT.

WAR DEPARTMENT,
Washington, October 1, 1870.

The following extracts, from the report of a board appointed to examine into the methods of keeping the records and transacting the clerical business of the War Department, are published for the strict observance of the bureaus and offices of the Department, from and after the 1st day of January next, and no departure from the system herein prescribed will be made without special authority. Application for information upon subjects referred to or omitted in this pamphlet, or for any special modification of its requirements, will be addressed to the chief clerk of the War Department.

WILLIAM W. BELKNAP,
Secretary of War.

CLASSIFICATION OF OFFICE BUSINESS.

All the clerical business of an executive bureau, or military office, is comprehended within the terms "letters received" and "letters sent;" and all action upon official papers is either of a record or executive character.

DEFINITION OF "LETTERS RECEIVED."

"Letters received" consist of written or printed communications coming into the bureau, whether in the guise of a formal letter, an indorsement upon a letter, a memorandum, a numbered or unnumbered circular, general or special order in any way relating to the business of the bureau, an unofficial or informal communication upon official matters, if it be necessary or proper to be recorded, a memorandum made in the office of any verbal communication of which a record should exist, and, generally, of any communication reaching the bureau to which future reference *may* become necessary or desirable.

DEFINITION OF "LETTERS SENT."

"Letters sent" consist of all communications of the foregoing character issued from the bureau.

RECEPTION AND DISTRIBUTION OF MAIL MATTER.

All communications received by mail or messengers should be opened, read, and pencil-marked for distribution to the proper officials by persons especially designated for the purpose, who should be familiar with the business of the bureaus and the particular duties of each of its officers and principal employés.

Such papers as are not of an urgent or special character should be folded, briefed, and recorded as herein described, after which they should be distributed for executive action as indicated by the receiver. Papers requiring immediate action should be briefed and recorded at the first opportunity.

The communications should be folded as nearly as possible to a uniform size, the standard being an ordinary-sized letter-sheet folded from bottom to top in three equal parts. Whenever a communication covers all sides of the sheet upon which it is written, leaving no room for briefing or indorsing, or where the paper can not be folded to a proper size, a half-sheet of letter-size paper may be fastened to it; but in no case should any loose wrapper be placed around an official paper. Loose wrappers on which briefs, indorsements, or office-marks have been placed by officials not belonging to the War Department should be fastened to the papers upon receipt in the bureau.

"BRIEFING" OF LETTERS RECEIVED.

A "brief" of every official communication received should be indorsed upon its first or upper fold, exhibiting the place where the letter was written, the date of the communication, the name or official designation of the writer, or the title of the Department, bureau, office, court, etc., whence the communication proceeds, and a synopsis of the contents or subject of the letter. Everything of importance should appear in the brief; but prolixity in the description of places, the titles and offices of persons, and in the summary of contents, should be avoided. For instance, in briefing communications from a large, well-known city, it is unnecessary to add the name of the State; in describing the writer, or a person named, no other title and offices than those immediately concerned in the letter need be given; and dates, names, titles, and offices, or mere incidentals of no importance should be omitted. In cases where the location of a person, office, or institution is permanent and well known, or where location is of no importance whatever, the brief need only exhibit the date, name of writer, and purport of the letter.

Communications from official personages on matters relating to the business of their offices should not be briefed in their individual names, but either by their official titles or the names of the offices of which they are in charge or in which they are serving. The annexed examples will serve to illustrate the proper method of briefing official communications.

Whenever the amount of business in a bureau is sufficient to warrant such a provision, a certain proportion of its clerical force should be habitually employed in briefing the communications received, thus insuring greater accuracy and expedition than could otherwise be secured.

No communication properly briefed should be again briefed in the same or any other office, upon any other fold of the paper; nor should any addition be made to a brief except to correct errors or supply omissions.

Indorsements, reports, or letters attached from time to time to the original communication should not be regarded as requiring any additional briefing.

The date of receipt of each communication should be noted in ink near the bottom of the briefing fold.

RECORDING OF LETTERS RECEIVED.

When a letter received has been briefed it should be entered in a record book kept for the purpose. The forms of the various record books for letters received are illustrated in the Appendix. The record books for the various descriptions of letters received should be classified as follows:

(1) *Applications for office*, embracing all communications received from or relating to applicants for appointment or employment in the public service.

(2) *Officers, agents, and employés*, embracing all communications received relating *individually* to persons employed in the public service by commission or appointment, under the direction of the bureau, from their original entry into the service to their final discharge therefrom.

(3) *Claims*, embracing all communications received relating to demands upon the United States for payment for supplies taken or furnished and for services rendered; and for the restoration of private property taken or used by the Government or its officers.

(4) *Contracts*, embracing all communications received relating to contracts or other agreements for supplies to be furnished, services to be rendered, or work to be performed on the public account.

(5) *Accounts and returns*, embracing all communications received relating to the sums on deposit in the national Treasury to the credit of the bureau, and of the amounts drawn therefrom to carry on the public service, and to the accounts and returns exacted from persons intrusted with or receiving public moneys for distribution or expenditure, or public property for use or issue to others, including the accounts and returns themselves.

(6) *General and miscellaneous*, embracing all communications received involving the issuance of suitable orders, instructions, and regulations for an efficient and economical administration of the public service; the preparation, procurement, and distribution of suitable official and professional publications; the preparation of yearly estimates of the sums required for the public service for the fiscal year ensuing; the procurement of needed supplies for the public service, and their distribution to the points where they are required for use or consumption; the creation, procurement, improvement, and preservation of necessary public buildings, grounds, and works; the disposition of surplus or unserviceable public property, and the preparation and submission of a yearly report of operations for the information of the proper authorities.

A record book for letters received should be large enough to contain the entries of one or more calendar years, but no such books should commence or terminate in any fractional part of a year.

Continuous numbers, beginning with the first and terminating with the last entry for a year, should be attached to the entries in the book and placed upon the papers.

Communications should be successively entered in the order of their receipt; but if the daily number of such communications be larger than one clerk can enter, the record book should be divided into two volumes—odd numbers being attached to the entries in one volume, and even numbers to the entries in the other. If, as is contemplated, the work of the entry clerk be restricted to a simple entry of the paper, the placing of the entry number upon it, and notation in the book of the action taken upon the papers entered, no more than two volumes are likely to be required for any one of the six prescribed classes of record books; but such books can be divided into as many volumes as may prove to be necessary, each of the volumes being distinguished by a letter of the alphabet, which will also be noted on the papers entered in the volume. For instance, should it be necessary to divide the record book of "*general and miscellaneous letters received*" for the year 1871 into four volumes, the thirty-fifth paper entered in the third volume would be known as "35, C, 1871," which designation should be noted in colored ink above, below, or between the spaces of the brief of contents, accompanied by some simple indication of the bureau, such as A. G., P. M. G., Eng., etc. It will not be necessary to add any notation of the particular class of record book in which a paper has been entered, as the subject of the communication will be a sufficient indication to any person familiar with the classification of the record books, and all papers which do not manifestly belong to any other set of books will necessarily be entered in the "*general and miscellaneous*" books of record.

No communication should be recorded in more than one record book in the same bureau, unless more than one class of record business is involved in it, in which case entries of so much of its subjects and the action upon it as relate to other record divisions may be made in the books of those divisions, and proper notations thereof placed upon the paper.

No communication exhibiting the notation of a previous entry should be again entered in the same class of record books, unless, for special reasons, it becomes necessary or desirable to transfer a remote entry to one of current date. All indorsements, reports, remarks, or directions attached to a communication that has been entered, sent from, and returned to the bureau should be regarded as a part of the original paper, and should not be separately recorded and numbered; and separate communications relating to one particular case, though independently recorded and numbered, should be collected and filed all together, both for the sake of convenience and to insure a full understanding of the case whenever taken up for action, notation being made on the subsequent papers, and against their entries on the record books, that they are filed with the first communication upon the case. Papers inclosed in a communication received should have a notation of the entry number assigned to such communication placed upon them, all useless fly-leaves being first taken off.

To insure proper indexing, a communication not received direct from the writer should be entered in the record book in the name of the last intermediate sender; the name of the writer then appearing in the body of the entry.

Should the number of cases falling under any one of the before-named classifications not justify their separation from the other records, that particular classification may be omitted, and the cases recorded under some other class. In the event stated, matters pertaining to classes 1, 2, 3, 4, 5 may be recorded in the same books as those of class 6

EXECUTIVE ACTION UPON LETTERS RECEIVED.

When communications received have been entered in the proper record books, and the required notations have been made upon them, they are to be distributed throughout the bureau for executive action; pencil memorandums of the distribution to be made in the record book at the time, and removed upon the return of the papers to the recorders.

The first executive action upon any case which has not manifestly arisen for the first time should be to ascertain from the records what has previously been done concerning it, and in all cases of importance inquiry should be made respecting the rules previously followed in similar cases.

Any information on the records of the bureau, or in possession of any official thereof, relating to a case, should be called for by the particular officer or clerk to whom it is referred for action, either verbally or by a written memorandum detached from the papers, and furnished in the same manner, no official reference or recording being necessary or desirable in communications between subdivisions of the same bureau. Inquiries of an oft-recurring nature should, as far as possible, be made and answered upon printed forms prepared for office use, thus saving time and insuring the same amount of information in each case, independently of the memory of inquirer and searcher. These memorandum reports should be preserved for future reference, being placed in an indorsed envelope and filed with the papers in the case; but they should not be permitted to leave the bureau.

A report upon any case required by a superior official from one of his assistants in the bureau should generally be adopted and used by him so far as to place or found his own remarks and views upon it; but should the superior officer prefer that the report and remarks upon any case should appear wholly over his own name or signature, the report of the assistant should be regarded as a memorandum for the information of his chief, and should not be recorded or sent out with the papers in the case.

Correspondence between the bureaus of the War Department with other executive bureaus maintaining intimate official relations with that Department, and with the Department itself, the Army, and others, should, whenever convenient, expeditious, and proper, be conducted by indorsement upon the papers pertaining to the case under consideration; but if the record of a case in the entry book be not regarded as sufficient; if it is not considered advisable to intrust the papers or any part of the information contained therein to other parties; if it be more convenient, useful, and proper to communicate by letter, order, circular, or memorandum, or if any other good reason exist, a departure from this general rule is allowable.

When indorsements are used they should be written, successively, crosswise upon the folds of the communication, additional sheets of paper being pasted on as required, and suitable margins being left on each fold for the purpose. Reports and remarks of considerable length may be written on seperate letter-sheets and fastened inside the communication, a note of the fact being made beneath the last indorsement. Simple references of papers by indorsement, as well as reference for "report" or "remark" only, should be made according to a set form of phraseology, to save the necessity of recording them at length in the books of letters sent.

Indorsements, as well as letters, addressed to public officers on the business of their offices, should designate them by their official titles rather than their individual names, as illustrated hereinafter.

Copies of original papers should not be unnecessarily multiplied. Except in special cases, the record kept in the bureau of original papers temporarily or permanently sent out is sufficient for reference. Originals referred to other executive bureaus, and not likely to be sent away from the seat of government, can always be referred to or recalled if required. Full copies of all the papers in a case need not be made when partial copies or extracts, covering the particular points involved at that stage of progress, will answer the purpose as well, or when the case can be sufficiently presented in a letter framed from the original papers and unaccompanied by copies.

Copies of papers, as well as originals, should be written on both sides of the paper used, unless it is probable that the matter contained therein is to be printed.

Communications addressed to the bureau upon matters which do not fall within its jurisdiction should be recorded and referred to the proper office, no acknowledgment of the receipt of such communications from the writer being required except in special cases.

Communications apparently referred for disposition to the bureau by persons whose public stations render them liable to be addressed upon various subjects by various parties, and which communications do not in themselves appear to require any correspondence with the writers, are not of necessity to be acknowledged or replied to at length, except upon request of the forwarder, or unless it be manifestly proper to communicate with the forwarder upon the subjects concerned.

Acknowledgments of communications received need not be sent except in special and important cases; nor need answer be made to communications upon matters which, since the date of the communication, and during its absence from the bureau, have been settled upon other papers, or otherwise.

Detached briefs, sometimes prepared by subordinates to save to their superiors the time and labor involved in the examination of a complicated case, set forth in numerous papers, should be terse and concise in language, informal in style, stripped of all mere verbiage, confined to the particular points of the case then before the bureau for action, and should not, except in special instances, be regarded as part of the official papers or the permanent records, but filed as memoranda.

Whenever a case requiring action extends through several papers, the papers should, with the aid of an elastic band or office tape, be always so arranged by the clerks into whose hands they come for action as to present to view the briefs of writers and contents of the principal communications in the order of their dates, the inclosures pertaining to each paper being contained within it, except such as it may be desirable to withdraw, indorse, and arrange among the principal papers.

Notations of the date or number of all letters, orders, circulars, memorandums, or other communications issued from the bureau, should be placed on the papers upon which such communications are based in small characters and in colored ink, upon the first or briefing fold of the paper, thus enabling an executive officer, or other person examining the paper, to see at a glance, or to ascertain, what action or attention the case has already received.

Communications referred by a superior to a subordinate officer, for such action as the subordinate may deem proper, do not require any formal indorsement or signature as authority for the latter to act upon them, but all instructions, calls for information, or information given, should be attested by the signature or initials of the superior officer or one of his assistants.

RECORDING OF LETTERS SENT.

A record book of letters sent, divided into as many volumes as may be necessary, should be kept in connection with the record books of letters received, in which should be recorded in full all communications issued from the bureau, except simple indorsements of reference for action, report, or remark, and regular series of orders, of which sets are separately kept on file. Should the business of any one class of records demand it, a separate book of letters sent may be kept for that class.

Such letters sent as are of a purely routine character, and of frequent recurrence, should be prepared upon printed forms, designated by numbers or otherwise, in which case only the manuscript portions of the letter, with the designation of the form affixed, need be recorded.

Brief descriptive headings should precede the entry of such indorsements as do not within themselves set forth the names of persons and things, or the subject concerned, sufficiently for indexing purposes.

To facilitate the dispatch of business, either the first draught of a communication, duly corrected, or a rough or press copy of the signed communication, should be retained for entry in the book of letters sent, and, after being recorded, such drafts or copies can be filed within the letters received on which they are based, or preserved, if desired in any other manner.

All names in the brief of an indorsement or report, or in the body of a communication, recorded in the letter book, which require to be indexed, should be underlined by the recorders.

The entry-marks of the letters received, upon which a communication issued from the bureau is based, should be noted in the margin of the record book of letters sent.

INDEXING.

A yearly alphabetical index should be kept up from day to day in connection with each record book of letters received and sent; but a separate index need not be kept for each volume of a book divided into volumes as before described. The index should contain the names of all persons and things appearing in the record book, as the writers, the receivers, or the subjects of the communications recorded therein, no name being entered more than once. Following each name in an index of letters received should appear the numbers of all communications received from or relating to the person or thing concerned (space being provided for the purpose), the numbers of the communications in which the name appears in the body of the letter, and not as the writer, being distinguished by the use of colored ink. In the indexes of letters sent the numbers should refer to the pages of the record book on which the communications are transcribed.

To facilitate searches for names under each letter of the alphabet, where the number of entries are great, the names may be arranged according to the first letter following the initial letter, under subdivisions corresponding with the five vowels of the alphabet.

A copious index of subjects of general interest, or involving principles applicable to similar cases likely to arise hereafter, should be compiled from individual cases after they have been recorded in the entry books and have received the action of the proper authorities. This index should extend to the business of the entire bureau, and should embrace the records of as many unbroken years as is consistent with convenience of size and handling. The design of this book of reference is to aid in securing uniform, just, and speedy decisions upon certain classes of cases of frequent occurrence, which might otherwise require, each of them, a lengthened search and study of principles, authorities, and precedents. Great care should be given to the preparation and keeping of this index.

Illustrative examples of the various kinds of indexes for record books of letters received are hereunto appended. These indexes should, when necessary, be kept by clerks especially assigned to that duty, to whom rough memorandums of names and entry numbers, in the order of their entry, should be handed by the recorders.

MEMORANDUM BOOKS.

Memorandum books, simple in design and inexpensive in character, may be used to aid in the dispatch of current business or for ready reference to particular classes of information, but they should not be multiplied beyond strict necessity, allowed to accumulate in course of time, or permitted to absorb much of the clerical labor of the bureau; nor should they be regarded as a part of the permanent records, and no file-numbers or notations connected with such books should be placed upon official papers.

HANDWRITING AND WRITING MATERIALS.

No other writing fluids than good black and red inks should be sanctioned, and copying ink should be used only for letter-presses.

Handwriting in record books and on official papers should be plain and of good size, flourishing and ornamental writing being especially avoided and forbidden. Proper names should always be written with especial care.

BRIEFING.

Class 1.

JAMES W. SMITH,
First Lieutenant, 12th Infantry.

ASSISTANT QUARTERMASTER.

By Senator NEWTON, Indiana.
Representative SINCLAIR, Indiana.
Judge TRIMBLE, Indiana.
Ex-Governor OLDHAM, Maine.
General Richard TOMPKINS et al.

(Three inclosures.)

[NOTE.—To be indexed under name of applicant; also under Q—"Quartermasters."]

MORTON S. JONES,
Minnesota.

FORAGE MASTER, FORT PEMBINA.

By Captain PLATT, A. Q. M.
Hon. G. S. HUDSON.
Postmaster HILL.
Citizens and Merchants of Pembina.

[NOTE.—To be indexed under name of applicant and under F—"Forage Masters."]

B. FRANKLIN HALL,
Late Sergeant, Massachusetts Volunteers.

CLERKSHIP, WAR DEPARTMENT.

By Senators and Representatives.
Officers of Regiment.
General LABAU, DEANE, et al.
G. W. SCHOULER, &c.

[NOTE.—To be indexed under H—"Hall," and C—"Clerkships."]

STEPHEN SHARPE,
New Hampshire.

COMMISSIONER, OHIO WAR CLAIMS.

By the Senators and Representatives, United States Officers, and principal State Officers of New Hampshire.

[NOTE.—To be indexed under S. and O.]

CLASS 2.

TUSCALOOSA,
January 20 1870.

ALABAMA, Western district of.

(United States attorney).

Requests that *Thos. H. Robinson*, Q. M. agent at Selma, be sent to him as a witness in case of "The United States vs. Geo. Hayfield and others."

[NOTE.—To be indexed under A, R, and H.]

ALSATIA, WISCONSIN,
September 13, 1870.

NORTH-GERMAN CONSULATE.

Requests information concerning Private *William Schmidt*, Company F, 97th Massachusetts Volunteers.

[One inclosure.]

[NOTE.—To be indexed under N and S.]

ST. LOUIS,
May 16, 1870.

SOUTHWEST, Department of.

(Medical director.)

Recommends transfer of Major *Charles Fisher*, Depot Commissary, to an eastern station, on account of ill-health.

[NOTE.—To be indexed under S and F.]

FEBRUARY 15, 1870.

QUARTERMASTER-GENERAL.

Recommends that Capt. *William S. Thompson*, post quartermaster at Portland, Oregon, be relieved by Capt. *Richard Belden*, A. Q. M., and ordered to report to the Quartermaster-General.

[NOTE.—To be indexed under Q, T, and B.]

17958——10

CLASS 2.

OCTOBER 29, 1870.

JUSTICE, Department of.

Opinion on application of Surgeon *Thomas Smilie*, U. S. Army, to be advanced in grade among the officers of his corps, that the applicant has no legal right to such advancement.

[NOTE.—To be indexed under J. and S.]

APRIL 30, 1870.

CLAIMS, Court of.

Requests address of Chaplain *William Goddard*, 30th Rhode Island Volunteers.

[NOTE.—To be indexed under C and G.]

NEW ORLEANS,
September 16, 1870.

LOUISIANA, State of.
(Levee Commission.)

Resolution requesting assignment of Major *Lawrence W. Abbott*, Corps of Engineers, to the work at "Northwest Pass" on account of his familiarity therewith.

[NOTE.—To be indexed under L.—("Louisiana" and "Levee Commission,") A. and N.]

FORT HUMBOLDT,
October 7, 1870.

NEVADA, District of.
(Judge-Advocate.)

Submits formal charges against Capt. *Lyman Bradford*, 40th Infantry, and recommends his trial by court-martial.

[NOTE.—To be indexed under N and B.]

CLASS 2.

CHEYENNE,
March 7, 1870.

WYOMING, Governor of.

Requests that Col. *Charles G. Gordon*, 15th Cavalry, be continued on duty in the Territory until Indian troubles are settled.

[NOTE.—To be indexed under W and G.]

FEBRUARY 29, 1870.
HOUSE OF REPRESENTATIVES.
(Committee on Reconstruction.)

Requests copy of report of Col. *Charles H. Lloyd*, U.S. Army, of his inspection tour in Alabama and Mississippi.

[NOTE.—To be indexed under H—"House of Representatives," R—"Reconstruction Committee," L, A, and M.]

BOSTON,
August 3, 1870.

ATLANTIC STEAMSHIP COMPANY.

Reports improper conduct of *John Smith*, clerk in equipment office, on steamer "Crystal Wave," July 27, 1870.

[NOTE.—To be indexed under A and S.]

JULY 19, 1870.

HENRY W. JOHNSON,
First Lieutenant, 6th Artillery.

PHILIP J. STETSON,
First Lieutenant, 12th Cavalry.

Apply for exchange of regiments after 1st of September next.

[NOTE.—To be indexed under J and S.]

CLASS 3.

TERRITORIAL STAGE COMPANY,
Atchison, Kansas.

Claim for horses impressed by United States military authorities during late war.

[Six inclosures.]

[NOTE.—To be indexed under name of the company only.]

JOSEPH SLAUGHTER.
Bullock County, Georgia.

Additional evidence in claim for beef-cattle taken for United States Army during the war, presented by *Littleton & Cook*, Washington.

[NOTE.—To be indexed under name of claimant.]

KNOXVILLE, City of,
North Carolina.

Application for restoration of *City Armory*, captured during late war.

[NOTE.—To be indexed under K—"Knoxville," and A—"Armory."]

INTERNATIONAL TRADING CO.,
Charleston.

Claim for cotton seized at Columbia and sold by the United States.

[Three inclosures.]

[NOTE.—To be indexed under name of the company, I, and place of capture, C.]

CLASS 3.

DR. JAMES WILSON YOUNG,
Allentown, Illinois.

Claim for medical services rendered at recruiting rendezvous before appointment in the medical staff; referred for remark by Senate Committee on Claims, Dec. 16, 1870.

[NOTE.—To be indexed under Y, S—"Senate," and C—"Claims Committee of Senate."]

MOORE & SKINNER,
Laporte, Minnesota.

Petition for additional allowance on contract for improvement of the *St. Joe Rapids;* referred by House Committee on Commerce, March 21, 1870.

[Two inclosures.]

[NOTE.—To be indexed under M—"Moore & Skinner," S—"Skinner & Moore," and "St. Joe Rapids," H—"House of Representatives," and C—"Commerce Committee."]

MISSOURI CAVALRY, Fourth Regiment.

Information relative to claim for veteran bounty; called for by House *Resolution,* July 14, 1870.

[NOTE.—To be indexed under M—"Missouri Cavalry," H—"House of Representatives," and R—"Resolutions of Congress."]

"BOONETOWN WEEKLY,"
Moore & Barton, proprietors.

Account for job printing for the military service in 1863.

[One inclosure.]

[NOTE.—To be indexed under name of journal, B, and names of proprietors, M and B.]

CLASS 3.

MRS. ELIZABETH JAMISON,
Rocky Creek, Virginia.

Claim for damages to property by United States troops referred by *Third Auditor* for information, Sept. 9, 1870.

[NOTE.—To be indexed under J and A—"Auditor, Third."]

THOS. J. SINGLETON, Heirs of,
Marshville, Louisiana.

Attention called to claim for rent of buildings occupied by United States, by Hon. *R. J. Saunders*, M. C., Feb. 17, 1870.

[NOTE.—To be indexed under name of claimant and presenter of claim.]

CLASS 4.

NEW YORK,
January 10, 1870.

GORDON IRON-WORKS COMPANY

with

Colonel *Stuart Thornton*, Corps of Engineers.

Contract for steam-dredge for western rivers.

SELMA, ALABAMA,
July 23, 1870.

DR. BEVERLY FORD

with

Surgeon *Chas. Johnson*, U. S. A.

Contract for medical services for the garrison at Selma till December 31, 1870.

CLASS 4.

BALTIMORE,
April 15, 1870.

SUNDRIES

to

Captain *Samuel Wilcox*, C. S.

Purchases of canned fruit and vegetables for sales to the Army.

FORT BARKER, IDAHO,
May 17, 1870.

JOHN TAYLOR & SON

with

Captain *Gillett M. Noyes*, A. Q. M.

Contract for transportation of military stores from Fort Barker to Camp McKelvey, Montana.

WASHINGTON,
June 20, 1870.

BROWN & SIMS

with

Richard Layton, disbursing cle. k.

Contract for stationery for next fiscal year.

LAWTONVILLE, FLORIDA,
March 14, 1870.

THOMAS GREENFIELD

to

Lieutenant *Gerald Reilly*, A. C. S.

Purchase of anti-scorbutics for the expeditionary force employed against Indians.

CLASS 4.

FORT CARTER, NEBR.,
October 10, 1870.

GEO. RUSSELL & JAS. S. TOWERS

with

Lieutenant *Sinclair Jackson*, A. C. S.

Contract to purchase hides of beef-cattle slaughtered at the post or in the vicinity.

FORT MARION, KANSAS,
March 14, 1870.

RICHARD SALTER & JOHN ROHR

with

Captain *Joseph Simpson*, A. Q. M.

Contract for lumber, brick, and stone for quartermaster's storehouses.

LITTLE RAPIDS, WIS.,
September 19, 1870.

RANSOM, Major *George H.*,
Corps of Engineers.

Reports delinquency of *Hardy & Sadlier*, contractors for blasting work, and recommends that suit be brought on their bond.

NEW YORK,
August 31, 1870.

STEAM COASTING CO.

and

PACIFIC TRANSPORTATION CO.

Give formal notice that existing agreement for transportation of troops and stores will be terminated September 30, 1870.

Class 4.

JUNCTION CITY, KANS.,
May 31, 1870.

JOSHUA RIDER AND J. S. HILL.

Proposal for supplying coal and wood to the quartermaster's department in Kansas.

PARIS, June 27, 1870.

FRANÇOIS BELLOTÉ.

Offers to furnish desiccated vegetables and concentrated meats for the use of the Army.

Class 5.

JUNE 25, 1871.

TREASURY DEPARTMENT.

Warrant for appropriations of the War Department for the fiscal year 1871–'72.

Received, Q. M. G. O., June 29, 1870.
Received, A. G. O., June 27, 1870.
Received, War Dep't, June 26, 1870.

NASHVILLE,
September 1, 1870.

SOUTHWEST—Military Division.
(Chief Commissary Sub.)

Estimate of subsistence funds for fiscal year 1871–'72.

[Three inclosures.]

Received, O. C. G. S., Sept. 5, 1870.

CLASS 5.

FORT JOHNSON, WYOMING,
February 8, 1870.

RICHARDS, Lieutenant *William G.*,
(Post Commissary.)

Account current for January, 1870.

[Seventeen inclosures.]

Received, O. C. G. S., February 20, 1870.

NEWPORT BARRACKS, KY.,
June 30, 1870.

LESLIE, Captain *Hamilton*,
(36th Infantry.)

Property return of detachment of recruits en route from Newport Barracks to Santa Fé for 2d quarter, 1870.

[Nine inclosures.]

[Received, Q. M. G. O., July 6, 1870.]

ST. LOUIS,
May 27, 1870.

LANGDON, Captain *Beverly T.*,
(Medical Storekeeper.)

Certificate of deposit for $327.49, on account of sales of medical and hospital property.

[One inclosure.]

Received, S. G. O., May 30, 1870.

WYANDOTTE, KANSAS,
February 28, 1870.

YOUNG, *Grandison W.*,
(late 1st Lieutenant 29th Infantry.)

Incloses receipt of Captain *Maxwell Stockton*, A. Q. M., for $79.63 deposited in settlement of his accounts with the Government.

[One inclosure.]

Received, Q. M. G. O., March 6, 1870.

CLASS 5.

MAY 14, 1870.

ADJUTANT GENERAL.

General Orders No. 60, directing that property returns, except for provisions, be hereafter rendered quarterly, instead of monthly.

Received, O. C. G. S., May 18, 1870.

JUNE 16, 1870.

ADJUTANT GENERAL.

General Orders No. 73, prescribing method of accountability for quartermaster's property, for post and garrison use, in charge of the guard.

Received, Q. M. G. O., June 18, 1870.

FORT LEAVENWORTH,
September 30, 1870.

DIXON, Lieutenant *Thomas Z.*,
R. Q. M., 11th Cavalry.

Explanations and additional vouchers for file with his money accounts for July, 1870.

[Eleven inclosures.]

PINE BLUFF, ARK.,
October 3, 1870.

MELVILLE, *Robt. Quincy,*
(late Paymaster of Volunteers).

Applies for settlement of his accounts under act of Congress of June 23, 1870.

[Twenty-three inclosures.]

Received, P. M. G. O., October 13, 1870.
Received, A. G. O., October 10, 1870.

CLASS 5.

JANUARY 27, 1870.

TREASURY DEPARTMENT.

Reports that remittances have been made to Major *Thomas Lincoln*, Engineers, for $5,000, and *James R. Hewlett*, engineer agent, for $480.50.

Received, Eng. Bureau, January 29, 1870.

NEW ALBANY, IND.,
February 29, 1870.

JENKINS, Captain *B. F.*,
Depot Quartermaster.

List of quartermaster's property sold by auction on the 24th, 25th, and 26th instant.

Received, Q. M. G. O., March 3, 1870.

Inventory and Inspection report
of
COMMISSARY PROPERTY,
for which
Lieutenant JOS. G. GOODWIN,
57th Infantry,
is responsible.

Inspected at *Camp Garnett*, Nev., on *August* 29, 1870.

Received, O. C. G. S., September 25, 1870.

SAN ANTONIO, TEXAS,
July 17, 1870.

FRONTIER, Department of the.

States, in reply to letter of June 29, that a board of survey is now investigating the loss and damage of ordnance stores turned over by Captain *Thos. Edwards*, Ordnance Corps, to Lieutenant *Evan Bradbury*, Post Quartermaster at Austin, for transportation to Lieutenant *Duncan McBride*, Ordnance Officer at Hunter Barracks.

CLASS 6.

FORT MUMFORD, KANS.,
March 8, 1870.

CAVALRY, 12th Regiment.
(Commanding Officer.)

Reports necessity for the return of some of the detached officers of his regiment before active operations begin.

[NOTE.—To be indexed under C—"Cavalry, 12th Regiment," and D—"Detached officers of 12th Cavalry."]

NORTH PLATTE CITY, NEBR.,
April 14, 1870.

PLATTE, Sub-District of.

Reports boundaries of *Fort Blaisdell Military Reservation*, and recommends that it be officially declared.

[Two inclosures.]

[NOTE.—To be indexed under B—"*Blaisdell*, Fort, Military Reservation," and P—"*Platte*, Sub-District."]

MAY 29, 1870.

FORT MURRAY, Post of.
(Commanding Officer.)

Reports conference with "*Buffalo Horn*" and other Indian chiefs at that post.

[NOTE.—To be indexed under B—"Buffalo Horn;" I—"Indian conference at Fort Murray," and M—"*Murray*, Indian conference at Fort."]

BOSTON,
October 9, 1870.

FORT ANDREW, Post of.
(Post Quartermaster.)

Requisition for stoves for use of the garrison.

[NOTE.—To be indexed under A—"*Andrew*, Fort;" R—"Requisitions for Q. M. stores," and S—"Stoves."]

CLASS 6.

WASHINGTON,
September 30, 1870.

RECORDS OF WAR DEPARTMENT.
(Board.)

Report and recommendations concerning records and business of War Department and Bureaus.

[NOTE.—To be indexed under B—"Board on Records, &c.;" R—"Records of War Department," and W—"War Department, Board on Records, &c."]

ST. LOUIS,
May 18, 1870.

TACTICS AND SMALL-ARMS,
(Board.)

Report on breech-loading small-arms for infantry, cavalry, and artillery.

[NOTE.—To be indexed under B—"Board on Small-arms" and "Breech-loading Small-arms;" S—"Small-arms Board," and T—"Tactics and Small-arms Board."]

RECORD BOOKS.

Application book.

File No.	Name.	Rank or residence.	Date of application.	Appointment desired.	By whom recommended.	Remarks.
347	Smith, John S	New York City	Jan. 14, 1870	Messenger	Hon. Thomas Brown, Joseph Street, Colonel Fletcher, Major Gale, and other officers of 72d Rhode Island Volunteers.	Withdrawn in person Mar. 11, 1870.
348	Barclay, Hon. W. D.	Michigan	Mar. 7, 1870	Commissioner New Jersey war claims.	Gov. Lytton, Senator Long, Judge Richards, and Geo. J. Smart.	Filed with appointment 698 of 1870.
349	Tarlton, Robert J	1st lieut. 26th Inf	Sept. 9, 1870	Quartermaster, commissary, paymaster.	Generals Jones, Taylor, Bishop; Senators Petit and Lyons; Rep's Farwell, O'Bryan, and others.	For "special attention" when vacancy occurs.
350	Crywell & Sons	Philadelphia	Nov. 11, 1870	Gover'm't auctioneers	Col. Randolph, Captain Jenkins, prominent merchants, and others.	Called for by War Dep't Dec. 10; received back Dec. 23; returned to War Dep't Dec. 28 (L. R., p. 379); rec'd back Dec. 31. Letter to applicants Jan. 4.
351	Munson, Jos. L	Omaha	Dec. 3, 1870	Post-trader, Fort Wolford, W. T.	Senators and Representatives of States; Delegate Ransom, Wyom.; commander and officers of posts.	Appointed for Fort Wilson Dec. 30; filed with 473 of 1870.

NOTE.—*Applications* only should be entered or retained on this book. The papers of an applicant receiving an appointment should be withdrawn and filed with or entered under the order or notice of appointment in the entry book of Class 2.
Applications for office need not be entered in any other book of letters received.

160

Record book—letters received.

Date of receipt and file number.	Name of writer.	Date and purport of communication.	Action.
		JANUARY 2.	
January 3........ (14)	War Department............	Refers application of *Jas. Thomson*, late Captain 40th Delaware Volunteers, for revocation of order of dismissal.	J. A. G. remark, Jan. 4; returned Jan. 11; Third Auditor, Jan. 17 (L. B., p. 79); received back Jan. 21; Q. M. G. report, Jan. 25; returned Feb. 1; Secretary of War, Feb. 11 (L. B., p. 183); received back, Feb. 25. See S. O. 48, par. 3, 1870.
		FORT MOULTRIE, *January* 1.	
January 4........ (15)	Dalton, Captain Richard, Corps of Engineers.	Acknowledges receipt of extract from report of Col. *Geo. W. Lawson*, 58th Infantry, on unfitness of work for quartering troops, and states what modifications can be made without impairing the defensive qualities of the fort.	Q. M. G., Jan. 5 (L. B., p. 39); returned Jan. 14; Chief of Ordnance, Jan. 18; received back Jan. 23; A. G., Jan. 29 (L. B., p. 56); returned Feb. 4 Filed with 579 of 1869.

NOTE.—This form of book to be used alone in classes 2 and 6, and in connection with other books of letters received in classes 3, 4, and 5; ample space should be left between the entries for all probable future notations of action taken.

Claims—letters received.

Date of receipts and file number.	Name of claimant or writer.	Date and subject of claim or letter.	Action.
		DETROIT, *January* 13.	
January 17...... (47)	Baldwin & Marshall.........	Ask if the law concerning balances of appropriations is held to debar the payment of their recently-allowed claim	Secretary of War, Jan. 18; returned Jan. 21; answered Jan. 22 (L. B., p. 53); Third Auditor, for file with papers in claim, Jan. 22.
		NEW YORK, *January* 21.	
January 25...... (48)	Ocean Navigation Co........	Claim for services rendered by steam-ship *Shooting Star* to United States steam-transport *Roanoke*, off Cape Hatteras, in 1865.	See page 46, Claims Register, 1870.
		JANUARY 28.	
January 29 (49)	State Department............	Refers communication of *Reginald Hopewood*, of England, asking instructions as to the manner of presenting a claim for damage to his property in Tennessee during the late war.	Q. M. G. report, Jan. 29; received back Jan. 31; A. G. report, Jan. 31; returned Feb. 5; applicant answered Feb. 6 (L. B., p. 121); filed with 329 of 1868.
		TEUTOSIA, WIS., *January* 15.	
February 6...... (50)	Friderichs, Carl H., late captain 63d Wisconsin Volunteers.	Claim for pay while out of service by summary dismissal.	See page 79, Claims Register, 1870.

161

Register of Claims.

File No.	Auditor's number.	Name of claimant.	Residence.	Nature of claim.	By whom presented or referred.	When received.	Amount claimed.	Amount allowed or recommended.	Action, disposition, and remarks.
276	1342	Territorial Stage Co.	Atchison, Kans.	Seizure of horses.	Third Auditor.	1870. Jan. 27	$14,982.70	$9,450.25	Chief Q. M. Dept. West, Feb. 4 (L. B., p.43); received Mar. 18; A. G. for information from records Army of the Frontier, April 11; returned April 18; Secretary of War, May 23 (L. B., p. 218).
293		Slaughter, Joseph	Bullock Co., Ga.	Beef cattle	Littleton & Cook, Washington.	Feb. 14	1,476.85	1,476.85	Additional evidence required Feb. 29 (L. B., p. 67); evidence received Mar. 27; Chief C. S. Southern Dept., April 21, to investigate loyalty; report received May 16; A. G. for address of Lieut. Philip Clayton, 6.1 Ky. Vols., May 30; letter to Lieut. Clayton, June 24 (L. B., p. 119); Third Auditor for settlement, Aug. 19.
314		International Trading Co.	Charleston, S. C.	Cotton sold by Government.	Thomas L. Atkins & Co.	Mar. 3	72,813.00		Papers withdrawn by attorneys May 3 for presentation to Ct. of Claims. See 643 of 1870.
325	482	Singleton, heirs of T. J.	Marksville, La.	Rent of buildings at New Orleans.	Hon. B. J. Saunders, M. C., and Third Auditor.	Mar. 31	427.37		Returned to Auditor April 14 (L. B., p. 78).
348		Missouri 4th Cavalry		Veteran bounty.	Adjutant-general of Mo.	May 26			Secretary of War with report, July 9 (L. B. p. 246); received back with report of P. M. General, Sept. 23; copies to House Military Committee, Dec. 19.
369	1763	Morton and Perkins	Bartonville, N. J.	Compensation for non-fulfillment of contract for Army clothing.	Second Comptroller.	July 19	28,047.32	5,000.00	J. A. General, Aug. 2 (L. B., p. 276); received back Sept. 3; Secretary of War, Sept. 9; request for $10,550.25 issued on settlement 1763, Oct. 15.
396		Knoxville, city of	North Carolina.	Restoration of armory.	General Joseph R. Preston.	Sept. 26			C. O. Dept. of Southwest report, Nov. 7; received back Dec. 16; application refused Jan. 8, 1871 (L. B., p. 16).

NOTE.—All claims and communications relating to claims, or on the subject of claims, should be entered in a book of letters received, of the ordinary form, and file-numbers assigned to them. Then such claims as require the administrative action of the Bureau should be set forth in this book as above, and a reference made in the book of letters received to the pages of this book on which the claims can be found. The file-numbers illustrated here are those of the letters-received book; the Auditor's numbers those of the settlement certificates issued in cases settled at the Treasury. The action on all claims not required to be spread on this book, and on all other communications, should be noted in the book of letters received. This book need not be indexed, as the index to the first entry of the cases in a book of letters received is sufficient.

17958——11

Contract letters received.

Date of receipt and file number.	Name of contractor or writer.	Date and subject of contract or letter.	Action.
Mar. 14... (74)	Bloomington Arms Company.	KINGS CROSS, MASS, *March* 12. Offer to purchase 10,000 *Springfield* muzzle-loading rifles at appraised value.	C. O. Springfield Armory remark, March 15; returned March 19, and offer declined March 20 (L. B., p. 317).
May 27... (75)	Slaughter, James G.	APRIL 10. Contract for *beef-cattle* at *Fort Fosdick* with Captain *Thomas L. Wyatt*, C. S.	See page 96, Contract Register, 1870.
June 3... (76)	Engineer Bureau.....	JUNE 2. Refers proposal of *William Hammersmith & Co.* to attach their patent *gun-shield* to the fortifications of the United States.	
June 29... (77)	Stansbury, Capt. R. T., Post Q. M.	OMAHA, *June* 24. Reports purchase of *fire extinguishers* for the Q. M. department at Omaha and Cheyenne from *Randall Fire Extinguisher Company*.	See page 137, Contract Register, 1870.
July 14... (78)	Campbell & Bell........	PITTSBURGH, *July* 11. Proposals for furnishing *iron head-blocks* and *iron railings* for the national cemeteries.	Inspector national cemeteries remark, July 15; received back July 27; answered July 30 (L. B., p. 465).

Register of contracts and purchases.

File.	Name of contractor or seller.	Place of delivery, performance, or sale.	Name of contracting officer.	Rank or office.	Date of contract or purchase.	Period.	Articles or services.	Quantities or time.	Price.	Date of transmittal to Treasury Department.	Action and remarks.
72	Winfield & Bro.	Baltimore	Fr. Skinner	Capt. and C.S.	1870. Jan. 11		Canned peaches	2,500 cans.	$1.12½	1870.	Returned to officer for size of cans Jan 15; received back Jan. 27.
79	Atlantic Steamship Company.	New York	Jas. W. Pringle	Major and Q. M.	June 15	1 year from July 1, 1870.	Transportation New York to Mobile.	Per ton. Per cub. yd. Per ton. Per cub. yd.	7.10 .75 5.25 .60	July 10	Returned to officer for amendment of certificate of responsibility of sureties June 27; received back July 6.
83	Wisewell & May	Philadelphia.	Chas. J. Huntington.	Medical purveyor.	July 17		Hospital knapsacks.	150.	14.50	Aug. 4	Contract terminated Sept. 16, and new contract made for improved knapsack at higher price (L. B., p. 34).
96	Jefferson Adams.	Cold Run	Wm. T. Varley	Lieut. of Ordnance.	Aug. 23	3 years from Sept. 1.	Superintendent gun foundry.	Per annum.	4,600.00	Nov. 16	
104	Benj. Van Dyke.	Boston	Rich'd A. Simms	Lieut. and sig. offi'r.	Sept. 9		Telescopes	12	25.00		Returned to Lieutenant Simms Sept. 18, to report authority for purchase; received back Sept. 25; Secretary of War Sept. 24 (L. B., p. 279); returned Sept. 30; letter to Lieutenant Simms Oct. 2 (L. B., p. 323).
123	Patrick O'Hagan.	Chicago	Ewing Preston	Capt. 29th Inf. R. O.	Sept. 16	Indefinite	Cooked rations for recruits.	Per ration	.28	Sept. 27	
	John Burley	Ft. Barker, Tex.	Sam'l S. Ferriss.	Li'ut. 11th Cavalry, post commissary.	Oct. 10		Beef cattle. Fresh beef. Hay. Corn.	700 head. 3,500 lbs. 75 tons.	.07 .11 18.00	Oct. 31	Returned to officer for verbal amendment Oct. 20; received back Oct. 29.
178	Dater & Timpson.	Washington	Thos. Fosdick	Disbursing clerk.	June 30	1 year	Stationery	375 bush.	.62	July 3	Annulled for violation of terms Oct. 24, 1870 (L. B., p. 286); revival refused Nov. 10 (L. B., p. 95).

Register of contracts and purchases—Continued.

File.	Name of contractor or seller.	Place of delivery, performance, or sale.	Name of contracting officer.	Bank or office.	Date of contract or purchase.	Period.	Articles or services.	Quantities or time.	Price.	Date of transmittal to Treasury Department.	Action and remarks.
187	National Submarine Company.	Devil's Pass, La.	Everton Giles	Lieut. Col. Engineers.	1870. May 14		Removal of rock	Per cub. yd.	$1.85	1870. June 16	Prosecution for non-fulfillment recommended Aug. 27 (L. B. p. 432); compromised Sept. 19 (L. B. 510); paper sent to War Department Nov. 29; see 276 of 1870.
198	Vulcan Iron Co.	Pittsburgh	Clayt'n Hotchkiss.	Major of Ordnance.	Aug. 10	6 months	20-pdr. breech-loading gun.	Per lb	.12	Aug. 27	

NOTE.—Contracts, reports of purchases, proposals, and offers will be entered in a book of letters received of the ordinary form, and a file number assigned to each. Contracts and purchases will then be set forth on this book, and a note made opposite their entry in the letter book, showing on which page of this register they are to be found. Contracts and purchases should be recorded briefly in the book of letters received, but proposals and offers should be stated sufficiently at length to afford an index of the articles and services proposed or offered. The two record books can be used in determining values at any time and place. The file numbers used on this register should be those of the first entry of the papers.

General and miscellaneous letters received.

Date of receipt and file number.	Name of writer.	Date and subject of letter.	Action.
Sept. 30 (561)	Northwest Military Division, commanding officer.	SEPTEMBER 20, 1870. Reports on Indians, post traders, means of transportation, subsistence stores, quarters, need of recruits, &c., in his command, as observed during his recent inspection tour, and submits recommendations.	Extracts for Interior Department, War Department, Q. M. Gen'l, C. G. Sub., Surg. Gen., Sup't Rect'g Service, Oct. 5 (L. B., pp. 249-286). Copy to Secretary of War for House Committee on Military Affairs, Dec. 27.
Oct. 15 (562)	Adjutant-General...	OCTOBER 14, 1870. Refers requisition of Captain Samuel Wilkins, Company H, Ninth Artillery, for ordnance stores.	Letter to C. O., Allegheny Arsenal, Oct. 16, and to Captain Wilkins' (L. B., p. 363).
Oct. 23 (563)	Post-Office Department.	OCTOBER 22, 1870. Refers for remark petition of officers and men at *Fort Grayson*, Texas, for increased mail facilities.	A. G. remark, October 24; returned Oct. 26; Q. M. G. report, Oct. 27; letter to P. M. G. Oct. 28.
Nov. 10 (564)	Cavalry School, commandant.	NOVEMBER 1, 1870. Report of trials of *Pringle's safety-bit*.	Referred to Q. M. G. Nov. 12; returned Nov. 15; letter to Pringle Nov. 18 (L. B. 638).

Record book—Letters sent.

Henry, Hon. Thos. J., Louisville. 437 (W. D.) 1870. 683 (W. D.) 1870.	WAR DEPARTMENT, *June* 16, 1870. SIR: I am directed by the Secretary of War to inform you, in reply to your letter of the 12th instant, that the application of Mrs. *Rebecca Harrison*, of Bentville, for the discharge of Corporal *Joseph Brown*, Co. M, 27th Infantry, has been duly considered by the Department, and that the same can not be granted without prejudice to the public interests. Very respectfully, your obedient servant, *Chief Clerk.*
Wyoming, Gov'r of. 79 (A. G. O.) 1870. See page 139.	Indorsement on application for continuance of Col. *Chas. G. Gordon* in that Territory. Respectfully referred by the General of the Army to the Commander of the Mil. Div. of the West, with authority to grant this application, if deemed compatible with the interests of the service and regarded as advisable in other respects. *Ass't Adj't Gen'l.* A. G. O., *March* 14, 1870.
Wilkins, Geo. B., 1st Lieut. 12th Inf'y. 63, 85 (Q. M. G.) 1870. Sec'y of War approved, May 20. See page 435.	REPORT: The case of this officer is respectfully submitted to the Quartermaster-General, with the report that it appears * * * * It is recommended that * * * * *. *Major and Q. M.* Q. M. G. O., *May* 18, 1870.
Engineer Officers. 743 (Eng.) 1870.	OFFICE CHIEF OF ENGINEERS, *June* 27, 1870. CIRCULAR: It is ordered by the Chief of Engineers that in future all *estimates* for funds forwarded to this office * * * * * *Capt. of Eng'rs, Bv't Lt. Col.*
Cavalry, C. O. 12th Reg't., Fort Richardson, Texas. 467 (Ord.) 1870. See page 296, Vol. I, 1869.	ORDNANCE OFFICE, *August* 14, 1870. SIR: The Chief of Ordnance requests * * * * * *Sharp's* breech-loading *Carbine* * * * * *. Very respectfully, *Major of Ordnance.*

OFFICE-MARKS, INDORSEMENTS, OFFICIAL ADDRESSES, INDEXES.

Illustrations of the office-marks upon communications and their inclosures.

```
746 (Eng.) 1870.
...........................................
       .
...........................................
...........................................
...........................................
===========
    (Three inclosures.)
FILE WITH 549 OF 1869.
Ans'd June 21, 1870.
See letter to.................June 30, 1870.
Copy of this, and answer of June 26,
1870, furnished to............July 18, 1870.
Submitted personally to the...........
August 27, 1870, and action deferred.
See letter to the..........................
Sept. 19, 1870.
   S. O. 316, par. 3, Oct. 20, 1870.
Received, Eng. Bureau, June 21, 1870.
```

```
           III.
       746 (Eng.) 1870.
Extract, as indicated by red ink brack-
ets within, furnished to..................
July 18, 1870.




[NOTE.—Inclosures should always be
numbered in the order of their date, or
in the order in which they should be
read.]
```

Illustrations of memorandum—Envelopes and indorsements.

```
          ENVELOPE.
       .
.............................(A. G.) 187...
Case of..................................
..........................................
..........................................
OFFICE MEMORANDA, BRIEFS,
         AND REPORTS.
Not to be taken from the files except
for reference, and not to be sent out of
the office.
```

Respectfully referred by the Department Commander to the Commanding-Officer of the District of the Plains, with directions to order a full investigation into the circumstances set forth herein by a competent staff officer serving in his command, whose report shall be forwarded to these headquarters accompanied by these papers.

Act'g Asst. Adjt. Gen'l.
H'dq'rs Dept. of the West, Sept. 29, 1870.

See report within.

Respectfully forwarded to Headquarters Military Division of the Northwest.

Brig. Gen'l Com'g.
H'dq'rs Dept. of the West, Oct. 14, 1870.

Respectfully returned by the Division Commander to the Commanding-Officer of the Department of the West. It is not deemed necessary or proper to apply to Headquarters of the Army, as recommended, for authority to establish a permanent military post at Whitestone Crossing, but suitable detachments of cavalry and infantry should be sent there next spring to remain till the following winter and the post quartermaster at Fort Wilson should be directed to forward requisitions for the necessary materials to provide them with temporary quarters. Suitable reports of the operations of these detachments are to be forwarded for the information of these headquarters.

Asst. Adjt. Gen'l.
H'dq'rs Mill. Div. Northwest, Oct. 28, 1870.

Official addresses.

To the SPEAKER
    of the House of Representatives,
        Washington.

To the PRESIDENT
    of the Senate,
        Washington.

To the CHAIRMAN,
    Committee on Military Affairs,
        United States Senate.

To the CHAIRMAN,
    Joint Select Committee on Ordnance,
        Washington.

To the CLERK
    of the House of Representatives,
        Washington.

To the PRESIDENT
    of the United States.

To the Honorable
    THE SECRETARY OF THE TREASURY.

To the Honorable
    THE ATTORNEY-GENERAL.

To the SECOND COMPTROLLER
    of the Treasury.

To the COMMISSIONER
    of the General Land Office.

To the
    COMMISSIONER OF PENSIONS.

To the CHIEF OF THE BUREAU
    of Yards and Docks,
        Navy Department.

To the CHIEF of the
    Bureau of Navigation,
        Navy Department.

To the PAYMASTER GENERAL
    of the Army.

To the COMMISSARY GENERAL
    of Subsistence.

To the CLERK of the
    Supreme Court of the District of Columbia,
        Washington.

To the ASSISTANT ATTORNEY GENERAL,
    United States Court of Claims,
        Washington.

To the GOVERNOR
    of the State of Nevada,
        Carson City.

To the SECRETARY OF STATE,
    State of New Jersey,
        Trenton.

To the SUPERINTENDENT OF PUBLIC INSTRUCTION,
    State of Illinois,
        Springfield.

To the CLERK OF THE DISTRICT COURT,
    Fourth Judicial District, State of Texas,
        San Antonio.

To the SURROGATE OF THE COUNTY OF KINGS,
        Brooklyn, New York.

To the MAYOR of the
    City of Louisville.

To the Treasurer of the
      Board of Public Works,
            Cincinnati.

To the Secretary
      of the Atlantic Woolen Mills,
            Westerly, Rhode Island.

To the President
      of the Interoceanic Steamship Co.,
            Wilmington, North Carolina.

To the Judge-Advocate,
      General Court-Martial,
            Fort Hamilton, New York.

To the Recorder of the
      Board on Tactics, Small Arms, and Equipments,
            Rock Island, Illinois.

To the Collector of Customs,
      Port of Philadelphia,
            Pennsylvania.

To the United States Attorney,
      Northern District of New York,
            Buffalo.

To the Commandant,
      United States Navy Yard,
            New London, Conn.

To the Commanding Officer,
      Post of Fort Greenleaf,
            Florida.

To the Depot Quartermaster,
      Fort Harker, Kansas.

To the Post Commissary,
      Jefferson Barracks, Missouri.

To the Assistant Adjutant-General,
      Headquarters, Department of the West,
            Fort Leavenworth, Kansas.

To the Chief Commissary of Subsistence,
      District of the Plains,
            Fort Gibson, Indian Territory.

To the Commanding Officer,
      Company C, 12th Regiment of Cavalry,
            Camp Mansfield, M. T.

Alphabetical vowel index.

Aa.

Adams, Capt. Chas. J.—3, 11, 14, 28, 59, 73, 91, 126.
Accounts of Civil Engineers—7, 43, 69.
Abbott, Geo. Wash.—15, 27, 34.

Ae.

Ahrens, Sam'l D.—16, 18, 72.
Aerial Navigation Co.—116, 243, 376.
Affrey, Surgeon Chas.—92, 111, 293.

Ai.

Aikenside, Joshua—142, 234.
Aides-de-Camp—68, 236.
Amerson, Col. Albert T.—83, 171, 216.
Allerton, William S.—41, 69, 82.

170

Ao.

Atwater, Gen'l Jons.—26, 249.
Appropriations for current fiscal year—76, 83.
Aspodel, Geo. C.—182, 246.
Annual Report—6, 54, 87.

Au.

Ayers, Cadet Jackson H.—46, 126.
"*Avalanche*." Steamer—154.
Augustus, Private Julius C.—35.
Austin Arsenal Lot—112.

INDEX LETTERS.

Congress	C.
House of Representatives	H.
United States Senate	S.
Committee on Appropriations, House of Representatives	A. and H.
Committee on Military Affairs, United States Senate.	M. and S.
President of the United States	P.
Department of State	S.
Department of Justice	J.
Solicitor of the Treasury	T.
General Land Office	L.
Comptrollers of Treasury	C.
Auditors of Treasury	A.
Bureau of Internal Revenue	I.
Navy Department Bureaus	N.
Commissary General of Subsistence	S.
Bureau of Refugees, Freedmen, etc.	F.
Bureau of Military Justice	J.
Supreme Court of the United States	S.
United States Minister to Great Britain	G.
United States Consul General at Montreal	M.
United States Commercial Agent at Port Stanley	P.
British Minister to the United States	B.
Foreign Consuls at Richmond	R.
United States and Mexican Claims Commission	M.
Commissioners for codifying the laws of the United States	C.
United States Coast Survey	C.
United States Internal Revenue Officers	I.
Assistant Treasurers of the United States	T.
Officers of United States Customs	C.
Officers of United States Public Land Service	L.
Officers of United States Indian Service	I.
Officers of United States Pension Service	P.
Headquarters of the Army	A.
Chief Quartermaster Department of the West	W.
Depot Paymaster at New York	N.
Post Commissary at Fort Wayne	W.
Board of Engineers on River and Harbor Improvements	R.
United States Arsenal at San Antonio	S.
Chief Signal Officer of the Army	S.
Regiments and Companies of Cavalry	C.
United States Military Academy	M.
Military Reservation of Fort Garland	G.
Military Post of Camp McGarry	M.
Major Generals	M.
Second lieutenants	L.
Assistant medical purveyors	M.
United States navy-yard at Mare Island	M.
United States East India Squadron	E.
Officers of United States courts, southern district of Ohio	O.
United States attorney, district of Vermont	V.

INDEX LETTERS—Continued.

Postmaster at Fort Wayne	F.
Special agents of the Post-Office Department	P.
Legislative, executive, and judicial officers of the State of Illinois	I.
Officers of city, town, or village of Bentonville	B.
Officers of Gordon Iron Works	G.
Alfred Bolter, proprietor of the Eagle Mills	B.
Benjamin Andrews, publisher of Weekly Review	A.
The New Haven Daily Record	R.
Owners of Steam-ship General Jackson	G.
Business firm of Garrett & Burnes	G and B.
Captain Smith, disbursing officer at Portland	S.
Captain Brown, commanding Company M 56th Infantry	B.
Major Jones, in charge of Snake River improvements	J.
Lieutenant Robinson, in charge of construction of Fort Hale	R.
Experimental board on iron gun-carriages	G.
Special commission on accouterments, equipments, and intrenching tools	A, E. and I.
Board on revision of forms in supply and staff departments	F and S.

Index words.

Abstract from record book of letters received.—**Army**, General of: Submits report of commanding officer Mil. Div. Northwest, of tour of inspection of his command. Indians on Sweetwater discontented and troublesome, and commanding officer Dep't of the West gone there on an expedition; post-traders, in some instances, abuse their privileges; allowance of transportation at Fort Berry insufficient; quarters at posts on the Blue Stone in bad condition; recommendation of commanding officer Dep't of the West for temporary increase of clothing allowance, approved; assignment of Major Leonidas Belden as depot quartermaster at Fort Columbia requested, an early return to their posts of all available detached officers recommended.

Army, General of.
Northwest, Mil. Div.
Inspection of Northwest Mil. Div.
Indian troubles in Div. of Northwest.
West, Dep't of.
Sweetwater River, expedition to.
Post-traders, abuses of.
Transportation at Fort Berry.
Berry, Fort, transportation at.
Quarters at Blue Stone posts.
Blue Stone posts, quarters at.
Clothing allowance in Div. Northwest.
Belden, Major Leonidas.
Quartermaster at Fort Columbia depot.
Columbia, Fort, quartermaster at depot.
Detached officers, Mil. Div. Northwest, return to stations.

Abstract.—**Military Academy**, superintendent of, requests information as to the legal and proper allowances to Board of Visitors.

Military Academy, Board of Visitors' allowances.
Allowances of Board of Visitors.
Visitors, Board of, allowances of.

Abstract.—War Department—Directs that the annual reports be prepared in narrative rather than tabular form; and that the substance of the sub-reports be embodied therein, except where necessary to keep the sub-report separate and entire.

War Department.
Annual Reports.
Reports (see "Annual Reports").
Tabular statements to be mainly omitted from annual reports.
Sub-reports of bureaus to be generally omitted from annual bureau reports.

Alphabetical reference book of decisions and precedents.

Accounts	Disbursing officers; when rendered—1870: 42, 168—1871: 67, 329. Army officers': various rules for settlement—1870: 42, 326, 474—1871: 23. (See "Clothing Accounts.") Settlement of suspended and disallowed, in Treasury Department—1870: 63, 75, 131—1871: 98, 146. (See "Returns.")
Bounty	Deserters'; various questions concerning rights and forfeitures—1870: 261, 576, 782—1871: 4, 33, 87. (See "Pay," "Allowance," "Emolument," etc.) Veteran; various questions relating thereto—1869: 15, 86, 193—1870: 231, 4, 96. (See "Missouri State Militia.")
Clothing Accounts	Volunteer; questions of settlement—1870: 11, 23, 306—1871: 2, 38. Regular; questions of settlement—1870: 43—1871: 181.
Contracts	How made, attested, reported, approved, etc—1870: 63, 76—1871: 41, 99. (See "Beef contracts.") For supplies at military posts; various rules and orders—1870: C 41, B 82, A 164—1871: 331, 487.
Commutation	Allowances of enlisted clerks and messengers—1870: 639, 817. (See "Clothing," "Fuel," "Quarters," "Rations.")
Deserters	Status of, when restored without trial, or charge removed—1870: B 58. (See "Bounty" and "Pay.") Apprehended and transported to depot or post; questions of cost—1870: 11, 36, 48, 325—1871: 264, 487.
Enlistment	Of minors; various rules, questions, and decisions—1870: 78, 138. (See "Discharge," "Minors," "Re-enlistment," etc.)
Funds	Public, in charge of disbursing officers; rules for keeping and for reporting at stated times, etc.—1870: 9, 100, 142—1871: 14, 63, 75. (See "Money.")
Guerrillas	Status of, as compared in various ways with organized forces—1870: 162, 431—1871: 123, 309.
Graves	(See "Cemeteries.")

MONEY AND PROPERTY ACCOUNTS, RETURNS, AND CORRESPONDENCE.

Letters received—accounts and returns.

Date of receipt and file number.	Name of writer.	Date and subject of letter.	Action.
Aug. 18 (176)	War Department	AUGUST 17, 1870. Refers copy of opinion of Attorney-General concerning effects of recent law upon unexpended balances of former appropriations.	Returned to Secretary of War Aug. 20 (L. B., p. 314); received back Aug. 24; circular to division, department, and depot quartermasters Aug. 25 (L. B., 379).
Sept. 11 (177)	Truman, Geo. H., 1st lieutenant 49th Infantry.	FORT BUXTON, DAK., August 31, 1870. Desires to know amount of suspension on his accounts, and to whom he shall pay a sum sufficient to admit of their settlement.	Third Auditor, Sept. 14 (L. B., p. 486); returned Sept. 15; returned to writer Sept. 23 (L. B., p. 499). Filed with 27 of 1870.
Oct. 25 (178)	Auditor, Third	OCTOBER 24, 1870. Recommends certain modifications of the property return, and incloses new form proposed by Captain *Thomas Johnson*, A. Q. M.	Referred to depot quartermasters, N. Y., Phil'a, and Pittsburgh, Oct. 30, for remark; received back Nov. 27; returned to Third Auditor Nov. 29 (L. B., p. 582); received back Dec. 3; Secretary of War, recommended, Dec. 5. See G. O. 153 of 1870.

REMARKS ON THE RECORD BOOKS OF MONEY AND PROPERTY ACCOUNTS, AND OF CORRESPONDENCE RELATING TO ACCOUNTS AND RETURNS.

Book 1 is designed to keep a correct account of all moneys coming into the Treasury to the credit of the bureau, either from regular appropriations or miscellaneous sources, and of all moneys drawn from the Treasury by requisition. An account should be kept with each head of appropriation. A balance struck at any time will show how much is yet in the Treasury subject to draft. An addition of the balances in the Treasury to the balances in possession of disbursing officers at date of last weekly report will show, with sufficient practical correctness, the financial resources of the bureau at any time of the year. Miscellaneous receipts, which revert into the Treasury and are not subject to draft, should not be entered on this ledger, or if entered for any reason, should be offset by an entry in the opposing column, so as to balance the account.

Book 2 is designed to exhibit a statement of the estimates of the disbursing officers of the bureau, together with the amounts allowed them. These estimates need not be recorded in any other book.

Book 3 is designed to keep an account of the receipt of the stated reports and returns from the officers responsible for public money or property, and of the disposition of such as are sent out from the bureau; also to show if any particular returns have not been received in proper season, or if any particular officers have failed to render their returns.

Book 4 is designed to keep an open debit and credit account with every officer receiving, responsible for, or expending public moneys. On one side the United States is to be credited with all sums coming into the possession of the disbursing officer from every source, as well as with all expenditures made by him that are, for the time being, suspended or disallowed; on the other side, the United States is to be debited with all moneys spent by him for whatever purpose, and with all suspensions or disallowances against him, when subsequently removed by refundment or explanation. The account may be balanced or closed at any time. Transfers of money between disbursing officers and others accountable for money or property should be entered singly, so that the entry in one officer's accounts may be checked when the funds are accounted for or reported by the other.

Book 5 is designed to separate the various expenditures of the disbursing officers, so as to show at any time what sums spent by them are chargeable to any designated head of appropriation; what has been spent for purposes not pertaining to the bureau, and what expenditures, not yet approved, can not, for the time being, be assigned to any particular appropriation.

Book 6 is designed to show the actual expenditures for the several distinct purposes of the bureau during the fiscal year. It is an auxiliary to Book 5.

Book 7 is designed to keep an accurate account with other bureaus and appropriations for which moneys have been expended that ought to be refunded.

Book 8 is designed to exhibit the sums received from sales of public property, and their distribution or disposition.

Book 9 is designed to keep an account of the weekly balances of funds in possession of disbursing officers.

In connection with the foregoing books, a book of letters received and of letters sent should be kept for the miscellaneous correspondence relating to money and property accountability in general or particular cases.

When a "request" for a remittance to a disbursing officer has been made, a statement thereof should be entered against the appropriation concerned in Book 1 and against the officer concerned in Book 4. When notice has been received that the remittance has left the Treasury, a check-mark should be placed against the two entries. When the disbursing officer takes up the amount on his money account, the check-marks should be crossed.

When a disbursing officer reports on his money account a transfer of funds to another officer, an entry of the same should be made in Book 4 on the account of each officer, giving the first officer credit for the amount and charging it to the receiving officer. When the latter officer takes up the amount, a check-mark should be placed against both entries.

When a disbursing officer acknowledges on his account the receipt of money from another officer, it should be entered as a credit on the account of the latter in Book 4, and as a charge on the account of the former. When the transferring officers subsequently reports the transfer, a check-mark should be placed against each entry.

When an officer makes report of a sale, and does not inclose a draft for the proceeds, the amount should be charged on his account in Book 4. If he afterward forward the proceeds, the charge on his personal account should be offset by an entry on the opposing side, and a check-mark placed against the several entries in Books 4 and 8. If he take up the proceeds on his next account-current, the check-marks should be made in the same manner.

This check system should be used in every recorded transaction affecting or relating to the responsibility for public money or property, and the foregoing illustrations will, it is thought, sufficiently indicate its utility and mode of operation to officials familiar with the subject of money and property accountability.

Whenever it appears that the public money has been received or expended by any officer with whom no account exists, his name and the particulars will at once be entered in Book 4, the absence of a check-mark being evidence that he has not yet accounted for the money, and its presence being an assurance that his account for it has been rendered. In like manner the name of an officer not previously accountable for public property will be entered in Book 3, with a check-mark under the name of the month in which a return should be rendered, and in the column assigned to the particular form of return required. Upon receipt of any particular return the check-mark can be crossed. An illustration is given of one month only, but the books should be ruled for the twelve months of the year. When returns are rendered at longer intervals than one mouth, places should be ruled for them under the month in which they are due.

No. 1.

The Treasury Department in account with the Quartermaster's Department.

Date.	From what source received or to whom remitted.	On what account.	Total. Dr. Dolls. Cts.	Total. Cr. Dolls. Cts.	Regular supplies. Dr. Dolls. Cts.	Regular supplies. Cr. Dolls. Cts.	Incidental expenses. Dr. Dolls. Cts.	Incidental expenses. Cr. Dolls. Cts.	Cavalry and artillery horses. Dr. Dolls. Cts.	Cavalry and artillery horses. Cr. Dolls. Cts.	Etc. Dr. Dolls. Cts.	Etc. Cr. Dolls. Cts.
July 20	War warrant No. 8	App'n for 1870–'71	12,000,000 00		4,500,000 00		1,000,000 00		800,000 00			
21	Col. W. Roberts, A. Q. M. Gen.	Estimate of funds.		245,765 00		143,260 00		45,460 00		10,000 00		
21	Lieut. J. Rankenflie, 8th Inf. A.A.Q.M.	Sales of property	168 00		93 00				75 00			
22	Capt. F. Taylor, A. Q. M.	Estimate of funds.		87,190 47		38,640 00		21,475 00		7,500 00		
23	Capt. John Schell, 2d Cav	Property lost	12 00		12 00							
23	Wm. Johnston, on treas. sett. No. 2367.	Claim for forage.		38 00		38 00						
25	Capt. M. Ball, 3d Inf., A.A. Q.M.	Estimate of funds.		4,728 13		2,000 00		183 00		1,800 00		
27	Treasury settlement No. 3416	Medical Dep't	219 45		219 45							

No. 2.

Register of estimates of funds.

When received.	By whom made.	For what month required.	Amount of estimate. Dolls.	Amount of estimate. Cts.	Amount allowed. Dolls.	Amount allowed. Cts.	Requisition applied for.
July 25	Capt. F. Taylor, A. Q. M.	February	75,860	42	68,225	00	January 26, 1870
July 27	Major Chas. Davis, C. S.	February	42,500	00	42,500	00	January 28, 1870
July 27	Lieut. Col. G. Tourniquet, Med. Purveyor.	February	3,842	00	3,500	00	January 28, 1870
July 28	Capt. Frank Schell, O. S. K.	February	5,418	66	5,418	66	January 30, 1870
July 28	Thos. J. Hunter, disbursing clerk	February	10,800	00	10,800	00	January 29, 1870

No. 3.

Register of money and property returns received.

File No.	From whom received.	Summary statement.	Report of persons.	Roll of enlisted men.	Report of stores &c.	JANUARY. Account current. When received.	When sent to Treasury.	Vol.	Remarks Page recorded.	Property returns. When received.	When sent to Treasury.	Vol.	Remarks Page recorded.
1534	Capt. F. Taylor, A. Q. M.	✓	✓			Feb. 14	M'ch 11	8	27	Feb. 18	Feb. 20		
1535	Lieut. G. Schneider, 9th Inf'y	✓	✓	✓		Feb. 5	Feb. 20	9	37	Feb. 4	Feb. 5		
1536	Col. W. Roberts, A. Q. M. G.			✓		M'ch 10	Ap'l 17	8	14				
1537	Major Charles Snow, Q. M.	✓	✓		✓	Feb. 15	M'ch 1	8	98	Feb. 28	M'ch 29		

No. 4.

Captain Francis Taylor, A. Q. M., in account with the United States.

Date.	Analysis book. No.	Page.	Debtor.	Amount. Dolls.	Cts.	Date.	Analysis book. No.	Page.	Creditor.	Amount. Dolls.	Cts.
July 1			To balance due on last settlement	$24,250	71	July 31			By amount of expenditures during the month	$98,276	21
22			To Treasury draft No. 1847	87,190	47	8			By transfers to Lieut. W. S. Jones, 2d Artillery, A. A. Q. M.	2,314	09
23		75	To transfer from Captain J. W. Smith, A. Q. M.	4,500	00	11			By transfers to Lieutenant H. Wood, 3d Cavalry, A. A. Q. M.	937	48
	4		To suspensions on money account for May, 1870	521	71		5	70	By removal of suspensions from money accounts for May, 1870.	521	74
25			To sale of public property	165	00	25			By certificate of deposit No. 783, Fourth National Bank, Cairo, Illinois	165	00
			To payment by Lieutenant Thomas Jenkins, 9th Infantry, to settle property accounts	9	42						
	5	39	To suspensions on money accounts for June, 1870	324	18						

No. 5.

Analysis book.

Account current.			Disbursing officer.	Total expenditures.		Fuel.		Forage.		Straw.		Stationery.		Incidental expenses.		Cavalry and artil'y horses.		Army transportation.		Barracks and quarters.		Clothing and equipage.		National cemeteries.		Medical Department.		Ordnance Department.	
Mo.	Abs.	Vou.		$	c.	$	c.	$	c.	$	c.	$	c.	$	c.	$	c.	$	c.	$	c.	$	c.	$	c.	$	c.	$	c.
May	A	1	Capt. F. Taylor, A. Q. M.	651	00	76	18	72	00					56	00			95	00	500	00								
May	A	2	do	72	00																			108	16				
May	A	3	do	108	16																								
May	A	4	do	38	29			38	29																				
May	A	5	do	214	93			46	99	20	99	38	29	47	12														
May	B	1	do	47	12											47	12													
May	B	2	do	96	38															96	38							14	75
May	B	3	do	42	19															13	16	29	03						
May	B	4	do	863	50											863	50					2	50			9	14	8	09
May	B	5	do	2	50																								
May	C	6	do	9	14																								
May	C	7	do	8	09																								
May	C	1	do	9	75																								
May	C	2	do	24	17																									17
May	C	3	do																											
			Allowed	2,187	27	76	18	111	46	99	29	38	29	966	62			204	54	531	53			117	30	17	89	24	17
May	A	4	Capt. F. Taylor, A. Q. M.	38	00	38	00								00					41	00								
May	B	6	do	75	00											75	00													
May	B	8	do	36	41															36	41								
May	B	2	do	275	08																	275	08						
May	C		do	97	25											24	00			18	00	36	00			19	25			
			Suspended	521	74	38	00							99	00			54	41	311	08			19	25			

No. 6.

Statement of approved disbursements from the appropriations for 1870–'71.

Analysis Book.		Month.	By whom disbursed.	Total amount.		Regular supplies.		Incidental expenses.		Cav'y and artillery horses.		Barracks and quarters.		Army transp'n.		&c.	
No.	Page.			Dolls.	Cts.	Dolls.	Cts.	Dolls.	Cts.	Dolls.	Cts.	Dolls.	Cts.	Dolls.	Cts.		
1	70	July, '70	Col. H. T. Waters, A. Q. M. G	1,453	08	251	06	142	15			56	27	379	11		
1	70	July, '70	Maj. C. D. Snow, Q. M	2,714	38	826	40	471	98	600	00	716	33	699	67		
2		July 22, '70	Requisition on treas., sett. No. 7821	864	00	478	00							386	00		

No. 7.

The Medical Department in account with the Quartermaster's Department.

DR.   CR.

In what month paid.	Analysis Book.		Expenditures.	Amount.		Date.	Refundments.	Amount.	
	No.	Page.		Dolls.	Cts.			Dolls.	Cts.
Aug	1	42	Capt. Francis Taylor, A. Q. M	17	89	Sept. 14	By treasury settlement No. 2946	17	89
Sept	2	18	Lt. G. Schneider, 9th Inf., A. A. Q. M	48	65	Oct. 1	" " 3329	287	29
July	1	4	Capt. M. Ball, 3d Inf., A. A. Q. M	287	29	" 8	" " 3147	48	65
	1	78	Major Chas. Snow, Q. M	8	55				
Aug	1	57	Lieut. Timothy Dexter, 4th Art., A. Q. M	92	33				

No. 8.

Record of sales of public property.

Date of sale	By whom sold.	Where sold.	Gross receipts.		Expenses of sale.		Net proceeds.		Regular supplies.		Incidental expenses.		Cavalry and artillery horses.		Barracks and quarters.		Army transportation.				Clothing and equipage.				Turned into Treasury.		Certificate of deposit.	
																	Draught animals.		Other means of transportation.		Clothing.		Equipage.				When received.	When sent to War Department.
			$	c.	$	c.	$	c.	$	c.	$	c.	$	c.	$	c.	$	c.	$	c.	$	c.	$	c.	$	c.		
July 25	Capt. F. Taylor, A.Q.M.	Nashville, Tenn.	180	00	15	00	165	00	40	00	...	...	60	00	35	00	22	00	...	...	...	...	14	00	...	...	Aug. 10	Aug. 15
July 28	Lt. G. Schneider, 9th Inf.	Fort Smith, Ark.	216	20	8	00	208	20	63	00	9	26	...	...	67	21	...	...	21	...	16	00	8	10	...	...	Aug. 30	Sept. 3

No. 9.

Statement of public funds in possession of officers of the Quartermaster's Department for the week ending July 23, 1870.

Report received.	Name of officer.	Station.	Amount on hand.		Where deposited.
			Dolls.	Cts.	
1870, Aug. 1	Col. George Gordon, A. Q. M. G.	San Francisco, Cal.	321,464	19	Sub-treasury, San Francisco, $321,425.08; office safe $17.11.
Aug. 3	Lt. Col. Dwight Foiley, D. Q. M. G.	Austin, Texas	86,524	06	Sub-treasury, N. O., $51,216.93; 1st Nat. Bk., Austin, $35,307.13.
Aug. 25	Major Robert Roe, Q. M.	Portland, Oregon	27,191	38	Sub-treasury, San Francisco, $8,040.00; 2d Nat. Bk., Portland, $19,191.38.

Exhibit B.

DECISIONS OR PRECEDENTS.

SAMPLES OF CARD-INDEX.

Claim—Information to prove or found a claim refused.

December 9, 1881, Hon. Mr. F. refers to the War Department letter from G., attorney-at-law, asking information in regard to service of M., who enlisted in Michigan regiment.

December 21, 1881, the Secretary of War (by indorsement to F.) states that while no information is furnished to individuals tending to found or prove a claim against the United States, such record as may be on file will be cheerfully furnished to any Department before which a case may be pending. The Secretary states that the regulation is of long standing, and its constant observance is considered necessary for the proper protection of the public interests. He also refers to the great labor involved in a compliance with the request of G., the number of the regiment not being given, and the names of the Michigan soldiers not being indexed at the Department, and the time required to comply with the request could not be spared, in view of the pressure upon the clerical force engaged in answering inquiries from the Pension Office respecting soldiers whose regiments and companies are known. (17765. W. D. 1881.)

Clerk as a witness before district court allowed pay.

In case of G., clerk, Surgeon-General's Office, who was granted twenty days' leave of absence without pay, upon being summoned to appear before the United States district court at Yankton, Dak., to testify on behalf of the United States, G. requested upon his return that leave with pay be substituted for leave without pay. The matter was referred to the First Comptroller for decision, who, on January 17, 1884, returned the papers, indorsed "G. is entitled to his salary for the time he was absent within." (5448. A. 1883.)

Decision not to be re-opened.

The Attorney-General decided that a final decision, upon a knowledge of the facts, by an officer authorized to decide on claims against the Government, is not to be re-opened and reviewed by his successors in office, except for the correction of mistakes, such as errors in calculation, etc. (See 14 Opin. Atty. Genl., p. 275.)

Executive Departments—General investigation of.

In the matter of investigation by committees of the House of Representatives, see the letter of President Jackson to Hon. Henry A. Wise, dated January 26, 1837, published on page 29 of House Report No. 194, Twenty-fourth Congress, second session (vol. 215), a document of 91 pages with an appendix of 154 pages. President Jackson refused the privilege to a committee of the House to make a general investigation of the Executive Departments without specific charges, on the ground, among others, that the use of the books, papers, etc., of the Departments for such purpose would interfere with the discharge of the public duties devolving upon the heads of the different Departments.

Executive functions at Washington and elsewhere.

In House Ex. Doc. 162, Forty-fourth Congress, first session, is published the message of President Grant of May 4, 1876, in response to the resolution of the House, declining to give the specific information called for, but giving a memorandum of the absence of the President of the United States from the national capital during each of the several administrations, and of public and executive acts performed during the time of such absence.

Holidays in District of Columbia.

The following are holidays in the District of Columbia: New Year's Day, Washington's Birthday, Fourth of July, Christmas Day, Thanksgiving Day, Inauguration Day. (See Revised Statutes of District of Columbia, section 993, page 116; see 20 United

States Statutes, page 277; see act of June 18, 1888, amending section 993, Revised Statutes of District of Columbia. Volume 22, United States Statutes, page 1, provides that whenever any day set apart as a legal holiday in the District of Columbia shall fall on the first day of the week, commonly called Sunday, then in such event the next succeeding day shall be a holiday within the District of Columbia.

Minor—When enlistment is void ab initio.

(5246. W. D. 1874.) July 11, 1874, upon the application for the discharge of M., a minor, the Secretary of War referred to previous decisions of the Department, in which it was held that the enlistment of a minor was void *ab initio* when sufficient evidence is furnished that the enlistment was without the consent of the parent or guardian.

"When sufficient evidence of the facts above referred to is furnished there can no longer be any justifiable grounds for retaining him in service or for punishing him for offenses against military law and discipline committed while so held. Not being legally an enlisted man he can not be guilty of desertion, and he should be discharged unconditionally; but this does not relieve him from the liability to answer for civil offenses before the proper courts and upon civil process."

Officer as a witness before district court.

June 23, 1884, upon the inquiry of Major M. in regard to his pay while attending as a witness before the district court of El Paso, Tex., before which he had been subpœnaed, the following indorsement was placed:

Respectfully returned to the commanding-general, Department of Texas, giving authority to Major M. to obey the subpœnas within mentioned for a reasonable time, providing his military services can be spared, and this without reduction from his current pay. In reference to the inquiry of Major M., in the last paragraph of the fourth indorsement, the Secretary of War is of opinion that there is no reason for giving duty-pay to an officer subpœnaed as a witness in a civil suit in which the Government is not concerned while the officer is on leave of absence. (2815 C 1884.)

Papers for Court of Claims—Rule.

July 23, 1875, the Attorney-General, in a letter to the Secretary of War, states that "immediately on receipt of petitions in cases in the Court of Claims a copy is sent to the proper Department with a report. It often happens that subsequently an order of the court is issued for copies of all, or some of the same papers already furnished this Department by you. In such cases, in order to save labor to your Department, instead of sending to this Department duplicates of the report to the court, it will be sufficient that you inform me of the papers sent to the court by you of which copies have already been furnished to this Department."

Papers—General Court Martial Record.

December 7, 1883, the Judge Advocate-General stated that he had been directed by the Adjutant-General to send a clerk of his bureau to Yankton, Dak., with a record of general court martial in the case of William S. Kelley, for the purpose of identifying the same before the United States district court at that place, and requested information as to the transportation and other expenses of said clerk.

This was returned to the Judge Advocate-General with the following indorsement:

"Upon conference with the proper official at the Department of Justice it is learned that the proper method to pursue in the matter within presented is as follows: The Judge Advocate-General should furnish the clerk who may be selected for the purpose with an official letter instructing him to proceed to Yankton and specifying for what purpose. The clerk should keep a careful itemized account of his necessary expenditures and upon his return should present the same properly certified to the Department of Justice, from which he will obtain reimbursement as provided by section 850 of the Revised Statutes."

Papers—original—not to be sent from Department.

Upon the request of the clerk of the House Committee on War Claims of April 17, 1876, addressed to the Commissary-General, requesting all papers in the claim of E., the Secretary of War declined "to permit these original papers to go from the Department, but copies may be furnished if call is regularly made on the head of the Department."

On December 14, 1881, a request was received from the clerk of the Senate Committee on Claims addressed to General M., for the papers in the case of the legal representatives of B, and a similar decision was made by the Secretary of War. (4002 W. D. 1876 and 12068 W. D. 1881.)

Papers—Originals or copies not to be furnished from files of House of Representatives unless consent of the House is first obtained.

See House Report No. 1, Forty-sixth Congress, first session, where a subpœna issued by a judge-advocate of a general court martial to the file clerk of the House of Representatives directing him to produce certain original papers, the House of Representatives resolved that before either original or copies of papers could be furnished the consent of the House must first be obtained.

Papers—Original—Sent to committees of Congress.

March 18, 1886, ordered that in sending original papers to the committees of Congress the attention of the committee will be invited to the fact that the accompanying papers are originals and pertain to the files of the War Department, and to request that while they remain in its custody they be kept inaccessible to persons other than members of the committee having the bill in charge, and that when they shall have served the purpose for which they are desired they be promptly returned to the Department.

Papers—Original—Rule as to furnishing.

December 1, 1876, the Secretary of War informed the Attorney-General by letter that "The rule of the Department is not to furnish original papers from its files, except in cases where they are to be used as evidence for the United States, and then only by the hands of a clerk of the Government, to be by him returned to the files when they are no longer required, and not to pass out of his possession." (11016 W. D. 1876.)

Papers—Privileged communications.

In case of civil suit for libel, McGhan vs. Clephane, the following questions were submitted to the Attorney-General for decision:
(1) Whether the head of a Department is bound in law to produce in court as evidence in private controversies the archives, records, or papers on file in such Department and relating to its administration.
(2) Whether the paper referred to within, if it be a letter addressed to the Assistant Secretary of War on a matter relating to the administration of said Department and to the public interest and not published by the writer to any other person, is or is not in the nature of a privileged communication which the head of the Department is or is not bound to produce under this process.
To which inquiries the Attorney-General replied as follows:
"Letters on file with the heads of Departments are privileged communications; unless their publication has been authorized no copies should be taken at private request and the production of the originals can not be compelled in a suit between individuals. It has been ruled that such communications can not be made the foundation of an action for libel. Then I think the head of a Department is bound not to produce a letter on file in his office.
"Such a letter as you describe is a privileged communication." (4595 W. D. 1876.)
The above decision was affirmed by Hon. A. B. Olin, justice supreme court, District of Columbia, in the following language:
* * * "I have come to the conclusion to deny this application to compel the production of this paper."

Pay of officers during the Revolutionary war.

For schedule of pay and emoluments of officers of the Revolutionary war prepared by chief clerk, Paymaster-General's Office, October 24, 1818. See vol. 1, American State Papers, Military Affairs, pages 793-796, inclusive. This table is much more complete than the one published in vol. 3 (fifth series), American Archives, page 1505. (Indorsement of P. M. G. of February 18, 1873, on 1276, W. D., 1873.)

Promotion of clerks—Grounds for recommendation to be stated.

In the matter of the recommendations of the Surgeon-General for promotion of C. and M. the papers were on June 1, 1882, returned by indorsement to the Surgeon-General: "The Secretary of War directs that in all recommendations for promotion the grounds of such recommendations should be briefly stated."

Reports.

(1) The President communicates information on the state of the Union to Congress under section 3, Article II of the Constitution.

(2) The heads of Departments are required to make annual reports of the expenditures of contingent funds under section 193, Revised Statutes.

(3) Section 194 requires an annual report of the names of clerks and other employés employed.

(4) The time of making annual reports is fixed by section 195, Revised Statutes.

(5) Section 196, Revised Statutes, prescribes the time when reports of the Department and reports of the chiefs of bureaus shall be furnished to the Public Printer.

(6) Sections 228, 229, 230, 231, and 232, Revised Statutes, prescribe certain reports which shall be made by the Secretary of War.

(7) Section 3788, Revised Statutes, provides in what manner the reports shall be printed.

Supplies for War Department and bureaus.

Extract from War Department indorsement to Quartermaster-General.

* * * "Such repairs of buildings as do not require immediate attention should be estimated for.

"Inasmuch as the appropriation for contingent expenses of the office of the Secretary of War, and the bureaus, buildings, and offices of the War Department must be disbursed under the direct supervision of the Secretary of War, the circular of June 28, 1883, will be adhered to, as it was the intention of Congress in making the appropriation for the contingent expenses of the War Department under one head, to centralize the purchase of supplies with a view of securing the lowest prices. In exceptional cases the chiefs of bureaus will be authorized to procure such special supplies as they may desire on report being made showing the reasons therefor." (3734. A. 1883.)

Titles to land—Secretary of War may employ and pay conveyancers to examine.

June 13, 1871, the question of the power of the Secretary of War in this connection being submitted to the Attorney-General for decision, Assistant Attorney-General Hill, on June 17, rendered the opinion which was approved by the Acting Attorney-General Bristow. Mr. Hill quotes previous opinions of the Attorney-Generals (11 Ops., 433, and 12 Ops., 416), holding that the Secretary of War had authority to employ and pay counsel for such services; and regarding the claim in question, that of B. for drawing and procuring the passage of an act through the Legislature of Connecticut ceding jurisdiction to the United States of the land bought, and examining the title to such land, which services the district attorney was not obliged to perform, and the Secretary of War was authorized to remunerate him for performing such services or else to employ other counsel, and the fee to be paid is a matter under the exclusive control of the Department which employed him. (12 Ops., 401.) Mr. Hill further holds that the act of June 22, 1870, relative to the employment of counsel, does not apply to such peculiar services as the examination of a title to land, such services generally requiring special and peculiar knowledge, etc.

After further reference to the law Mr. Hill says, "construing this provision of the section with the previous one, strengthens my conclusion that the services of a conveyancer are not included within its terms, and that therefore the Secretary of War may, in his discretion, employ conveyancers to examine titles notwithstanding the provisions of this act."

Transportation of public property by "private parties."

The post-quartermaster at Fort Monroe reports that the commanding officer of the arsenal there has turned over to him, for shipment to New York, 49,000 pounds of iron skids, which will have to be transported to destination by private parties, and requests an interpretation of the law in this case, and whether General Orders 65, A. G. O., 1884, fourth page, applies to shipments of this character.

The Quartermaster-General is of the opinion that the inviting of bids by posters and circular letters would be sufficient advertisement in the meaning of the law for small quantities of freight. In this case the amount is less than 25 tons of freight, and where very considerable quantities are to be transported advertisements in newspapers should be resorted to.

This was indorsed as follows:

"The Secretary of War concurs in the views of the Quartermaster-General.

"For the purpose of this act a corporation or person conducting the business of transportation in such manner as to be regarded in law as a 'common carrier' is not a private party. A common carrier may in general be defined as one who undertakes for hire to carry persons or goods for all who choose to employ him, not one who only does it occasionally. The Secretary of War thinks, however, that a private schooner not having an established route or stated points of departure and arrival should be regarded as a 'private party' within the meaning of the act." (4625 A 1884.)

War Department—Building burned.

On Saturday evening, November 8, 1800, the War Department building, with the records and files, was consumed by fire. (See Order Book, vol. 1, p. 1, and Miscellaneous Letters, vol. 1, p. 63, and American State Papers, Misc., vol. 1, p. 232.)

On Thursday, August 22, 1814, the War and State Department records and files were removed, and it is presumed that the buildings were burned by the British forces on August 24, 1814. (Reports of Congress, vol. 1, p. 417.)

November 9, 1814, the Secretary of War reported to the Speaker of the House that all the books of record had been saved, and that no papers of any kind were lost except recommendations for appointment in the Army, and letters received more than seven years previous. (Reports to Congress, vol. 1, p. 310, and American State Papers, Misc., vol. 2, p. 250.)

February 14, 1815, the Senate passed a bill making an appropriation of $500,000 for repairing or rebuilding the public buildings in the city of Washington, which was signed by the Speaker of the House on February 15, 1815, and approved by the President on the same day. (See Senate and House Journals, third session, Thirteenth Congress, p. 352 and pp. 652 and 676.)

War of rebellion—Date of opening and closing.

The following is an extract from letter of the Adjutant-General, dated February 24, 1883, to General C.:
* * * "The 15th of April, 1861, is usually held to be the date on which the war opened. The Supreme Court of the United States has decided that the war of the rebellion closed on August 20, 1866, the date on which the President issued his proclamation declaring the insurrection at an end." (517, A. G. O., 1883. See sec. 2, act of June 23, 1870, 16 Stats., p. 167.) In all States except Texas on April 2, 1866 (9 Wallace, 56), and in Texas, August 20, 1866 (12 Wallace, 700).

War of rebellion—Number of prisoners, Union and Confederate, and deaths of.

July 19, 1866, the Secretary of War, in a letter to the Speaker of the House of Representatives, stated that it appears from the report of the Commissary-General of Prisoners that 26,436 deaths of rebel prisoners of war are reported, and 22,576 Union soldiers are reported as having died in Southern prisons. The reports also show that 220,000 rebel prisoners were held in the North, and 126,940 Union prisoners were held in the South. (See House Ex. Doc. 152, first session, Thirty-ninth Congress.)

War of rebellion—Strength of Army.

A statement of the strength of the Army at various dates is published on page 102, message and documents (Thirty-ninth Congress, first session) War Department, part 3, 1865-'66, being report of the provost-marshal-general. This report shows that the highest number of men borne on the rolls of the Army was 1,000,516, May 1, 1865. (See report of the Adjutant-General on 9876—W. D., 1878.)

The total number of men furnished for the Union Army during the war, reduced to a three years' standard, was 2,135,605. Number in rebel service can not be stated with accuracy. (See 10272, W. D., 1878.)

INDEX TO DECISIONS OR PRECEDENTS.

Advertisements by circulars or posters. (*See* Transportation.)
Annual reports. (*See* Reports.)
Appropriation for rebuilding War Department. (*See* War.)
Army officer as witness before district court. (*See* Officer.)
Army, strength of during late war. (*See* War.)
Building, War Department, burned. (*See* War.)
Bureaus, call addressed to, for original papers. (*See* Papers.)
Bureaus of War Department. (*See* Supplies.)
Clerks, recommendation for promotion must state grounds. (*See* Promotion.)
Common carriers defined. (*See* Transportation.)
Congress, original papers to committees of. (*See* Papers.)
Contingent fund, War Department, to be expended under direct supervision of the Secretary of War. (*See* Supplies.)
Controversies, production of papers. (*See* Papers.)
Conveyancers may be employed by the Secretary of War to examine titles to land. (*See* Titles.)
Court of Claims, papers for. (*See* Papers.)
Court-martial record. (*See* papers.)
Deaths of prisoners. (*See* War.)
Departments, investigation of. (*See* Executive.)
Discharge of minor. (*See* Minor.)
District of Columbia. (*See* Holidays.)
Enlistment of minor. (*See* Minor.)
Expenses of clerk in charge of papers before court. (*See* Papers.)
Fire, War Department building burned. (*See* War.)
House of Representatives, original papers from files. (*See* Papers.)
Information to found or prove a claim refused. (*See* Claim.)
Investigation of Executive Departments. (*See* Executive.)
Land, conveyancers may be employed by Secretary of War to examine title to. (*See* Titles.)
Letter transmitting original papers to Congress. (*See* Papers.)
Letters, what are privileged communications. (*See* Papers.)
Official letters, what are privileged communications. (*See* Papers.)
Original papers from files of House of Representatives. (*See* Papers.)
Original papers not to be sent from Department. (*See* Papers.)
Original papers to committees of Congress. (*See* Papers.)
Original papers, when furnished. (*See* Papers.)
Pay to clerk, a witness before district court. (*See* Clerk.)
Pay status of officer, a witness before district court. (*See* Officer.)
Posters, advertisement by. (*See* Transportation.)
Presidents, absence of, from Washington. (*See* Executive.)
President declines to permit investigation of Executive Departments without specific charges. (*See* Executive.)
Prisoners during late war. (*See* War.)
Private controversies, production of papers. (*See* Papers.)
Private parties, construction of works. (*See* Transportation.)
Privileged communications. (*See* Papers.)
Public property, transportation of, by "private parties." (*See* Transportation.)
Rebellion, strength of the Army. (*See* War.)
Rebellion, war of, date of opening and closing. (*See* War.)
Records and files burned. (*See* War.)
Records saved except those for seven years prior to 1814. (*See* War.)
Review of decision. (*See* Decision.)
Revolution, pay of officers during. (*See* Pay.)
Rule as to original papers to be used as evidence. (*See* Papers.)
Rule as to papers for Court of Claims. (*See* Papers.)
Salary of a clerk as witness before district court. (*See* Clerk.)
Salary of officer, witness before district court. (*See* Officer.)
Witness before district court. (*See* Clerk.)
Witness before district court. (*See* Officer.)

Exhibit C.

LIST OF SUBJECTS.

The following list of subjects has been taken from the index book of letters received in the office of the Secretary of War for the year 1888.

The subjects are here arranged by principal subjects and subdivisions thereof. The words in bold-face type in the column of "subjects" are the principal subjects under which record cards should be filed. The words in italics, in same column, are the subdivisions, and these words will follow the principal subject at the head of the record cards.

It will be seen that this is not a complete list, but it suggests a comparatively easy way to insert other subjects or subdivisions at their proper places.

In practice the brief on the paper will be copied on the record card, and the paper charged and sent at once to the proper person. Then the caption of the card, viz: The principal subjects and subdivisions followed by proper name will be determined, and inserted at the top of the card with the aid of a list like this; then the proper cross reference cards will be prepared. Of course, as explained in the body of the report, the number of cross reference cards will be largely reduced by a careful arrangement of subjects. When there are several subdivisions of a principal subject, and one of them represents a class about which there is a large correspondence, it may become necessary to insert it in the list of principal subjects and except it from the subdivisions. Thus, "Bridge" falls under the principal subject "Engineering;" the amount of business falling under the title "Bridge" may make it desirable to have a subject devoted to that title. So with "Railroads," they fall under the subject "Transportation," but it may in practice be necessary to have a subject "Railroad" instead of that word being a subdivision of the subject "Transportation."

Subject.	Subdivision.	Subject.	Subdivision.
Attorney	Agents, powers of.	*Artillery*	See Army.
Absence	Leaves.	**Auctions**	Auctioneers.
Accounts	Balances, checks, depositories, interest, national banks, Treasury drafts.	*Auctioneers*	See Auctions.
		Army Dispensaries.	See Medical.
		Balances	See Accounts.
Advertising and Accounts.	See Advertisements.	*Balloons*	See Aerial vessels.
		Bands	See Music.
Advertisements	Advertising and accounts.	*Beef*	See Subsistence.
Aerial Vessels	Air ships, balloons, flying machines.	*Biographical Annals.*	See Books.
		Blanks	
Agents	See Attorneys.	**Boards**	Boards of survey.
Aides-de-Camp	See Army.	*Boards of Survey*	See Boards.
Air Ships	See Aerial vessels.	*Boats*	See Vessels.
Allotments	See Appropriations.	*Bonds of Indemnity.*	See Bonds.
Ammunition	Cartridges, percussion fuse, powder, primers, projectiles, shells, shot.	**Bonds**	Bondsmen, bonds of indemnity, surety company.
Animals	See Transportation.	*Bondsmen*	See Bonds.
Annual Reports		**Books***	Biographical Annals, Century Magazine, Congressional Directory, Congressional Globe, Directories, Manual, Manual of Strategy, Rebellion Records.
Anonymous			
Appropriations	Allotments, deficiencies, estimates, incidental expenses.		
Aqueterra	See Medicines.		
Aqueduct	See Engineering.	*Bran*	See Forage.
Archives	See Records.	*Brass*	See Metals.
Arlington (Res'n)	See Lands.	*Breakwaters*	See Engineering.
Arms	Cannon, carbines, guns, Gatling guns, gun-carriages, gun-sights, Hotchkiss gun, howitzers, mitrailleuse, muskets, revolvers, rifles, Rubén repeating rifle, shotguns, swords.	*Bread*	See Subsistence.
		Bridges	See Engineering.
		British subjects	See Foreign.
		Bugles	See Music.
		Buildings	Army building, foundries, hotels, kilns, mantels, observatories, plumbing, rooms, saloons, sheds, urinals.
Army	Aide-de-camp, artillery, cavalry, chaplains, enlisted men, infantry, lieutenancies, non-commissioned officers, officers, officers deceased, officers retired, rank, retired-list, soldiers.		
		Copper	See Metals.
		Canals	See Engineering.
		Cannon	See Arms.
		Carbines	See Arms.
Army Building	See Buildings.	*Cartridges*	See Ammunition.
Army Regulations	See Regulations.	*Cattle*	See Subsistence.

*It may be preferable to embrace books in a subdivision of "Publications," and thus include "Newspapers" and "Pamphlets" in the same subdivision.

Subject.	Subdivision.	Subject.	Subdivision.
Cavalry	See Army.	Fire	Fire-extinguishers, fire-plugs, perfect hand fire-extinguishers.
Cemeteries	Headstones.		
Century Magazine	See Books.		
Chaplains	See Army.	Fish	Salmon fishing, salmon cannery, salmon-packing station, fishways.
Checks	See Accounts.		
Cholera	See Medical.		
Christmas	See Holidays.	Fishways	See Fish.
Circulars	See Orders.	Flags	Flag-staff, colors.
Claims	Claim division.	Flag-staffs	See Flags.
Claim division	See Claims.	Flour	See Subsistence.
Clerks	See Employés.	Flumes	See Engineering.
Clothing	Collars, epaulets, gauntlets, gloves, helmets, kersey, leggings, mittens, shoes, uniform.	Flying-machines	See Aerial vessels.
		Forage	Bran, hay, straw.
		Foreign	British subjects, Dutch army, foreign countries, French army, German army, Peruvian troops.
Coal	See Fuel.		
Collars	See Clothing.		
Colleges		Foreign countries	See Foreign.
Colors	See Flags.	Foremen	See Employés.
Confederate archives.	See Records.	Fortifications	See Forts.
		Forts	Fortifications.
Congressional Directory.	See Books.	Foundries	See Buildings.
		Frauds	Stealing.
Congressional Globe	See Books.	French army	See Foreign.
Congress	Senate, House of Representatives.	Freight	Express.
		Fuel	Coal.
Copyists	See Employés.	Funeral expenses	
Courts-martial	See Courts.	Furniture	Desks, book-shelves.
Courts	Courts-martial.	Guns	See Arms.
Cows	See Subsistence.	Gas	Gas-fixtures.
Cyclostyle	See Stationery.	Gas-fixtures	See Gas.
Dams	See Engineering.	Gatling guns	See Arms.
Decoration Day	Memorial day.	Gauntlets	See Clothing.
Deficiencies	See Appropriations.	Gentian (Med.)	See Medical.
Depositories	See Accounts.	German army	See Foreign.
Desertion	Deserters.	Gloves	See Clothing.
Deserters*	See Desertion.	Gauges	See Instruments.
Desks	See Furniture.	Gun-carriages	See Arms.
Dikes	See Engineering.	Gun-sights	See Arms.
Directories	See Books.	Hams	See Subsistence.
Dispensaries, Army	See Medical.	Harbors	See Engineers.
Ditches	See Engineering.	Haversacks	See Equipments.
Docks	See Engineering.	Hay	See Forage.
Draughtsmen	See Employés.	Headstones	See Cemeteries.
Draw (iron bridge)	See Engineering.	Hektographs	See Stationery.
Drayage	See Transportation.	Helmets	See Clothing.
Dredging	See Engineering.	Horses	See Transportation.
Dredges	See Engineering.	Hospitals	See Medical.
Drums	See Music.	Hospital stewards	See Medical.
Dutch army	See Foreign.	Hospital Corps	See Medical.
Dynamite sky-rocket	See Explosives.	Hotels	See Buildings.
Eight-hour law	See Law.	Hotchkiss gun	See Arms.
Electricity	Electric lights.	House of Representatives.	See Congress.
Electric lights	See Electricity.		
Embalming	See Medical.	Howitzer	See Arms.
Employés	Clerks, copyists, draughtsmen, foremen, interpreters, labor, laborers, messengers, overseers, Q. M. agents, watchmen.	Hydraulic mining	See Engineering.
		Hydraulic excavation.	See Engineering.
		Homes	Soldiers' homes, veterans' homes.
Engineers	See Engineering.	Holidays	Christmas.
Enlisted men	See Army.	Iron	See Metals.
Envelopes	See Stationery.	Ice	
Epaulets	See Clothing.	Ice machines	See Machines.
Equipments	Haversack, knives, saddles, waist-belt.	Incidental expenses	See Appropriations.
		Indians	Indian agencies, Indian reservations, Indian Territory.
Estimates	See Appropriations.		
Extra-duty pay	See Pay.	Indian agencies	See Indians.
Explosives	Dynamite sky-rocket.	Indian reservations	See Indians.
Express	See Freight.	Indian reservation boundaries.	See Indians.
Engineering	Aqueduct, breakwaters, bridges, canals, dams, dikes, ditches, docks, draw-bridge, dredging, dredges, engineers, flumes, harbors, hydraulic mining, jetties, levees, locks, piers, piles, rivers and harbors, riprap stone, rivers, roads.		
		Indian Territory	See Indians.
		Infantry	See Army.
		Ink	See Stationery.
		Inspections	Inspectors.
		Instruments	Microscopes, gauges.
		Interest	See Accounts.
		Interpreters	See Employés.
File-boxes	See Stationery.	Inventions	
Fire-extinguishers	See Fire.	Jetties	See Engineering.
Fire-plugs	See Fire.	Journeys	See Transportation.

*This subject and subdivision might be included in the subject "Army."

Subject.	Subdivision.	Subject.	Subdivision.
Jurors	See Law.	Perfect hand fire-extinguisher.	See Fire.
Kersey	See Clothing.	Pencils	See Stationery.
Kilns	See Building.	Percussion fuse	See Ammunition.
Knives	See Equipments.	Peruvian troops	See Foreign.
Knights	See Societies.	Petroleum	See Oil.
Laborers	See Employés.	Photographs	See Pictures.
Lands	Arlington.	Pictures	Photographs, portraits.
Lathes	See Tools.	Piers	See Engineering.
Law	Statutes, Revised Statutes, law books, eight-hour law, jurors, notaries public.	Piles	See Engineering.
		Plumbing	See Building.
		Ponies	See Transportation.
Law books	See Law.	Portraits	See Pictures.
Leaves	See Absence.	Postage	Postage-stamps, postal notes.
Leggings	See Clothing.	Postage-stamps	See Postage.
Levees	See Engineering.	Postal-notes	See Postage.
Lieutenancies	See Army.	Post	Post funds, post-offices, postmasters, post traders, post schools.
Liquor.			
Litters	See Medical.		
Locks and dams	See Engineering.	Post-offices	See Post.
Memorial Day	See Decoration Day.	Postmasters	See Post.
Machines	Copying-presses, ice-machines.	Post traders	See Post.
		Post schools	See Post.
Macaroni	See Subsistence.	Potatoes	See Subsistence.
Mails		Powers of attorney	See Attorney.
Mantels	See Buildings.	Presses, copying	See Machines.
Manual	See Books.	Primers	See Ammunition.
Manual of Strategy	See Books.	Printing	Printers.
Mares	See Transportation.	Printers	See Printing.
Medals		Prisoners	Prisoners of war.
Meats	See Subsistence.	Prisoners of war	See Prisoners.
Measles	See Medical.	Projectiles	See Ammunition.
Medical	Attendants, aqueterra, medical books, medical certificates, dispensaries, embalming, gentian, hospital, hospital corps, hospital steward, litters, medicines, measles, nurses, salve or ointment, vaccine virus, cholera, yellow fever.	Publications	
		Public animals	See Transportation.
		Powder	See Ammunition.
		Quartermaster's agents.	See Employés.
		Quarters.	
		Railroads	See Transportation.
		Rank	See Army.
		Rations	See Subsistence.
		Rebellion Records	See Books.
Medical attendants	See Medical.	Rebel Archives	See Records.
Medical books	See Medical.	Records	Archives, Confederate Archives, Rebel Archives.
Medical certificates	See Medical.		
Medical supplies	See Medical.	Revolutionary war	See War.
Medicines	See Medical.	Retired-list	See Army.
Memoranda		Reunions	See Societies.
Messengers	See Employés.	Revolvers	See Arms.
Metals	Brass, copper, iron.	Rifles	See Arms.
Microscopes	See Instruments.	Rivers and harbors	See Engineering.
Mileage	See Transportation.	Riprap stones	See Engineering.
Militia.		Rivers	See Engineering.
Mineral oil	See Oil.	Roads	See Engineering.
Mittens	See Clothing.	Rooms	See Buildings.
Mitrailleuse	See Arms.	Rogue River war	See War.
Mules	See Transportation.	Ruben repeating rifles.	See Arms.
Music	Bands, bugles, drums, trumpets.	Rules and regulations.	See Regulations.
Muskets	See Arms.		
Museums		Regulations	Army regulations, Rules and regulations.
National Banks	See Accounts.		
Naval	Naval vessels, naval veterans, Naval War College.	Saloons	See Buildings.
		Saddles	See Equipments.
		Salve or ointment	See Medical.
Naval vessels	See Naval.	Salmon packing stations.	See Fish.
Naval veterans	See Naval		
Naval War College	See Naval.	Salmon fishing	See Fish.
Newspapers		Salmon cannery	See Fish.
Notaries public	See Law.	Schools	School teachers.
Nurses	See Medical.	School teachers	See Schools.
Oaken book-shelves	See Furniture.	Senate	See Congress.
Observatories	See Buildings.	Sheds	See Buildings.
Officers of the Army	See Army.	Shells	See Ammunition.
Officers deceased	See Army.	Shoes	See Clothing.
Officers non-com'd	See Army.	Shot-guns	See Arms.
Officers retired	See Army.	Shot	See Ammunition.
Oil	Mineral oil, petroleum.	Signal	Signal Corps, Signal Service, signal stations, signal stores.
Omnibuses	See Transportation.		
Orders	Circulars.		
Ordnance stores	See Ordnance.		
Ordnance	Stores.	Signal corps	See Signal.
Overseers	See Employés.	Signal stations	See Signal.
Pay and allowances	See Pay.	Signal Service	See Signal.
Pay	Extra duty, allowances.	Signal stores	See Signal.

Subject.	Subdivision.	Subject	Subdivision.
Signals	*See* Signal.	*Telegraph Operators.*	*See* Telegraph.
Sleeping-car accommodations.	*See* Transportation.	*Telegraphical Sig.-Code.*	*See* Telegraph.
Societies	Knights, Reunions.	*Tobacco Supply*	*See* Subsistence.
Soldiers	*See* Army.	**Tools**	Lathes.
Soldiers' Home	*See* Home.	**Transportation**	Animals, drayage, horses, journeys, mares, mileage, mules, omnibuses, ponies, public animals, railroads, sleeping-cars, street-cars, wagons.
Stationery	Cyclostyle, envelopes, file-boxes, hektographs, ink, pencils.		
Statistics.			
Statutes, Revised	*See* Law.		
Statutes	*See* Law.		
States and Territories.		*Treasury drafts*	*See* Accounts.
		Trumpets	*See* Music.
Stealing	*See* Frauds.	*Tug-boats*	*See* Vessels.
Steamers	*See* Vessels.	*Uniforms*	*See* Clothing.
Straw	*See* Forage.	*Urinals*	*See* Buildings.
Street cars	*See* Transportation.	*Vaccine virus*	*See* Medical.
Subsistence	Beef, bread, cattle, cows, flour, hams, meats, potatoes, rations, macaroni, stores, Subsistence Department, tobacco, vegetables, yeast powder.	*Vegetables*	*See* Subsistence.
		Vessels	Boats, steamers, tug-boats, wrecks.
		Veterans' Home	*See* Home.
		Waist belt	*See* Equipments.
Subsistence stores	*See* Subsistence.	*Wagons*	*See* Transportation.
Subsistence department.	*See* Subsistence.	**Wars**	Revolutionary, Rogue River War.
Swords	*See* Arms.	**Water**	
Targets		*Watchman*	*See* Employés.
Taxes		*Wrecks*	*See* Vessels.
Telephones		*Yellow fever*	*See* Medical.
Telegrams	*See* Telegraph.	*Yeast powder*	*See* Subsistence.
Telegraph	Telegraph operators, telegrams, telegraphical signal code.		

EXHIBIT D.

SPECIMENS OF CROSS-REFERENCE CARDS. SIZE, 3½ INCHES WIDE BY 8 INCHES LONG.

(1)

Tit	1889.

TITCOMB, G. W.

Record card No. 6, 1889.
Date. Dec. 29, 1888.
Subject: Papers—copy.
Page......[of book after record cards are bound.]

NOTE.—As the name of the writer is entered on the head (or index) line of the record card, which is filed under the subject concerning which he writes, experience may demonstrate that cross-references for the name of the writer will seldom be necessary

Cross-reference card.
Letters—Office of Secretary of War.

(2)

Fis	1889.

FISK, ARCHIE C

Record card No. 6, 1889.
Date, Dec. 29, 1888.
Subject: Papers—copy.
Page......[of book after record cards are bound.]

Cross-reference card.
Letters—Office of Secretary of War.

(3)

| Spe | 1889. |

SPEED, CAPT. FREDK.

Record card No. 6, 1889.
Date, Dec. 29, 1888.
Subject: Papers—copy.
Page...........[of book after record cards are bound.]

Cross-reference card.
Letters—Office Secretary of War.

SPECIMEN OF RECORD CARD. SIZE, 8 INCHES WIDE BY 10 INCHES LONG

(4)

Papers.	Copy.	Titcomb, G. W.
Office Secretary of War.	No. 6.	1889.

Return to Record Division, room 235, as soon as read. If a copy is desired it must be made at once, so this card can be returned to the files.
Date: Denver, Colo., Dec. 29, 1888.
From G. W. Titcomb.
Subject: On behalf of Archie C. Fisk, requests copy of cartel for exchange of prisoners, Feb. 1865, Vicksburg; and findings of court-martial, case of Capt. Fredk. Speed.

Number of inclosures.
Received Jan. 3, 1889.   Sent to A. G. Jan. 3, 1889.
Acknowledged   , 1889.   Received back (with one inclo.) Jan. 22, 1889.
                                Bureau office mark, 6140, A. G. O., 1888.
Action: Jan. 23, letter to Mr. T. to state purpose for which copy is intended.
Feb. 8, reply received, dated Feb. 4, that copy is requested for historical purposes.

The blank spaces outside of lines must not be written on; it is for binding purposes.

(5)

Ohi	1887.

OHIO RIVER R. R. CO.

Record card No. 1409, 1887.

Date, March 20, 1887.

Subject, bridge over Great Kanawha River.

Page......[of book after record cards are bound].

Cross-reference card.

Letters—Office Secretary of War.

17958——13

(6)

Tho	1887.

THOMPSON, GEORGE W.

Prest. O. R. R. R. Co.

Record card No. 1409, 1887

Date, March 20, 1887.

Subject, bridge over Great Kanawha River.

Page......[of book after record cards are bound].

Cross-reference card.

Letters—Office Secretary of War.

FACE OF SPECIMEN "RECORD CARD."

(7)

Bridge.　　　　　　　　Great Kanawha River.　　　　　　　Geo. W. Thompson.
Office Secretary of War. No. 1409. 1887.
Return to Record Division, room 235, as soon as read.
If a copy is desired it must be made at once, so this card can be returned to the files.
Date, Parkersburg, W. Va., March 20, 1887.
From Ohio River R. R. Co., Geo. W. Thompson, prest.
Subject, submits plans and drawings of proposed bridge across Great Kanawha River below Falls.

No. of enclosures 25.
Received Mch. 25, 1887.　　　　　　　　　　　　　　Sent to C. of E. Mch. 25, 1887.
Acknowledged ———— —, 188 .　　　　　　　　　　Received back Mch. 25, 1887.
　　　　　　　　　　　　　　　　　　　　　　　　Bureau office mark 1297 Eng. 1887.
　　　　　　　　　　　　　　　　　　　　　　　　　　　　　　111

Action: Mch. 25. C. of E. recommends that board be convened to report on plans and location.
Mch. 26. Approved.　　　　　　　　　　　　　　　　　　　C. of E. Mch. 26.
Rec'd back Apl. 21.

　　　　　　　　　　　　　　　　　　　　　　　　　　　W. D. Apl. 27, 1887.
　The report of the Board of Engineers, the recommendations of Col. Craighill and the Chief of Engineers are approved. The papers are respectfully referred to the Chief of Engineers and the Acting Judge Advocate-General to prepare the plans and papers in duplicate for the approval of the Secretary of War. Duplicates of the report of the board and Col. Craighill's letter should be submitted.
　　By order of the acting S. of W.:　　　　　　　　　　JOHN TWEEDALE, C. C.

Rec'd back June 6 from J. A. G. with papers prepared for execution.

REVERSE OF SPECIMEN "RECORD CARD."

(8)

W. D. June 15, 1887.

Resp'y ref'd to the C. of E. for file in his office. One copy of the within instrument being sent to Mr. George W. Thompson, Prest. Ohio River R. R. Co.

By order of the acting S. of W.:

JOHN TWEEDALE, C. C.

[Inclosure No. 2.]

[Circular.]

WAR DEPARTMENT,
Washington City, February 9, 1889.

In the matter of briefing and entering "letters received" and recording "letters sent" and indorsements in the respective bureaus and offices of the War Department, attention is invited to the case entitled "Salaries and fees of United States consuls," published on pages 25 to 37, inclusive, of volume 1 of the Report of the Select Committee of the United States Senate, appointed under Senate resolution of March 3, 1887, to inquire into and examine the methods of business and work in the Executive Departments, etc.

With this case as a sample to be followed, chiefs of bureaus are requested to have an actual case selected, such as will show the average action or work upon cases in their respective bureaus or offices, then to have a history of the case prepared by the clerk in charge showing in minute detail (including copies of briefs, office marks, indorsements, letters, entries in record and index books, etc.), the action from and including the receipt of the case in the office, through its various courses to and including its final disposition, in like manner as is shown in the case mentioned.

This history having been prepared as required, chiefs of bureaus will cause an investigation of the subject to be made, and having thereupon decided whether any unnecessary work has been done or any persons have been employed on the work more than were needed, and what possible improvements can be made in the methods adopted, they will apply the appropriate remedy and make report of their action to the Secretary of War, and transmit therewith a copy of the history of each case made up as above directed.

By order of the Secretary of War:

JOHN TWEEDALE,
Chief Clerk.

[Inclosure No. 3.]

[Circular.]

WAR DEPARTMENT,
Washington City, February 13, 1889.

(1) Letters and other papers received at the War Department or any of its bureaus will, unless otherwise directed, be at once sent to the offices to which they pertain without instructions, each chief of a bureau being responsible that the mail sent to him is promptly acted upon, and report made to the Secretary of War in cases requiring his action, or to which he should reply. When acted upon by the Secretary, the proper notation will be made and the papers sent to the office to which the subject-matter pertains, unless instructions to the contrary are given; and, generally, only such papers will be filed in the office of the Secretary of War as do not pertain to the business of any of the subordinate bureaus. This rule will also apply to the filing of papers in the bureaus and offices of the Department. Only such papers will be filed in a given bureau or office as clearly belong to its business and are within the jurisdiction of the chief thereof.

(2) Where there are several record divisions in one bureau, the action on a paper should only be noted on the books of the division to which the business pertains; this to avoid duplication of entries, and to prevent the obliteration of briefs by date and other stamps.

(3) Before a paper which is acted upon by the Secretary of War is filed, as directed in paragraph 1, it should be sent to any chief of a bureau who has expressed an opinion or made a recommendation thereon, in order that he may be informed of the action taken.

(4) A paper submitted for the action of the Secretary of War will be so prepared that the last indorsement or report shall contain, in the fewest possible words, a summary of the case, unless this appears in some report on the same or an accompanying paper to which reference is made. It should also show the question to be decided, and conclude with an opinion or recommendation. When necessary, the law, orders, or customs of the service governing in like cases will be stated, and the case made complete in itself, so that reference to previous papers will only be necessary to afford more definite information upon matters already summarized in the report. As papers submitted in person can be orally explained, it will be sufficient, in the majority of such cases, to indorse on each an opinion or recommendation, omitting the other requirements of this paragraph.

(5) Where it is evident that it will be necessary to send the report of the bureau officer with the reply of the Secretary of War, the report should be separate from the papers or a copy of it submitted.

(6) The subject of correspondence will be indicated by the writer in the upper left-hand corner of the first page of the letter or report, the "subject" not to exceed three or four words.

(7) Chiefs of bureaus are authorized to decide cases properly within the scope of their authority in their own names. When existing regulations or orders require certain cases to be submitted to the Secretary of War for his action, but in which there is no difference of opinion, no doubt as to the facts, law, or regulations, *where the amount involved does not exceed* $500, when the decision of the Secretary of War can be distinctly foreseen, or the principles of which have been previously determined, chiefs of bureaus are authorized to decide such cases and sign the decision "By authority of the Secretary of War;" provided any case so decided pertains to the particular class of business over which the chief of the bureau who decides the case has jurisdiction.

(8) All cases decided by the Secretary of War, or in which he has given orders, will be signed either by the Secretary or "By order of the Secretary of War," and all such cases must be noted or recorded in the office of the Secretary, except orders affecting the *personnel* of the Army (officers and enlisted men) and the movement of troops.

(9) Chiefs of bureaus are authorized to correspond with any military officer upon the business of their respective bureaus, forwarding the same, or a copy, through or to any commander who should be informed of the contents thereof.

The Secretary of War requests chiefs of bureaus to see that the requirements of this circular are fully complied with.

By order of the Secretary of War:

JOHN TWEEDALE,
Chief Clerk.

[Inclosure No. 4.]

WAR DEPARTMENT—ASSIGNMENT OF BUSINESS.

Accounts:
    For advertising and job printing: S. of W.
    Of bonded Pacific railroads for Army transportation: Q. M. G.
    Of National Homes for Disabled Volunteer Soldiers: S. of W.
    Of officers in Quartermaster's Department: Q. M. G.
Accounts current for subsistence funds: C. G. S.
Advertising accounts: S. of W.
Advertising for subsistence supplies or services: C. G. S.
Advertisements: S. of W.
Animals, public, recovery of lost or sto'en: Q. M. G.
Appointment of clerks, messengers, etc.: S. of W.
Appointments in Quartermaster's Department, applications for: Q. M. G.
Aqueduct (Washington): C. of E.
Armory. (*See* National Armory.)
Army:
    Claims for quartermaster stores taken for use of, during the rebellion: Q. M. G.
    Contingencies: S. of W.
    Estimates for subsistence of: C. G. S.
    Matters relating to discipline of: I. G.
    Matters relating to instruction of: I. G.
    Inspections of personnel or materiel of: I. G.
    Register, compilation of: A. G.
    Subsistence of: C. G. S.
    Transportation: Q. M. G.
    Payments to, record of: P. M. G.
Arsenals: C. of O.
Artificial limbs: S. G.
    Transportation for invalid pensioners journeying to procure: Q. M. G.
Assignment:
    Of commissary sergeants to stations: C. G. S.
    Of medical officers: S. G.
    Of officers of Quartermaster's Department: Q. M. G.
Attorneys, registration of to prosecute claims: S. of W.
Auditor. (*See* Second Comptroller, etc.)

Back pay, claims for. (*See* Claims.)
Bake-ovens (post and field), providing and repairing of: C. G. S.
Balances to credit of disbursing officers standing three years or more, notices of: S. of W.
Barracks and quarters, construction, repair, purchase, or hire of: Q. M. G.
Blank books, Quartermaster's Department: Q. M. G.
Blank forms, Subsistence Department: C. G. S.
Blank forms, Inspection Department: I. G.
Blanks, distribution to the Army: A. G.
Blanks and general orders for Pay Department: P. M. G.
Board of Engineers: C. of E.
Boards, retiring: A. G.
Boards of Survey:
    On quartermasters' stores: Q. M. G.
    On subsistence supplies: C. G. S.
    Preliminary to action of an inspector: I. G.
Bonds:
    Drafting of: J. A. G.
    Official and others given to the United States: J. A. G.
    (*See* Paymasters' bonds.)
Books:
    Company and regimental: A. G.
    Hospital, and medical records: S. G.
Books of request for transportation: Q. M. G.
Books and blanks, distribution to the Army: A. G.
Boots, shoes, etc., manufactured at the military prison: Q. M. G.
Bounty and back pay, payment of Treasury certificates for: P. M. G.
Bounty and claims: A. G.
Bridges:
    Examination of legal papers relating to erection of: J. A. G.
    Hire, construction or purchase of: Q. M. G.
    Over navigable waters: C. of E.
    And roads (military): C. of E.
Buildings. (*See* Public buildings.)
Cables. (*See* Telegraph lines.)
Calls from Department of Justice, answers to: A. G. and J. A. G.
Camp, sites for: Q. M. G.
Canals: C. of E.
Cantonments, sites for: Q. M. G.
Car tickets, issue of: Q. M. G.
Cemeteries. (*See* National cemeteries and post cemeteries.)
Certificates of deposit: S. of W.
Certificates of deposits of funds pertaining to the appropriations for the Quartermaster's
    Department received from sales to officers and soldiers, sales at auction, and other
    sources: Q. M. G.
Changes of stations of officers of Quartermaster's Department: Q. M. G.
Charges and specifications, preparation and revision of: J. A. G.
Charts. (*See* Maps.)
Circulars (*see* Orders), distribution of, etc.: Q. M. G.
Civil departments. (*See* Departments.)
Civil law. (*See* Military and civil law.)
Claims:
    Furnishing to Second Comptroller, Second Auditor, Adjutant-General, Quarter-
        master-General, and Commissioner of Pensions abstracts of proceedings of courts-
        martial and other information from the records required in settlement of claims
        for back pay, bounty, pensions, and witness fees: J. A. G.
    Before War Department: S. of W.
    Disputed, for mileage: P. M. G.
    For commutation of rations of enlisted men on furlough; traveling; competitors
        rifle competitions; prisoners of war, and ordnance sergeants, or others on duty
        where subsistence in kind is not furnished: C. G. S.
    For extra-duty pay: Q. M. G.
    For losses of personal property, act of March 3, 1885: S. of W.
    For payment of subsistence supplies or property: C. G. S.
    For private horses: Q. M. G.
    For quartermaster's stores taken or furnished for use of the U. S. Army during the
        rebellion, under act of July 4, 1864: Q. M. G.
    For rail, water, or stage transportation: Q. M. G.

Claims—Continued.
    For re-imbursement of expenses incurred for subsistence of enlisted men: C. G. S.
    For tolls and telegrams: Q. M. G.
    In connection with buildings, structures, repairs, post cemeteries, sites for military posts, camps, cantonments, etc., etc.: Q. M. G.
    Miscellaneous, arising out of the rebellion: A. G.
    Miscellaneous, based on certified accounts known as "regular purchase vouchers:" Q. M. G.
    Of officers and soldiers to rank, pay, promotion, and other military rights, etc: J. A. G.
    Pertaining to medical matters: S. G.
    (*See* Soldier claims.)
Clerks, messengers, etc., appointment, promotion, reduction, discharge, and transfer of: S. of W.
Climatology, matters relating to: C. S. O.
Clothing and equipage supplies, procurement and distribution of, and claims connected therewith: Q. M. G.
Clothing, issue and distribution of, under special orders of the Secretary of War, as required for the militia of the States and Territories: Q. M. G.
Collections by paymasters, record of: P. M. G.
Commissary sergeants:
    Applications and recommendations for appointment of: C. G. S.
    Assignment of: C. G. S.
    Reports and records of: C. G. S.
Commutation to enlisted men of the line of the Army engaged in the construction and repair of telegraph lines connected with the Signal Service: C. S. O.
Commutation of fuel: Q. M. G.
Commutation of quarters:
    (1) Determining whether the officer was on duty and entitled to quarters: A. G.
    (2) Determining whether public quarters were available: Q. M. G.
    (3) Payments of commutation of quarters: P. M. G.
Commutations of rations:
    Of enlisted men on furlough and traveling, claims for: C. G. S.
    Of prisoners of war, claims for payment of: C. G. S.
Companies, record of payments to: P. M. G.
Company record books, supplying of: Q. M. G.
Comptroller. (*See* Second Comptroller, etc., and Claims.)
Confederate archives: A. G.
Contingencies of the Army: S. of W.
Contracting for subsistence supplies or services: C. G. S.
Contracts for transportation, preparation, and revision of: Q. M. G.
Corps of Engineers:
    Personnel of officers and employés of the: C. of E.
    Publications of the: C. of E.
Correction of records relating to officers and enlisted men: A. G.
Courts of inquiry and courts-martial:
    (1) Reviewing and reporting upon proceedings of: J. A. G.
    (2) Publishing findings and sentence of: A. G.
    (3) Recording, filing, etc., record of proceedings of: J. A. G.
    (*See* Records of courts-martial.)
Deeds, drafting of: J. A. G.
Departments of Justice, answers to calls from: A. G. and J. A. G.
Departments:
    Discontinued geographical, records of: A. G.
    Transportation of property for the civil, of the Government: Q. M. G.
Depositories. (*See* Government depositories.)
Deposits by enlisted men, record of: P. M. G.
Deserters, rewards for apprehension of, etc.: Q. M. G.
Desertion, removal of charge of: A. G.
Detachments, payments to: P. M. G.
Detail of enlisted men of Signal Corps as signalmen: C. S. O.
Disbursing officers:
    Balances to credit of. (*See* Balances.)
    Of the Quartermaster's Department, examination of estimates from: Q. M. G.
    Of the Subsistence Department, estimates from: C. G. S.
Discharge, certificates in lieu of: A. G.
Discharge of clerks, messengers, etc.: S. of W.

Discipline of Army, matters relating to: I. G.
Districts, discontinued geographical, records of: A. G.
Divisions, discontinued geographical, records of: A. G.
Drafts paid, notices of: S. of W.
Drainage, structures for: Q. M. G.
Duties and conduct. (*See* Military duties.)
Emergency purchases of subsistence supplies or services: C. G. S.
Engineer depot and post at Willets Point: C. of E.
Engineer School of Application: C. of E.
Engineer troops: C. of E.
Engineers:
    Board of: C. of E.
    Publications of the Corps of: C. of E.
Enlisted men:
    Claims for reimbursement of expenses incurred in subsistence of: C. G. S.
    Claims for commutation of rations while on furlough, travelling: C. G. S.
    Commutation to, engaged as repairmen on telegraph lines connected with Signal Service: C. S. O.
    Detailing, of Signal Corps as signalmen: C. S. O.
    Enlistment, promotion, transfer, discharge, retirement, certificates of disability, and final statements of deceased soldiers: A. G.
    Record of deposits by: P. M. G.
    Record of payments to, on discharge: P. M. G.
Estimates:
    For appropriations: S. of W.
    From disbursing officers for quartermaster's funds: Q. M. G.
    From disbursing officers for subsistence funds: C. G. S.
    Of appropriations for subsistence of the Army: C. G. S.
    And bills from Public Printer: S. of W.
Expenses:
    For interments of officers and soldiers: Q. M. G.
    Incident to pursuit of lost or stolen public animals: Q. M. G.
    Incurred in subsistence of enlisted men, claims for reimbursement of: C. G. S.
Extra duty during the Mexican war and the war of the rebellion: Q. M. G.
Extra duty pay, claims for: Q. M. G.
Forms, distribution of, etc.: Q. M. G.
Fortifications, surveys for; location, plans, construction, care, repair, modification, supervision of buildings or works within, or exterior to: C. of E.
Fuel, commutation of fuel for officers and soldiers: Q. M. G.
Funds:
    Estimates received from disbursing officers for quartermaster's: Q. M. G.
    Estimates received from disbursing officers for subsistence: C. G. S.
    Monthly accounts of receipts and disbursements rendered by paymasters, and forwarded to Second Auditor: P. M. G.
    Record of, sent to paymasters: P. M. G.
    Weekly and monthly statement of, for comparison with Treasury records: Q. M. G. and C. G. S.
Furlough, claims for commutation of rations of enlisted men on: C. G. S.
Garfield Hospital, accounts of: S. of W.
General, general courts-martial, and special orders and circulars: A. G.
Gettysburgh, monument and memorial tablets of regular Army at: C. of E.
Government depositories, notification of changes in: S. of W.
Harbor lines, establishment of: C. of E.
Horses:
    Claims for private, turned into regiments: Q. M. G.
    Claims for, lost by officers and soldiers: Q. M. G.
Hospital:
    Books and medical records: S. G.
    Corps: S. G.
    Supplies: S. G.
Hospitals, payments to: P. M. G.
Hospitals and hospital stewards' quarters:
    Plans and specifications for: S. G.
    Report and recommendation upon, and construction, repair, hire, or purchase of: Q. M. G.
Indebted railroads, transportation for Army over: Q. M. G.
Indebtedness, inquiries as to: S. G.

Insane soldiers—admission to Government Hospital: A. G.
Inspection of South Pass jetties: C. of E.
Inspection reports on subsistence supplies: C. G. S. and I. G.
Inspections:
    Of colleges, etc., where officers are detailed as professors: I. G.
    Of money accounts of officers disbursing public funds: I. G.
    Of personnel or materiel of the Army, matters relating to: I. G.
Instruction of the Army, matters relating to: I. G.
Instruments for military surveys: C. of E.
Interments of officers and soldiers, expenses of: Q. M. G.
Inventory and inspection reports of quartermaster's stores: Q. M. G.
Investigations, making special report upon any military subject when called upon by the
    Secretary of War or major-general commanding the Army: I. G.
Job printing accounts: S. of W.
July 4, 1864, act of. (See Quartermaster's stores.)
Jurisdiction over military reservations. (See Military reservations.)
Justice, Department of, answers to calls from: A. G. and J. A. G.
Kind and quality of articles for rations and sales: C. G. S. and I. G.
Laboratory: S. G.
Land-grant railroads, transportation accounts of Army over: Q. M. G.
Land. (See Military reservations.)
Law. (See Military and civil law.)
Libraries at military posts, supplying newspapers to: Q. M. G.
Library of Surgeon-General's Office: S. G.
Library of the War Department: S. of W.
Licenses, drafting of: J. A. G.
Lost public animals, recovery of: Q. M. G.
Maps and charts, preparation and publication of: C. of E.
Medical Museum: S. G.
Medical officers:
    Assignment of: S. G.
    Reports and returns of: S. G.
Medical records and hospital books: S. G.
Medical supplies: S. G.
Memorial tablets of the regular Army at Gettysburgh, Pa.: C. of E.
Meteorological instruments and apparatus, etc.: C. S. O.
Meteorology, matters relating to: C. S. O.
Mexican war and war of the rebellion, extra duty during: Q. M. G.
Mileage:
    Disputed claims for: P. M. G.
    Record of payments of: P. M. G.
Military Academy, appointment of cadets, reports of Boards of Visitors, etc.: A. G.
Military bridges and roads: C. of E.
Military courts. (See Courts of inquiry, etc.)
Military duties and conduct, matters relating to proper performance of: I. G.
Military posts:
    Sites for: Q. M. G.
    Supplying newspapers to libraries at: Q. M. G.
Military prison at Fort Leavenworth, Kans.:
    Correspondence and orders: A. G.
    Manufacture of boots, shoes, barrack chairs, and corn brooms from material purchased
        under contract by the commandant of the prison, under direction of the Quarter-
        master-General: Q. M. G.
Military prisoners, applications for pardon or mitigation of sentence of: J. A. G.
Military reconnoissances: C. of E.
Military reservations (see A. R. 1772):
    Public lands purchased, appropriated, or designed for:
        Permanent military fortifications, and lands acquired in connection with improve-
            ments of rivers and harbors: C. of E.
        Armories, arsenals, and ordnance depots: C. of O.
        Barracks, posts, cantonments, or for other military uses: Q. M. G.
    Rights of the Government and others on, and relative to extent of jurisdiction over:
        J. A. G.
Military signaling (by flag, torch, lantern, heliograph, etc.): C. S. O. (See also Signal-
    ing.)
Military surveys, instruments for: C. of E.
Military and civil law, preparing reports relative to: J. A. G.

Militia, clothing and equipage for. (*See* Clothing and equipage.)
Miscellaneous claims arising out of the rebellion: A. G.
Money accounts of officers disbursing public funds, inspection of: I. G.
Monroe, Fort, wharf at: C. of E.
Monument at Washington's headquarters, Newburgh, N. Y.: C. of E.
Monuments and memorial tablets of regular Army at Gettysburgh, Pa.: C. of E.
Movement of troops: A. G.
Museum (Medical): S. G.
Muster-rolls of the regular Army and volunteer forces: A. G.
National armory, matters relating to: C. of O.
National cemeteries, matters relating to: Q. M. G.
National Homes for Disabled Volunteer Soldiers, accounts of: S. of W.
Navigable waters:
    Bridges over: C. of E.
    Riparian rights of the United States and others in: J. A. G.
Newspapers for libraries at military posts: Q. M. G.
Non-commissioned staff, record of payments to: P. M. G.
Notices of drafts paid: S. of W.
Notifications of changes in Government depositories: S. of W.
Office of Commissary-General of Subsistence, estimates for: C. G. S.
Officers:
    Appointment, promotion, transfer, details, leaves, resignation, and retirement: A. G.
    Record of payments to: P. M. G.
    Record of stoppages against: P. M. G.
Officers of Quartermaster Department:
    Changes of station of: Q. M. G.
    Returns of: Q. M. G.
Officers and soldiers:
    Expenses for interments of: Q. M. G.
    Commutation of fuel for: Q. M. G. (*See also* commutation of quarters.)
Orders, general, general courts-martial and special: A. G.
Ordnance depots, matters relating to: C. of O.
Ordnance sergeants, claims of commutation of rations for: C. G. S.
Ordnance soldiers, enlistment, promotion, and discharge of: C. of O.
Ordnance and ordnance stores for the Army, the militia, colleges, the Executive Departments, or individuals, whether they be applications for proposals to purchase, offers to sell, inventions, or generally anything on the subject: C. of O.
Ovens. (*See* Bake-ovens.)
Pacific railroads, accounts for the transportation of the Army over bonded: Q. M. G.
Pay-roll of the employés of the Qurtermaster-General's Office: Q. M. G.
Paymaster:
    Separate accounts with each: P. M. G.
    Record of collections by: P. M. G.
Paymasters' bonds, submitted to the Secretary of War, and, if approved by him, are sent by the Paymaster-General to the Second Comptroller for file in his office: P. M. G.
Payments to the Army, record of: P. M. G.
Pensioners, invalid, transportation for, journeying to procure artificial limbs: Q. M. G.
Pensions, information relating to: A. G. and S. G.
Personal property, claims for losses of—act of March 3, 1885: S. of W.
Personnel:
    Of the Army, conduct and management of: I. G.
    Of officers of the Quartermaster's Department: Q. M. G.
    Of officers and employés of the Corps of Engineers: C. of E.
Post cemeteries, care of: Q. M. G.
Post quartermaster seargeants, applications for appointment and assignment of, etc.: Q. M. G.
Posts. (*See* Military posts.)
Powder depots, matters relating to: C. of O.
Printed matter, distribution of: Q. M. G.
Prison. (*See* Military Prison.)
Prisoners. (*See* Military prisoners.)
Prisoners of war:
    Claims for commutation of rations of: C. G. S.
    Records of: A. G.
Proceedings of courts-martial, etc. (*See* Courts of inquiry, etc.)
Promotion of clerks, messengers, etc.: S. of W.

Property, transportation for the civil departments of the Government: Q. M. G.
Public buildings and grounds: C. of E.
Public funds. (*See* Funds.)
Public Printer, estimates and bills from: S. of W.
Publications of the Corps of Engineers: C. of E.
Quality of articles for rations and for sales: C. G. S.
Quartermaster's Department:
    Certificates of deposits for funds pertaining to appropriations for the: Q. M. G.
    Examination of accounts of officers in: Q. M. G.
    Personnel of officers of: Q. M. G.
    Reimbursement of expenses incurred on account of: Q. M. G.
    Returns of officers of: Q. M. G.
Quartermaster's stores:
    Claims for such taken or furnished to the U. S. Army during the rebellion, under act of July 4, 1864: Q. M. G.
    Examination of returns of: Q. M. G.
    Inventory and inspection reports of such as are no longer fit for use: Q. M. G.
Quarters, construction, etc., of: (*See* Barracks and quarters, Commutation of quarters.)
Railroads. (*See* Pacific railroads.)
Rations, kind and quality of: C. G. S. (*See* Commutation of rations.)
Rebellion:
    Claims for quartermaster stores taken during the war of the: Q. M. G.
    Distribution of official records of the: S. of W.
Rebellion and Mexican war, extra duty during: Q. M. G.
Reconnoissance and surveys: C. of E.
Record books. (*See* Company record books.)
Records:
    Of Federal and Confederate prisoners of war, discontinued geographical divisions, departments and districts, army corps, divisions, brigades, camps, and depots: A. G.
    Of volunteer forces: A. G.
    Relating to officers and enlisted men, correction of: A. G.
Records of courts-martial, furnishing copies to be used as evidence in courts and by committees of Congress: J. A. G.
Records of proceedings of courts-martial, furnishing copies to parties tried: J. A. G.
Records of the Rebellion:
    Distribution of: S. of W.
    Subscriptions to: S. of W.
Recruiting parties and recruits, subsistence of: C. G. S.
Recruiting service relating to the regular Army: A. G.
Recruiting service relating to volunteer forces, State quotas and credits, drafted men, substitutes, bounties and claims, accounts of mustering and disbursing officers, A. G.
Reduction of clerks, messengers, etc.: S. of W.
Regulations and tactics, construction and issue of: A. G.
Re-muster of officers: A. G.
Repairs to buildings for use of Army: Q. M. G.
Reports:
    Of military operations and battles, on bills before Congress: A. G.
    Of military operations, of battles, of inspections, on some claims to Congress, to Department of Justice and Court of Claims: A. G.
Reports and returns of medical officers: S. G.
Requisitions:
    For funds: S. of W.
    For funds to be sent to paymasters: P. M. G.
    For subsistence supplies and blank forms: C. G. S.
Reservations. (*See* Military reservations.)
Returns:
    Of officers for clothing and equipage received, issued, and transferred, examination of: Q. M. G.
    Of officers of the Quartermaster's Department: Q. M. G.
    Of quartermaster's stores, examination of: Q. M. G.
    Of subsistence stores and property: C. G. S.
    Of posts, regiments, departments, and divisions, militia, deserters, casualties, deceased soldiers, and recruiting: A. G.
    Regimental and post, of volunteer forces: A. G.
Rewards for apprehension of deserters: Q. M. G.

Rifle competitions, claims of competitors for commutation of rations: C. G. S.
Riparian rights of the United States, the several States and individuals in navigable waters: J. A. G.
River and harbor works, sites for: C. of E.
River and harbor works and canals: C. of E.
Roads and bridges in Yellowstone Park: C. of E.
Rolls, muster, of the regular Army and volunteer forces: A. G.
Salary of officers, record of: P. M. G.
Sales at auction and other sources, certificates of deposits for funds pertaining to appropriations for the Quartermaster's Department received from: Q. M. G.
Sales to officers and soldiers, certificates of deposits for funds pertaining to appropriations for the Quartermaster's Department, received from: Q. M. G.
Sales, kind and quality of articles for: C. G. S.
Second Comptroller and Second Auditor, replies to inquiries from, relative to payments made to officers and enlisted men both of the regular Army and volunteer forces in the Florida, Mexican, and rebellion wars: P. M. G.
Secret service accounts: S. of W.
Sergeants. (See Post quartermaster sergeants.)
Settlement certificates: S. of W.
Sewerage, structures for: Q. M. G.
Shooting galleries, hire, purchase, construction, etc., of: Q. M. G.
Signal equipments and stores, requisitions for: C. S. O.
Signal Service, all matters relating to, including civil and military force and fiscal questions connected with: C. S. O.
Signal stations, establishment, maintenance, or discontinuance of: C. S. O.
Signaling, instruction in, and other matters relating to: C. S. O.
Signalmen, detail of enlisted men of Signal Corps as: C. S. O.
Sites:
    For military posts: Q. M. G.
    For river and harbor works: C. of E.
    And reservations for permanent works: C. of E.
Soldier claims, cases known as being claims for private horses: Q. M. G.
Soldiers and officers, expenses of interments of: Q. M. G.
Soldiers' Home:
    Transportation for: Q. M. G.
    Monthly requests of commissioners to withdraw money from the permanent fund: S. of W.
South-Pass jetties, inspection of: C. of E.
Specifications and charges, preparation and revision of: J. A. G.
Stables, hire, construction, purchase, etc., of: Q. M. G.
Statements, weekly and monthly, of funds: Q. M. G. and C. G. S.
Stationery for War Department and its bureaus: S. of W.
Stations of officers of the Quartermaster's Department, changes of: Q. M. G.
Stolen public animals, recovery of: Q. M. G.
Stoppages against officers, record of: P. M. G.
Store-houses, purchase, construction, hire, etc., of: Q. M. G.
Storms, observations and reports of: C. S. O.
Street-car tickets, issue of: Q. M. G.
Structures for the Army, erection of: Q. M. G.
Subsistence of the Army:
    Estimates for: C. G. S.
    Matters relating to: C. G. S.
Subsistence of enlisted men, claims for expenses incurred in: C. G. S.
Subsistence of recruiting parties and recruits: C. G. S.
Subsistence Department, employment and compensation of civilians in: C. G. S.
Subsistence funds:
    Accounts-current for: C. G. S.
    Estimates from disbursing officers for: C. G. S.
    Weekly and monthly statements of: C. G. S.
Subsistence funds or supplies, all papers connected with the settlement of an officer's accountability for: C. G. S.
Subsistence stores and property:
    Purchase, issue, sale, and transfer of: C. G. S.
    Returns of: C. G. S.
Subsistence supplies:
    Boards of survey and inspection reports on: C. G. S.
    Requisitions for: C. G. S.

Subsistence supplies or property, claims for payment of: C. G. S.
Subsistence supplies or services:
    Advertising and contracting for: C. G. S.
    Emergency purchases of: C. G. S.
Supplies for the Army, character, quality, and adequacy of: I. G.
Supplies for War Department and Bureaus, including stationery, miscellaneous supplies, fuel, ice, etc.: S. of W.
Supplies (Quartermaster), distribution to the Army: Q. M. G.
Surgeon-General's office, library of: S. G.
Surveys and military reconnoissances: C. of E.
Surveys (military), instruments for: C. of E.
Tactics, construction and issue of: A. G.
Target ranges, hire, purchase, construction, etc., of: Q. M. G.
Telegrams, claims for: Q. M. G.
Telegraph lines:
    Construction, operation, maintenance, equipment, and repair of United States military or sea-coast telegraph lines and cables (and telephone lines): C. S. O.
Providing operators and repairmen for: C. S. O.
Telephone lines. (*See* Telegraph lines.)
Tolls, claims for: Q. M. G.
Torpedoes and instruction therein: C. of E.
Transportation: Q. M. G.
    Books of requests for: Q. M. G.
Transportation accounts of the Army over land-grant railroads: Q. M. G.
Transportation claims of Army during the rebellion: Q. M. G.
Transportation contracts, preparation and revision of: Q. M. G.
Transportation for invalid pensioners journeying to procure artificial limbs: Q. M. G.
Transportation of property for the civil departments of the Government: Q. M. G.
Transportation for the Soldiers' Home: Q. M. G.
Treasury certificates for bounty and back pay, payment of: P. M. G.
Trusses and appliances: S. G.
Uniform, outfit, and supplies of the Army, matters relating to: I. G.
Vessels owned by the Quartermaster's Department: Q. M. G.
Volunteer forces, records of: A. G.
Volunteers in Florida, Mexican, and rebellion wars, record of payments to: P. M. G.
Vouchers for advertising and job printing: S. of W.
Vouchers, regular purchase, certified accounts known as: Q. M. G.
War Department, library of: S. of W.
Washington Aqueduct: C. of E.
Washington Monument: C. of E.
Washington's Headquarters, Newburgh, N. Y., Monument at: C. of E.
Water supply, structures for: Q. M. G.
Weekly and monthly statements of Subsistence funds: C. G. S.
    Of Quartermaster funds: Q. M. G.
Wharf at Fort Monroe: C. of E.
Wharves, hire, construction, purchase, etc., of: Q. M. G.
Willets Point, Engineer depot and post at: C. of E.
Witness fees. (*See* Claims.)
Works (permanent), sites and reservations for: C. of E.
Wrecks, removal of: C. of E.
Yellowstone Park, roads and bridges in: C. of E.

    The foregoing assignment of business will be observed in all the offices and bureaus of this Department.

                                                        WM. C. ENDICOTT,
                                                          Secretary of War.

WAR DEPARTMENT, *February* 13, 1889.

[Inclosure No. 5.]

[Circular.]

WAR DEPARTMENT,
Washington City, February 9, 1889.

The classes of work falling within the jurisdiction of the several bureaus of the Department are being arranged from the statements made by chiefs of bureaus, and will soon be published for distribution. In connection therewith, each chief of a bureau is requested to have a list prepared of the classes of papers acted upon in the several divisions of his bureau, noting thereon the name of the person who acts upon each item. This list to be arranged for easy reference, and copies distributed to the several record divisions in his bureau, in order that duplication of entries may be avoided and it may be definitely known where to send papers after they are entered. Lists to be corrected from time to time when necessary.

By order of the Secretary of War:

JOHN TWEEDALE,
Chief Clerk.

INDEX.

	Page.
Abbreviations, list of	134
Accounts of supply division paid by disbursing clerk W. D. and audited by 1st Auditor	85
Regulations for	85
To be inspected by officer of the I. G. Department	86
Accountable requisition, consolidated form for	73
Acknowledgments of receipt in certain cases, recommended	122
Blank letter forms in certain cases, specimens of	122–123
Postal-card of	122
Action of S. W. on recommendations of Board on Business Methods:	
Discontinuing letters of request on settlement certificates	15
Approving rules and regulations of W. D	15
Concerning certs. of deposit	30
In letter to Sec. of the Treasury June 21, 1888	30
By circular of June 21, 1888	30
By instructions	30
By orders of June 18, 1888	30
By revoking Par. 1608 A. R.	30
Concerning Army paymasters' collections	32
On printing of card index of 164th N. Y. Vols	45
On credit requisitions	48, 72
In consolidating deposit lists in W. D	72
Discontinuing duplicate requisitions on Public Printer	74
Referring proposed circular on administration to bureau officers for report	79
Establishing half-hourly mail service	81
Relieving Capt. Hoyt from supply division and assigning Mr. Thorp to charge	86
Rescinding circular requiring daily reports of work	89
In indorsement approving report of Board on Correspondence	137
In circular February 15, 1889, to carry out report of Board on Correspondence	138
In circular of February 9 and 13, 1889, relating to correspondence	196
On report of board (except as to correspondence) in letter to chairman of Senate select committee, January 23, 1889	1, 8
Transmitting report of Board on Correspondence and recommending appropriation for blanks for printing of report of board; also for payment to a Board on Business Methods	90
Authorizing the Q. M. G. to sign by order of the Secretary of War	76
Establishing supply division, July 21, 1884	84
As to assignment of business to the bureaus	206
"Action on papers," definition of	90
Adjutant-General, remarks of, on report of board on card-index record of rolls	43
Views of, on administration and course of papers	77
Administration—Appendix 8	74
Letter of Q. M. G. of August 22, 1873, as to disposing of cases by him, and signing by order of the S. of W	75
Suggestion of Q. M. G. approved September 9, 1873	75, 76
Views of present Q. M. G. as to unnecessary routine in correspondence	76
Proposed extension of order of September 9, 1873, to other bureaus, and papers to be signed "By authority of the S. of W."	77
Those "by Order of the S. of W." to be recorded in his office	77
Chiefs of bureaus should correspond with military commanders on business of bureau	77
Views of A. G. as to change of regulations, so that papers may be sent by dept. commander direct to bureau	77

Page.

Administration—Appendix 8—Continued.
   Views of Q. M. G., C. G. S., and G. of O 77, 78
   Chiefs of bureaus should report G. O. and A. R. to be amended to conform to
      proposed circular 78
   Proposed amended circular 78, 79
      Papers to be sent direct from office of S. of W. to bureau 79
      Report to be made to S. of W. in cases requiring his action 79
      Papers to be filed in office to which they pertain 79
      What papers submitted to S. of W. should show subject to be indicated
         in upper left-hand corner of paper 79
      Chiefs of bureaus to decide certain cases in their own names, signing "By
         authority of the Secretary of War" 79
      Cases decided by S. of W., how signed 79
      Chiefs of bureaus to correspond with mil. commanders or staff officers on
         business of bureau 79
   Suggestions from bureaus on circular called for, and detailed statement of
      classes of work belonging to bureau 79
   And list of orders or A. R. requiring amendment to conform to this circular. 79
Alphabetical arrangement of card-index record of rolls 34
   Arrangement of cards of rolls by regiment and State not approved by A. G.. 44
   Lists preferred 136
Appendix No. 1. Requests for requisitions and settlement certificates 13
    2. Rules and Regulations W. D. June 4, 1888 15
    3. Certificates of deposit 16
    4. Army paymaster's collections 31
    5. Card-index record of rolls of Vol. army 33
    6. Credit requisitions 46
    7. Requisitions on Public Printer 73
    8. Administration 74
    9. Messenger service 80
   10. Supply division 82
   11. Daily reports of work 86
   12. Correspondence 89
Appointments to fill vacancies 109
Army paymaster's collections, App. 4 31
   Funds in, pertaining to other appropriations than "pay, &c., of the Army,"
      mostly covered into the Treasury and drawn out by long routine de-
      scribed 31
   Letter of P. M. G. to Q. M. G 31
   Endorsements of Q. M. G. and S. of W 31–32
   Settlement cert. prepared by 2d Aud 32
   Sent to 2d Compt., returned to S. of W. and P. M. G. and Q. M. G 32
   Transfer and counter requisitions and sending to 2nd Aud., 3rd Aud.,
      and warrant div., etc 32
   P. M. G. should designate appropriation on cert. of deposit 32
   Views of board approved by S. of W. June 22, 1888 32
Army Regulations, G. O. revoking par. 1608 of 30
   Conflict in, as to certs. of deposit 24
   Relating to certs. of deposit given 26
   Necessary changes in, to conform to proposed circular to be reported by bu-
      reau officers 79
Assignment of business 197–205
Assistant Secretary needed in W. D 7, 11
Automatic dating and numbering machine 41
Blank letter forms in certain cases 123
Blue pencil, underscoring parts of letter with 118
Board on Business Methods, report of, transmitted to Congress by letter of S. of
      W. January 23, 1889 1
   Scope of, how duties of members of were performed 7
   Report of, as to correspondence transmitted to Congress 89
   Order appointing 9
   Object of 9
   Suggestions invited to 11
   Decides to investigate matters by topics, and report on each separately 11
   Recess of 11
   Delayed, by what causes 11

	Page.
Board on Business Methods, etc.—Continued.	
Care of, in making recommendations for change	11
Reasons for recommendations of, fully stated	11
Printing of report of	89
Visits certain corporations, etc	116, 117
(See Recommendations of.)	
Book. (See Charge book.)	
Books, in Req. Div. to be discontinued	24, 30
Of certificates of deposit in Q. M. G. O. to be consolidated	24
In office of C. G. S. of record of certificates of deposit	21
In P. M. G. O. of certificates of deposit	22
In S. G. O. of certificates of deposit	22
In C. S. O. of certificates of deposit	23
(See Record books, letters received and letters sent.)	
Brief cards, notations on	119
Briefing and indexing, instructions relative to	119
Briefing of papers, rules for	119
Brower Bros., N. Y. City, cabinet letter files manufactured by	135
Business, assignment of	197–205
Should be disposed of with promptness, with least entries possible, etc	9
Present method of transacting, as illustrated in the transfer of the steamer Success	100–109
Pension case of Thos. W. Taylor	110–116
Houses. (See Corporations, etc.)	
(See Item of, Reduction of.)	
Bureau, correspondence of chief of, with mil. commander or staff officer	79
Statement of classes of work belonging to each to be made	79
Chiefs of should have authority to dispose of certain papers and sign by authority of Secretary of War	79
Bureau officers, reports of, on papers submitted to S. of W	74, 79
Reports of, as to amendments to proposed circular on administration	79
To report necessary changes in A. R. and orders to make them conform to proposed circular	79
Bureaus, chiefs of, to extend asssistance to the Board on Business Methods	10
Classes of work falling to, to be stated	79
Heads of, attention of, invited to R. S. 173, 174, and 175	87
Separate appropriation for office contingencies for, prior to 1883	82
Bureaus, W. D., to prepare accountable requisitions	72, 73
Cabinet files suggested	135
Calls for information from vol. rolls and records, No. of, unanswered July 1, 1888	42
Calls, No. of, for information from rolls received in A. G. O	36
From records, no record of, kept in P. M. G. O	41
Cameron, Amberg & Co., cabinet letter files manufactured by	135
Card, index record of rolls of volunteer army, App. 5	33
When work of, was commenced	33
Method of making, pursued	33
Size of form of, used	33
Contains all the information on the rolls except name of paymaster	33
Completed and under way	33
Arrangement of	33
Use made of	33
Printing of, recommended	33
Should be arranged in one alphabetical series for regiment	33
Objections to printing answered	34
Publications already made of military records	34
Of soldiers by States, by W. D., and by Congress	34
Advantages of printing	34
Alphabetical series for state	34
Regimental registers discontinued, and reasons therefor	34
Discontinuance of reg. registers recommended by Senate select committee	34
Extract from report of Senate committee recommending the system, alphabetical arrangement by regiment and State, and printing of	34
Number of rolls in A. G. O	35
Of men in vol. army and of cards required	35
Pages in printed copy of	35
Cost of printing and binding	35

17958——14

	Page.
Card, index record of rolls of volunteer army, App. 5—Continued.	
Printing of, of 164th N. Y. Vols. recommended to test cost and utility	35
Cylinder for placing rolls on, recommended	35
Recommended when full military history is called for	35
And to be in copying ink and press copy sent in answer to call	35
Such cards to be filed and future answers to be made from them	36
Objections because such cards not compared considered	36
Calls for information from rolls received in 1884-5-6 and duplication work in answering such calls	36
Estimate of time required to complete	36
Number of clerks required by law to be engaged on rolls, regiments to be carded	36
Number of clerks saved by	36
Table showing average calls answered by one clerk monthly in 1884 to 1887	36
Work required in answering calls	37
When 20 regiments are carded one clerk can be spared for work on	37
Falling off of calls after printing of	37
Number of men now engaged on	37
Number of, which can be completed in a year	37
Table showing progress of work on basis given	37
Number of clerks required to complete, in a given time falling off of calls when, are printed and gain thereby	38, 39, 40
Necessity for something to save rolls	41
Time rolls will last	41
180 men should be put on work of	41
Work done on card index in Record and Pension Div., S. G. O	41
Transfer of certain records to S. G. O. suggested	41
Pension Record Div., A. G. O., employs 9 men who could be employed in answering calls if they could be answered promptly	41
Record not required if calls answered promptly	41
No record of calls kept in P. M. G. O	41
Automatic dating and numbering stamp	41
Discontinuance of Record and Pension Div. recommended	41
Number of unanswered calls July 1, 1888	42
The work should be brought up to within a week	42
Sample of card, Exhibit A	42, 43
Remarks of A. G. on Report of Board on	43
Does not concur in recommendation for printing and reasons given; time required for reading proof; rolls do not give complete information	43
May be erroneous and corrected by other records; might not be accepted by auditing officers as official basis for action	44
The information for settlement of soldier's claim should be furnished officially by W. D. and not taken from printed records	44
The printing of the 164th N. Y. Vols. not advised; one alphabetical series for regiments and States not advised; no special objection to cylinders suggested, but advantages considered doubtful; carding of full military histories and furnishing press copies in answer to calls not approved; objections to stated	44
Addition to force as suggested advisable	45
Reduction of business in answering calls can not be anticipated	45
Large number of calls in last five m'nths; proposed transfer of records to S. G. O. not approved	45
Record and Pension Div. necessary if inquiries of members of Congress and others are to be answered	45
Order of S. of W. of January 18, 1889, for printing 300 copies of; of the 164th N. Y. Vols. to test value of printing; how to be distributed, and reports to be made as to value of book	45
Card Index Record. Sample of	42, 43
Card Index Record system, advantages of	6
Recommended	133
Compared with present system of keeping the records	133
Arrangement by subjects	124
Form and style of card index	124
In use in Record and Pension Division, S. G. O	125
In lieu of letters-received books, advantages of	119
Should be of same size in each bureau	111
Slight danger of losing the cards	124

	Page.
Card index blanks for use of searchers	132
Card index briefs, adoption of, recommended	121
Object of	122
Specimen of	121
Card index of decisions, etc	133
(*See* Decisions.)	
Card index, samples of (Ex. B.)	180–85
Card-record book	124
Card record. (*See* Record Card.)	
Cards. (*See* Office Mail Cards.)	
Certificates of deposit, Appendix 3	16
How, arise; issued in duplicate; embrace two classes of public fund	17
Should not be confounded with receipts for funds deposited to credit of an officer	17
Course of business pursued with, traced by steps	17
What, must show on face	17
Copy of face of	17
Stamp and endorsement on	18
Receipt of, at office of S. of W	18
Record of in Req. Div	18
In docket book	18
In record of	19
Sent in to Q. M. G	19
Action on, in Q. M. G. O	19
Entry of, in Q. M. G. O	19
Form of record book of, in Q. M. G. O	20, 21
Similar routine of, in other bureaus	21
In office of C. G. S	21
In office of P. M. G	22
In office of P. M. G. arising under stoppage circular and under paymaster's collections	22
In S. G. O	22
In office of C. of O	23
In office of C. of E	23
In Signal Office	23
Duplication of work in	23
Recommendations concerning	24
Should be forwarded from Treasury to S. of W. without wrapper, endorsement or signature of C. C.; then sent without entry to bureau to be stamped and entered; appropriation to be designated in bureau, but no signature required; then forwarded to Treasury Dept.; should not remain in W. D. more than two days; not to be recorded in letters received or sent; two record books of, in Req. Div. should be discontinued; two books of, in Q. M. G. O. to be consolidated	24
Proposed new form of	25
Number of, received in office of S. of W. in 1887	24
Defects of Army Regs. concerning	24
Proceeds of sales of Government property, Exhibit A, sections of the A. R. relating to such sales	25
Statement of number of, received in Req. Div. in 1887, Exhibit B	26
Paragraphs of A. R. concerning, given, Exhibit C	26
Action of S. and W. and Secretary of Treasury on recommendations of board concerning	28, 29, 30
Charge book, in connection with keeping record cards	132
Number of lines to page of	132
Sample of	133
Charging papers withdrawn from files	99, 132
Chief clerks to supervise the work of other clerks (Sec. 173, R. S.), shall revise the distribution of work from time to time, and make any monthly report of and defects in business methods (Sec. 174, R. S.)	86
When monthly reports of, received duty of superior officers to take action to remedy defects pointed out (Sec. 175, R. S.)	86
Chief of Ordnance, views of, on correspondence	78
Chiefs of Bureaus. (*See* Bureaus.)	
Chief Signal Officer, recommendations of, relative to keeping the records in Signal Office	121

	Page.
Circular to chiefs of bureaus requiring history of a case to ascertain if unnecessary work is done	110
Circular, W. D., April 4, 1888, inviting suggestions to be sent to the Board on Business Methods	10
April 19, 1888, discontinuing letters of request on settlement certificates	15
August 9, 1888, discontinuing separate requests for accountable requisitions	72
September 11, 1888, discontinuing duplicate requisitions on Public Printer	74
Proposed, on administration	78
Proposed, amended, on administration	137
July 21, 1884, providing for supply div., W. D	84
February 19, 1885, regulations for accounting for supplies furnished supply div	84
April 25, 1845, requiring monthly reports and reports of unauthorized absences of clerks	86
April 23, 1887, requiring daily reports of work	87
January 21, 1889, rescinding cir. of April 23, 1887	89
(See Orders.)	
February 15, 1889, to carry out report of board as to correspondence	138
February 9, 1889, as to tracing of cases to show course of business by chiefs of bureaus	196
February 13, 1889, on administration	196
February 9, 1889, as to assignment of business to the bureaus	206
Classes of work falling to each bureau to be reported	79
Clerks, distribution of labor among	87
Daily statement of absence of, required to be kept by President Polk	87
Absence of, to be reported	87
Daily reports from, required	87
Definition of	90
Pay of, for overtime	11
Remarks upon work performed by low-grade and high-grade	109
Remarks upon useful employment of	109
Statement as to non-payments of debts by, required	87
Cockrell, Hon. F. M., chairman senate select committee. (See Senate Select Committee.)	
Collections of Army Paymasters. (See Army Paymasters' Collections.)	
Colored pencil, use of, recommended	118, 136
Commercial houses. (See Corporations.)	
Commissary-General of Subsistence, views of, on correspondence	78
Commission on business methods recommended for Treasury and W. D.	10
What, should do, and what action should be taken on report of	10
Committee on Business Methods. (See Commission; Board on Business Methods.)	
Comparison of cards with rolls not necessary	36
Communications, returning of by indorsement	116
Conclusions of the board on the subject of correspondence	137
Corporation and commercial establishments visited by the Board on Business Methods	116–117
And Government Departments, difference in manner of acting on correspondence by, and remarks thereon	116–117
Correspondence, difference in manner of acting on, by corporations and Government Departments, with causes of difference and table of contrast	116–117
Report on	89–205
Credit requisitions, Appendix No. 6	46
Letter of Secretary of Treasury and recommendation of Treasury board that the W. D. make out its own, hereafter	46
Prepared in 2d and 3d Auditor's Offices no reason why W. D. should not prepare its own	46
Consolidated form for, recommended to save labor	46
Explanation of form	47
Advantages of proposed form of	47
Consolidation of letter of request, accountable requisition, and accountable warrant recommended	47
Letter of request and requisition consolidated in W. D	48
Form of proposed consolidated deposit list, requisition, and warrant, Exhibit A	48
Copies of six deposit lists, Exhibits B, E, H, L, O, and R	50, 53, 56, 59, 62, 65
Copies of six requisitions, Exhibits C, F, I, M, P, and S	51, 54, 57, 60, 63, 66

                                     213

                                                                            Page.
Credit requisitions, Appendix No. 6—Continued.
    Copies of six warrants, Exhibits D, G, K, N, Q, and T 52, 55, 58, 61, 64, 67
    Form of credit req. Q. M. G., Exhibit U   68
    Form of accountable req., Exhibit V   69
    Form of accountable warrant, Exhibit W   70
    Form of consolidated request, accountable requisition, and accountable war-
        rant, Exhibit X   71
    Letter of S. of W. to Sec. of Treasury as to W. D. making out its own, and
        enclosing copy of report of board on circular, August 9, 1888, consol-
        idating, with request for   72
    Form of consolidated, to be prepared in bureaus   72
    Consolidated form of deposit lists adopted by W. D   73
Cross-reference cards, recommended   123
    File-boxes for   131
    Kind of paper for   131
    Manner of indexing names on   132
    Specimens of   190
Cylinders for rolls, no special objection to, by A. G   44
Daily reports, Appendix 11   86
    Of absences directed by the President to be kept by heads of bureaus   87
    Shall not contain statements of work in reply to oral inquiries   87
    Work reported under   87
    Voluminous character of   88
    Chief S. O. invites attention to expense of making, and waste of time   88
    Unsatisfactory return of   88
    Objections to, by the C. C., S. G. O   88
    Order requiring, too literally construed; recommendation that circular requir-
        ing, be rescinded   89
    W. D. circular, January 21, 1889, rescinding circular requiring   89
Debts, statement of complaints as to non-payment of, by clerks required by the
        President in 1845   87
Decisions, need of index of   124
    Preserving searches of   134
    Or precedents, card index of   133
    Advantages of card index of   133
    Books made up of card indexes of   134
    Present manner of keeping record of, too slow for time of war   137
    Proposed card index of   133
    Size, style, and copies of card index of   134
    Or precedents, list of 180–185
Definition of "Action on papers," "Clerks," "Department," "Important
        papers," "Information of value," "Mail," "Letters," "Papers," and
        "Recorded" or "Recording"   90
Delay in handling papers, remedying of. (See Taylor.)
"Department," definition of   90
Departments. (See Government Departments.)
Deposit lists, consolidated form for copies of   48
Disbursing officer's receipts not certificates of deposit   17
Drafts of important letters   117
Duplication of entries to be avoided 117–119
    Effect of order of February 13 on duplication   118
Duplication of work, Army paymaster's collections   31
    To be avoided   10
    Certificates of deposit   23
Employés, retired-list for   12
    Salaries of 11, 12
    Superannuated, letters of Chas. J. Folger and John Sherman, Secretaries of
        the Treasury, concerning hardship of discharge of   12
Equitable Life Assurance Society, N. Y   116
Exceptions in practice, being table of letters and papers not recorded 92–98
File-boxes for cross-reference cards   131
    Cases for record cards   131
Files, manner of keeping record of papers withdrawn from 99, 132
    Saving of space in the   135
First Auditor audits account of disbursing clerk W. D. for supply div   85

	Page.
Form of certificate of deposit	17
New, of accountable requisitions	73
Of books of registry of cert. of dep	18, 19, 20, 21, 22, 23
New, of C. of D. proposed	28, 29
Of paymasters' collections	31
Of card-index record of soldier	42
New consolidated, of credit requisitions	48, 71
(See Credit Requisitions, Exhibits A to X.)	
Of acknowledgments	122, 123
Of card-index brief	121
Of record card	130, 131
Of card-record charge book	133
Of briefs	144–158
Of record books	159–167
Of indorsements, office marks, official addresses, and indexes	167–172
Of books of money and property accounts, returns, and correspondence	172–179
Of cross-reference cards	190, 191
Of record card	192–195
Frech, Jacob, clerk Class IV, S. G. O. Appointed on Board on Business Methods	9
Full military history. (See Military History.)	
Government Departments. (See Treasury Dept; War Department.)	
Departments and corporations, difference in manner of acting on papers by, and remarks thereon	116–117
Property. (See Proceeds of.)	
Greeley, Edwin S., of New York	116
Half-hourly collection and delivery of mail	108–109
Advantages of, demonstrated	116
Handwriting shall be plain and of good size, and flourishes, etc., forbidden	91
Hoyt, Captain, C. H., in charge of supply div	87
Duties of	84
Recommendation that he be relieved	85
Relieved from charge of supply div. January 10, 1889	86
"Important papers," definition of	90
Indexing, instructions relative to	119
Of names on cross reference cards	132
(See Briefing.)	
Index-record cards. (See Record Cards.)	
Indorsing of letters	117
Indorsements, formal, not necessary in certain cases	137
Notations of simple	136
"Information of value," definition of	90
Ink, necessity of, that will last indefinitely	117
(See Red Ink.)	
Inspector General's Department, officer from, to inspect books and accounts of supply division	86
"Instructions for keeping the records," etc. (published October 1, 1870), provisions of, in regard to official papers	91
Instructions, etc., relative to record divisions	119
Item of business, tracing of an	100–116
Traced, relative to cert. of deposit	16
To Army paymaster's collections	31
Pension claims of Thos. W. Taylor	101–116
Transfer of the steamer *Success*	100–109
Laws concerning proceeds of Government property given	25
Legislation necessary to carry out reformed methods should be prepared and submitted to Congress	10
Letter forms. (See Blanks.)	
Letters, average number received per day in Secretary's Office	132
Definition of	90
Complimentary closing of replies to	135
Drafts of important letters	134
Form and style of replies to	134
Nature of, and action on those requiring immediate attention	135
Returning of, by indorsement	135
Underscoring of, with blue pencil	118
(See Papers.)	

                                                                                Page.
Letters—Continued.
    Received, definition of..   91
    Number of pages of record of, and lines recorded of, in 1888 126–130
    Record card book of...   130
    Table of papers not recorded 93–98
    Sent...   91
    Definition of   91
    Printed forms for..   123
    Number of pages of record of, in 1888.. 126–130
    Record card book of..   130
    Recording in permanent books of important   117
    Table of letters and papers not recorded 93–98
Lines in charge book, numbering of   132
Lists alphabetically arranged preferred   136
Mail, definition of   90
    First action upon receipt of   118
    Half-hourly collection and delivery of.. 108–109
    Advantages of half-hourly collection and delivery demonstrated 108–109
    Marking of, with initials of office to which it pertains........................   118
    Mail arrangement in the offices of the Metroplitan Ins. Co..................   136
    Chutes for W. D. building, recommended.......................................   136
        Diagram of...   136
    Delivery, half-hourly, recommended...   81
Messenger service, Appendix No. 9, automatic system to secure frequent commu-
        nication between offices recommended.......................................   80
    Delay in communication at present illustrated   80
    Delay of three days in paper passing through six hands.....................   80
    Half-hourly mail delivery recommended..   80
    Method of, described   80
    Advantages of system proposed...   81
    Office mail cards described, and how to be used..............................   81
    W. D. orders, January 18, 1889, providing for half-hourly mail service in
        bureaus and between bureaus and office of S. of W.....................   81
Method of entering and acting on papers until action thereon is completed, as
        shown by tracing an actual case...100–116
Methods of Government Departments and corporations, etc........................   116
    Remarks upon old and new methods...   137
Metropolitan Life Insurance Co., N. Y., pneumatic tubes in offices of, for con-
        veyance of mail   136
    Village telephone in offices of..   136
Military commanders, chiefs of bureaus to correspond with......................   79
    History, full, carding of, not approved by A. G..............................   44
    Records of soldiers, publications made of......................................   34
    Records, when full, required, card index should be made..................   35
Monthly reports, required by act of 1842   86
    The President directs that, be transmitted to him   86
    What they shall contain   86
    W. D. circular April 25, 1845, requiring the, provided for by law shall be reg-
        ularly made, and shall include statement of unauthorized absences of
        clerks   87
    Written, of chief clerks not made from December, 1851, to April, 1887.......   87
Mutual Reserve Fund Life Association, N. Y   116
Names, manner of indexing on cross-reference cards   136
New England Mutual Life Insurance Co., Boston   116
New York Mutual Life Insurance Co..   116
Notations of simple indorsements   136
Office mail cards   81
Orders, January 18, 1889, establishing half-hourly messenger service   81
    January 10, 1889, relieving Capt. Hoyt from charge of supply div., and as-
        signing M. R. Thorp   86
    Appointing Board on Business Methods..   9
    Discontinuing record-books of certs. of deposit in req. div   30
    Printing of card-index record of 104 N. Y. Vols..............................   45
    Establishing half-hourly mail service...   81
    (*See* Circulars.)

	Page.
Papers, administrative action on proposed circular	74
Amended circular	78
To be signed by Q. M. G. "by order of the Secretary of War"	76
Views of A. G., Q. M. G., C. G. S., and C. of O. on course of, and action on	77, 78
Administrative action on circular issued directing how, shall be acted on, what, shall be sent direct to bureaus, how submitted to S. of W., subject to be indicated in upper left-hand corner, when to be signed "by authority" or "by order" of the S. of W., chiefs of bureaus to correspond with military commanders	78, 79
Action on, pertaining to several bureaus	136
Awaiting final action	133
Circular to chiefs of bureaus requiring minute history of case to ascertain if unnecessary work is done in handling	110
Definition of "papers," "action on papers," and "important papers"	90
Delay in handling, remedying of	90
Description of, which it is recommended be not recorded	99
Keeping record of, withdrawn from files	99
Manner of briefing and recording of	117–119
Method of entering and acting on, as illustrated by actual case	100–109, 110–116
Moving of, by messenger service half-hourly	81
Numbering of	132
Pertaining to several bureaus	136
Reasons for necessity of recording, important	117
What is to be done when, are charged to a person for six days	132
Paymaster's collections, certificates of deposit arising under	22
(*See* Army Paymaster's Collections.)	
Pay to clerks for overtime work	11
Pechin, Maurice, detailed for duty as clerk on Board on Business Methods	9
Stenographer and clerk to board	12
Penmanship. (*See* Handwriting.)	
Pencil. (*See* Blue Pencil.)	
Pennsylvania Railroad Company	116
Pension record division, A. G. O., discontinuance of, recommended	41
Recommendation of discontinuance of, not approved by A. G	45
Polk, President, letter of, as to duty of clerks, reports to be made, etc	86
Postal-card of acknowledgment to persons who rarely write to Department, form of	122
Precedents. (*See* Card Index of Decisions and Precedents.)	
President, The, letter of, to S. of W., April 11, 1845, requesting that the monthly reports required by law be regularly sent to, and directing that daily statements as to services and absences of clerks be kept by heads of bureaus; also a statement of complaints as to non-payment of debts by clerks	86
Press copy card-index record should be sent in answer to call for information	35
Illegibility of, after lapse of time	117
Filing of, with letter	117
Printing of card-index record of rolls	34
Rolls of 164th N. Y. Vols	35
Of rolls not approved by A. G	43, 44
Report of Board on Business Methods	89
Proceeds of Government property, laws concerning, given	25
Prolixity should be avoided	91
Public Printer, duplicate requisitions on. (*See* Requisitions on Public Printer.)	
Publications made of military records of soldiers by States, W. D., and Congress	34
Q. M. G. letter of August 22, 1873, as to disposition of papers by, and signing by order of the S. of W	75
Authority to, to sign by order of the S. of W	76
Views of, on correspondence and administration	76, 77
Receipts for funds deposited by a disbursing officer not same as certificates of deposit	17
Recommendations of the Board on Business Methods	1–11
Clerks should be paid for overtime	11
Salaries of clerks should be increased	11
Additional stenographer needed	12
That requests for requisitions on settlement certificates be discontinued	13
Concerning certificates of deposit	23, 24
Concerning army paymaster's collections	32

	Page.
Recommendations of the Board on Business Methods—Continued.	
In regard to card-index record of rolls of vol. army, printing of	33-34
Alphabetical arrangement of	33, 34, 44
Printing of 164th N. Y. Vols	35, 44, 45
Cylinders for rolls	35, 44
Card index to be made when full military history called for; press copy of to be sent in answer to call; filing of, and future answers to be made from card-index record	35, 44
180 men should be employed on card-index	41
Transfer of records to S. G. O	41, 45
Discontinuance of record and pension div., A. G. O	41, 45
Automatic dating and numbering stamp	41
Work of answering calls should be brought up to within a week	42
That the W. D. make out its own credit req.; new form of credit req.	46
Consolidated form of deposit lists	48, 49
Duplicate requisitions on Public Printer should be discontinued	73
Bureau officers should report amendments required to make A. R. and orders conform to proposed circular	79
In proposed circular on administration that classes of work falling to bureau be stated	79
To extend authority given to Q. M. G. to sign by order of S. of W. to other bureaus, and to be "By authority of the Secretary of War"	79
That the supply div be placed in charge of a clerk with $10,000 bond and Capt. Hoyt be relieved; that salary of chief of supply div. be $2,400 and the same for other chiefs of divisions	85
That daily reports of work be discontinued	89
That certain classes of papers mentioned be not recorded	99
That searchers be required to keep a memorandum book to ascertain if any papers need not be recorded, to be compiled once a year	99
That acknowledgment of receipt of letters be sent in certain cases	122
That card-index briefs be made of certain cases described	121
That card-index system be adopted	133
Record and pension div., A. G. O	42
Discontinuance of, recommended	42
Necessary if inquiries as to claims are to be answered	45
Record books, introductions to, showing purposes for which kept, sample of	119
Card book of letters received and letters sent	124
Cards.	
Advantages of, enumerated	124
Arrangement by subjects	124
Charge book in connection with	132
Compared with present system of keeping the records	124
File cases for	131
Form and style of	130
How long to be withdrawn from files	132
In lieu of letters-received books	119
In use in record and pension div., S. G. O	125
Index of names on	132
Numbering of	132
One clerk to be in charge of	132
Should be of same size in each bureau	134
Slight danger of losing the cards	124-125
Specimens of (Exhibit D)	192-194-195
Temporary file of record cards of cases awaiting final action	133
What they combine	124
What is to be recorded on	123
(See Card Index System, Cross Reference Cards, Decisions, Card Index of, and Card Index Briefs.)	
Divisions, consolidation of, and reasons therefor	119
"Recorded" or "Recording," definition of	91
Record and pension div. of the S. G. O., card-index system in use in	125
Recording of papers, description of papers which it is recommended be not recorded	90
Only important papers should be recorded	117
Searchers to keep a memorandum to ascertain what papers need not be recorded	99, 117

Recording of papers, etc.—Continued.
    Table of papers not at present recorded:
        Letters received 92–95
        Letters sent 96–98
    Papers that do not require recording, as provided in "Instructions for keeping the records," etc. (1870) 92
    Present system too slow for time of war 118
    Table of papers excepted from recording 92–98
    Value of system of recording, as shown by actual case 118
Recording of simple indorsements 136
Red ink ruling on papers to be discontinued 136
Reduction of business by printing of card index record of rolls 36–41
    Can not be anticipated by A. G. 45
Regimental register of rolls of vol. army discontinued 34
Regulations of the Army. (See Army Regulations.)
Replies to letters, form of 134 134
    Complimentary closing of 134
Report of Board on Business Methods. (See Board on Business Methods.)
    Of classes of work falling to each bureau 79
Reports required as to value of printed card index records of rolls .. 45
    Of bureau officers to S. of W. on papers submitted 74, 79
    As to amendments to proposed circular on administration, as to amendments to A. R., and orders to make them conform to proposed circular 79
    (See Daily and Monthly Reports.)
Requests for requisitions on settlement certificates, report on 13
    Considered useless and disuse of, recommended 13
    Circular discontinuing 15
    (See also Settlement Certificates.)
Requisitions. (See Requests for, on Settlement Certificates, Settlement Requisitions, Credit Requisitions.)
    On settlement certificate, copy of 14
    (See also Settlement Certificates.)
    On Public Printer, Appendix 7 73
    Duplicate, required by W. D. Order of March 28, 1864, considered unnecessary since bureaus are in one building, and discontinuance recommended 73
    W. D. circular discontinuing duplicate, press copy of, to be retained in bureau. 74
    Division, office of S. of W., statement of certs. of deposit received in, in 1887. 24
Retired list for employés of W. D 12
Rolls of vol. army, methods of reproduction of, considered by Senate select committee 34
    Number of 35
    Necessity for doing something to save 41
    Time, will last 41
    No. of calls from 36
    Condition of 34, 41
    Do not give complete information, and may be erroneous 44
    Printed card-index record of, might not be accepted as proper evidence 44
    (See also Card Index Record of.)
Routine in Army paymaster's collections described 31
Rules and regulations, W. D., June 4, 1888 15
Salaries in W. D., recommendations of S. of W. as to, in letter to Senate committee 6, 7
    In W. D. inadequate 11, 12
    Of chiefs of divisions should be $2,400 85
Sample card-index record 42, 43
Search, preservation of result of 136
Searchers to keep a memorandum book, recommended 99
Secretary of Treasury, letter of, on credit requisitions 46
    Letter of, on certificates of deposit 30
Secretary's action, noting record of, in Secretary's Office 136
Senate Select Committee on Business Methods in Departments, letter of chairman of, to S. of W 9
    Extract from report of, as to appointment of commissions in Treasury Dept. and W. D 10
    Recommends Discontinuance of Vol. Army Register 34
    Extract of report of, recommending card-index for rolls of vol. army 34
    Consider methods of reproduction of rolls 34

	Page.
Settlement certificates, definitions of	13
Course of business pursued with	13
Letters for request for requisition on, useless	13
Copy of	14
Copy of request for requisition on	14
Copy of requisition on	14
Circular discontinuing requests for requisitions on	15
Settlement requisition, copy of	14
(*See also* Settlement Certificates.)	
Signal Office, recommendation in regard to transacting business in, but not yet for the other bureaus	120
Sloane, W. & J., New York	116
Southern Pacific Railroad Company	116
Special cases	117
Staff officers, chiefs of bureaus to correspond with	79
Stationery, method of purchase of, prior to 1882 and after	82
Table showing purchase of	83
Chief clerk in charge of purchase of, up to July 21, 1884	83
Regulations for accounting for	83
Stenographer, another required in office of S. of W	7
Stenographers, two required in Secretary's Office W. D	12
Stoppage circular, certificates of deposit arising under	22
Stores. (*See* Corporations.)	
*Subject, illustration of arrangement by subject in card index	124
Of correspondence to be indicated in upper left-hand corner of paper	79
Subjects, list of, of letters received in 1888 (Exhibit C)	186
Steamer *Success*, transfer of, showing method of entering and acting on papers	100–109
Remarks upon manner of disposing of this case	106–109
Success. (*See* Steamer *Success*.)	
Suggestions invited to be sent to Board on Business Methods	11
Superannuated employés, retired-list for, recommended	12
Hardship of discharge of, views of Secretary of Treasury in regard to discharge of	12
(*See also* Employés and Clerks.)	
Supplies. (*See* Supply Division.)	
Supply division (Appendix 10)	82
Stationery prior to 1882 given to bidder whose total bid for all items was lowest	82
May 22, 1882, samples required, and each item separately passed upon and award made accordingly	82
Separate appropriation for each bureau prior to 1883	82
Miscellaneous supplies then purchased by each bureau without advertisement	82
Two appropriations, stationery and miscellaneous supplies by act of March 3, 1883, and put under S. of W	82
The method adopted in 1882, for stationery applied then to purchase of miscellaneous supplies	82
Tables showing expenditures for miscellaneous supplies, 1884 to 1888, and stationery, 1882 to 1888, showing saving under new system	83
C. C. under S. of W. had charge of purchase of mis. supplies and stationery up to July 21, 1884, cause of change of system	83
Supply division formed, W. D. circular, July 21, 1884	84
Duties of officer in charge of	84
Capt. Hoyt, A. A. Q. M., in charge of	84
Accounts of, paid by disbursing clerk W. D	85
Quartermaster's accounts are audited by 3rd Aud	85
But the accounts of this division go to 1st Aud., who does not audit Q. M. accounts, and to overcome this difficulty circular was issued that after accounts were passed upon by the Q. M. G. they should be filed in office of the S. of W	85
W. D. circular, February 19, 1885, as to accounts of, the reason for assigning Army officer in charge, that he should account under A. R. if Q. M. Dept. fails	85
Recommendation that a clerk be placed in charge under proper bond	85
Salaries of similar clerks in other Departments	85
Salary should be $2,400, and same to other chiefs of divisions	85

	Page.
Supply division (Appendix 10)—Continued.	
W. D. orders, January 10, 1889, relieving Capt. Hoyt in charge of supply div. and assigning M. R. Thorp to charge of	86
Bond of $10,000 required, duties of chief of	86
Books and accounts of, to be examined by officer of the I. G. Department	86
Surgeon-General's Office. Record and pension div. of, method of business and work accomplished in, stated in letter of S. of W	5
Card-index system in record and pension div. of	6
Card-index system in use in	125
Table of letters and papers not required to be recorded	92–98
Taylor, Thos. W., pension claim of, showing delay which will be remedied by order of January 18, 1889, and circular of February 9, 1889	109–116
Remarks upon this case	115
Telephone service in offices of Metropolitan Insurance Co., N. Y., advantages of	136
Temporary file for papers awaiting final action	133
Thorp, M. R., assigned to charge of supply div	86
Tolman, L. W., chief of req. div., appointed on Board of Business Methods	9
Topics, the board decides to consider matters to be inquired into by	10
List of, considered by board and acted upon	11
Transfer of certain records in A. G. O. to S. G. O. suggested	41
Not approved by A. G	45
Treasury Department, more briefings, records, &c., in, than necessary, commission recommended to be appointed in	9
Letters of Secretaries of, concerning discharge of superanuated employés in	12
Tweedale, John, C. C., W. D., appointed on Board on Business Methods	9
Unanswered mail, ascertaining delay of action on	136
Vacancies, manner of filling	109
Vol. army, number of men in	35
(*See* Rolls of, and Volunteer Rolls.)	
Volunteer rolls, card-index record of	137
Wannamaker, John, of Philadelphia	116
War Department, more briefings, records, &c., in than necessary, commission recomended to be appointed in	9
Rules and regulations of, June 4, 1888	15
Number of employés in	11
Amount of money disbursed in, annually	11
Superannuated employés in, should be retired	12
Washington City, not a commercial city, affords little opportunity for Dept. employés to enter into other business	12
"Your obedient servant," omission of	135

www.ingramcontent.com/pod-product-compliance
Lightning Source LLC
Chambersburg PA
CBHW031812230426
43669CB00009B/1112